CLINT EASTWOOD

CLINT EASTWOOD

A Biography

Sara Anson Vaux

GREENWOOD BIOGRAPHIES

AN IMPRINT OF ABC-CLIO, LLC
Santa Barbara, California • Denver, Colorado • Oxford, England

1/28/15
LN
$37.00

Library of Congress Cataloging-in-Publication Data

Vaux, Sara Anson.
 Clint Eastwood : a biography / Sara Anson Vaux.
  pages cm — (Greenwood biographies)
 Includes bibliographical references and index.
 ISBN 978-1-4408-2997-0 (hardback) — ISBN 978-1-4408-2998-7 (ebook)
1. Eastwood, Clint, 1930– 2. Motion picture actors and actresses—United
States—Biography. 3. Motion picture producers and directors—
United States—Biography. I. Title.
 PN2287.E37V38   2014
 791.4302'8092—dc23
 [B]   2014017772

ISBN: 978-1-4408-2997-0
EISBN: 978-1-4408-2998-7

18 17 16 15 14   1 2 3 4 5

This book is also available on the World Wide Web as an eBook.
Visit www.abc-clio.com for details.

Greenwood
An Imprint of ABC-CLIO, LLC

ABC-CLIO, LLC
130 Cremona Drive, P.O. Box 1911
Santa Barbara, California 93116-1911

This book is printed on acid-free paper ∞

Manufactured in the United States of America

CONTENTS

CONTENTS

SERIES FOREWORD

In response to school and library needs, ABC-CLIO publishes this distinguished series of full-length biographies specifically for student use. Prepared by field experts and professionals, these engaging biographies are tailored for students who need challenging yet accessible biographies. Ideal for school assignments and student research, the length, format, and subject areas are designed to meet educators' requirements and students' interests.

ABC-CLIO offers an extensive selection of biographies spanning all curriculum-related subject areas including social studies, the sciences, literature and the arts, history and politics, and popular culture, covering public figures and famous personalities from all time periods and backgrounds, both historic and contemporary, who have made an impact on American and/or world culture. The subjects of these biographies were chosen based on comprehensive feedback from librarians and educators. Consideration was given to both curriculum relevance and inherent interest. Readers will find a wide array of subject choices from fascinating entertainers like Miley Cyrus and Lady Gaga to inspiring leaders like John F. Kennedy and Nelson Mandela, from the greatest athletes of our time like Michael Jordan and

Muhammad Ali to the most amazing success stories of our day like J.K. Rowling and Oprah.

While the emphasis is on fact, not glorification, the books are meant to be fun to read. Each volume provides in-depth information about the subject's life from birth through childhood, the teen years, and adulthood. A thorough account relates family background and education, traces personal and professional influences, and explores struggles, accomplishments, and contributions. A timeline highlights the most significant life events against an historical perspective. Bibliographies supplement the reference value of each volume.

PREFACE

Until I saw *Unforgiven* when it first appeared in theaters, I only knew Clint Eastwood through snatches of movies I caught while my boys were watching them on TV. The first one I remember is *Firefox*. When I commented upon the dark screen and the strange persona of the protagonist played by Eastwood, I received a long lecture from my sons about the actor's contributions to the mythology of the American (male) hero. With *Unforgiven*, I realized that as a director (and as an actor who plays it low), Eastwood was a sage cultural analyst who was not afraid to challenge myths of a "pure" West for "just" conquerors or to expose the devastations that ecological disasters and economic greed have visited upon men, women, and children.

Apart from Christopher Frayling, Laurence Knapp, and Kent Jones, American Eastwood analysts have focused largely upon his depiction of the American male, his private life, or the plot details of his many movies. French critics, writing from a broad film background that includes classical American cinema (including Westerns), approach his films from a philosophical and humanistic as well as a cinematic perspective. Michael Henry Wilson's astute interviews, Noël Simsolo's art-centered approach, and recently, essays in the French journal

NUNC that look at Eastwood as deeply invested in the social, political, and ethical health of American society, grasp the foundational
agenda of a sophisticated director. My book *The Ethical Vision of Clint
Eastwood* (Eerdmans, 2012) offers an up-to-date analysis of Eastwood's
most probing movies from an ethical and "religious" perspective little
encountered by American audiences (although when I finished it,
Hereafter was not available for study and *J. Edgar* had not yet reached
theaters).

In the current Greenwood Biographies series, I have presented far
more information on Eastwood's personal life—the origins of his love
for music, particularly jazz; his major television role in *Rawhide*; his
breakthrough role as the Man with No Name in the Spaghetti Westerns; the establishment of his studio Malpaso, which allowed him creative freedom for his projects; the cultural shock of his role in Dirty
Harry; his rise to superstardom; his romantic adventures; and, gradu-
ally, the shaping of a cinematic artist who is almost universally recog-
nized as one of America's finest directors.

My analysis of Eastwood's "iconic" movies (that is, those that mark
his identity as a major director) arises at key moments as his life story
unfolds. As Chicago filmmaker and critic Michael Smith writes on his
blog whitecitycinema.com, I claim that Eastwood's body of work is
highly unified even though he has never had a hand in writing scripts
and is notorious for shooting his screenplays without rewrites.

The director himself has insisted since the first *Dirty Harry* (Don
Siegel, 1971) appeared that he works with stories, not from a political agenda. Nonetheless, the spectator should regard authors' protesta-
tions about their own work with a good deal of caution. Certain stories,
certain ways of filming, elicit thoughtful responses. For instance, as I
have studied four decades of Eastwood movies, I have observed that
he consistently engages with the social fabric of American society: the
(false) myths of cultural superiority that permeate a large portion of
Hollywood movies; the marginalization of increasing numbers of non-
white, non-rich persons; and the moral dilemmas in which everyday
people find themselves. He could have made other choices for cinematography, music, and casting. He could have sanitized his Westerns, as
literally thousands of movie and TV directors did before him. But he
did not.

Eastwood the director stays close to his individual characters—their mystifying, specific, human sufferings and joys. He mobilizes darkness and light to create emerging meanings—soft darkness for affection; hard darkness or bright light for evil. The stories often unfold at a deliberate pace; the director includes sequences that deepen the human dimension of a character rather than editing to emphasize a character with broad strokes or move the movie along at a breakneck pace. His use of music (particularly his own—think of *Mystic River* or *Million Dollar Baby*) subtly creates a meditative mood.

My personal favorites among the movies Eastwood has directed are *Unforgiven*—and then *Million Dollar Baby, Changeling, Mystic River, The Outlaw Josey Wales, Bird,* and *Invictus,* in that order. I am also insanely loyal to the Spaghetti Westerns, with Eastwood the actor at his ironic yet intense best, made with Sergio Leone, a director from whom he learned many of his directing skills. I did not like his August 2012 speech before the Republican National Committee. But then we are talking about at least three images—director, actor, and public figure—that only partly define Clint Eastwood. Sometimes newscasters, critics, and even our own friends confuse or even conflate the images. This book is aimed in part to help you explore the origins of these and many other characteristics of a complicated American cultural icon.

ACKNOWLEDGMENTS

Alex Thimons, graduate student in Screen Cultures in Northwestern University's Department of Radio/TV/Film, modestly declined credit for his contributions to the volume. Credit he must have, though, for star devotion to the meticulous details of fact-checking, locating bibliographic details, and writing up parts of the early Clint biography. We brainstormed for months over warm drinks at the Unicorn, Evanston's prime coffeehouse, home to students, professors, writers, and musicians. Bob Jewett of Heidelberg University and now Lincoln, Nebraska, launched my early Eastwood investigations. Ken Vaux remains my prime debate partner when he is not slaving over a hot stove to prepare my meals while I write.

Kindly note that parts of the following chapters have been adapted from my book on Eastwood's movies, *The Ethical Vision of Clint Eastwood* (Eerdmans, 2012). In turn, *Ethical Vision*'s early chapters contain material from *The Common Review: Eastwood Issue*, published by The Great Books Foundation, 2009.

TIMELINE: EVENTS IN THE LIFE OF CLINT EASTWOOD

May 31, 1930	Clint Eastwood born in San Francisco, CA.
Spring 1949	Graduates high school in Oakland, CA.
Spring 1951	Drafted into the army, Eastwood teaches swimming in California.
September 30, 1951	Survives a plane crash on a flight back from Washington to his base in California and swims to shore.
Summer 1953	Discharged from the army.
December 19, 1953	Marries Maggie Johnson.
April 1954	Universal offers Eastwood a contract, which would last until October 1955.
January 9, 1959	*Rawhide* premieres; it would run until 1966.
June 17, 1964	Daughter with Roxanne Tunis, Kimber, is born.
Summer 1964	Films his first Spaghetti Western with Sergio Leone, known in English as A *Fistful of Dollars*, followed by two others in 1965 and 1966.
1967	Leone's and Eastwood's Spaghetti Westerns released in the United States.

May 16, 1968	First child with his wife Maggie, Kyle, is born.
August 3, 1968	*Hang 'Em High*, the first film produced under Eastwood's new Malpaso banner, is released.
November 12, 1971	*Play Misty for Me*, Eastwood's first film as a director, is released, as are *The Beguiled* and the major hit *Dirty Harry*, both directed by Don Siegel.
May 22, 1972	Alison Eastwood, Clint's daughter with Maggie, is born.
April 19, 1973	*High Plains Drifter*, Eastwood's first Western as a director, is released in the United States.
June 30, 1976	*The Outlaw Josey Wales* is released in the United States.
December 20, 1978	*Every Which Way But Loose*, one of Eastwood's few full-on comedies, is released. It is wildly successful at the box office.
1979	Maggie and Clint legally separate. They divorce in 1984.
May 1985	*Pale Rider* shows as a competition entry in the Cannes Film Festival.
March 21, 1986	Scott, Eastwood's son with Jacelyn Reeves, is born.
February 2, 1988	Kathryn, Eastwood's daughter with Reeves, is born.
April 8, 1986	Elected mayor of Carmel, California.
May 1988	*Bird* shows in competition at Cannes; Forest Whitaker wins Best Actor at the festival.
August 3, 1992	*Unforgiven* is released; it would go on to win four Academy Awards, including two for Eastwood (as director and producer).
August 7, 1993	Francesca, Eastwood's daughter with Frances Fisher, is born.
May 1994	Eastwood is president of the jury at the Cannes Film Festival.
March 31, 1996	Eastwood gets married for the second time, to Dina Ruiz.

September 24, 1996	Eastwood settles final lawsuit filed by ex-partner Sondra Locke, out of court.
December 12, 1996	Morgan, Eastwood's daughter with Dina, is born.
May 2003	*Mystic River* shows in competition at Cannes; it would go on to win two Academy Awards.
December 14, 2004	*Million Dollar Baby* is released in the United States; it would go on to win four Academy Awards, including two more for Eastwood (as director and producer).
Fall 2006	Within two months, Eastwood releases two war-themed films: *Flags of Our Fathers* and *Letters from Iwo Jima*.
Fall 2008	Eastwood again releases two films in the same calendar year: *Changeling* (a competition entry earlier in the year at Cannes) and *Gran Torino*.
February 25, 2009	The Cannes Film Festival presents Eastwood with an extremely rare honorary Palme D'Or, for lifetime achievement.
December 11, 2009	*Invictus* is released in the United States.
October 15, 2010	*Hereafter* is released in the United States.
November 9, 2011	*J. Edgar* is released in the United States.
February 5, 2012	Eastwood appears in "Halftime in America," an advertisement for Chrysler that premiered during the halftime of Superbowl XLVI.
August 30, 2012	Eastwood speaks to an empty chair, meant to represent President Obama, during the Republic National Convention during which Mitt Romney was given his party's nomination for president.
October 22, 2013	Wife Dina files for divorce.
June 20, 2014	Eastwood's latest film, *Jersey Boys*, was released June 20, 2014. *American Sniper* is due out in 2015, and Eastwood also has announced that he will direct a remake of *A Star Is Born*.

Chapter 1

CLINT'S LIFE STORY: THE ICON TAKES SHAPE

ALL THE LITTLE ICONS

Let's begin neither at the beginning nor at the end, but somewhere in the middle—with *The Outlaw Josey Wales*, or rather, with the idea of "Josey Wales," the main character from an immensely popular 1976 movie admired, even adored, by film lovers across the political spectrum. The film's poster, adapted for the DVD cover, features a weathered cowboy adorned with a leather hat and a squint and two monstrous six-guns strapped across his chest. There it was, not a torn poster discarded in a corner of a dusty record shop in Paris or a worn DVD filed away in a movie buff's study in London or Chicago, but an image blown up Times-Square size to cover the back wall of a massive convention center in Tampa, Florida. In walked the 6'4" epitome of American masculinity and "exceptionalism," the actor made famous some four decades earlier as the Man with No Name and Dirty Harry (and Josey Wales), the idol of the small-government folks, arguably the most recognizable face in the entire world, an Oscar-crowned director—Clint Eastwood! The crowd went wild.

I will leave you hanging a few more minutes while I describe the weirdness of what happened next. Then I will unroll the happenings, people, cultural forces, and the like that makes any public appearance by flinty Clint a major media event. Be prepared: he grew up rather poor. He and his folks lived in their car off and on while he was growing up and his dad looked for work. He loved jazz from his teenage years. He was an athlete, a handy trait for an actor who performed his own stunts until he was at least 70. He prefers small government but makes movies that show what happens when a country fails its most vulnerable citizens. He is a philosopher, a cinephile, and a genius.

By August of 2012, Clint Eastwood had receded from tabloid fascination with his multiple romances, brief dip into politics as mayor of Carmel, California, and critical adulation for *Unforgiven* in 1992 and string of successes that began with *Mystic River* and *Million Dollar Baby* in 2003 and 2004. He was, as he liked to say, monogamous now, and he had to tend to other responsibilities such as acknowledging

Early in his career, Clint displayed his considerable musical gifts. (Paramount Pictures/Photofest)

and caring for the seven children acquired over the years. He was active on the golf circuit, fortunately for a fellow golfer whose life he saved earlier this year. His wife Dina enfolded him along with some of their children into some part of her new reality show. Moreover, and somewhat mysteriously, the Academy of Motion Pictures and American audiences had largely overlooked his last four movies, *Changeling* (2008), *Invictus* (2009), *Hereafter* (2010), and *J. Edgar* (2011). Time to relax, maybe to retire, as he had threatened since *Unforgiven*, when he was a mere 62.

But now he was back in the spotlight. The planners of the Republican National Convention (RNC) had selected him to introduce the guest of honor; the audience at the RNC had gathered in Tampa to choose—and crown—their nominee for president of the United States of America, Mitt Romney. In the United States alone, over 30 million people tuned in on their televisions, and untold others listened, streamed, or watched worldwide (Gorman 2012). What happened next offers a lesson in the ways large entities (corporations, governmental organizations, and political parties) take advantage of cultural icons to serve their own purposes. We have to wonder what RNC convention planners were thinking, however, when they selected a universally known but highly contradictory cultural representative to anchor their ambitious political agenda.

To understand the wattage of this event, and Eastwood's presence, let me lay some background for the role of political conventions in American electoral life. National party conventions hardly hold the interest in the 21st century that they enjoyed in 1952 when Dwight D. Eisenhower was tapped to run for the Republicans and Adlai Stevenson for the Democrats, or in 1960, when Republicans chose Richard Nixon and Democrats, John F. Kennedy. Only four years before 2012, though, the 2008 contest between Barack Obama and Hillary Clinton for the Democrats' nomination had sparked considerable theatrics, and conventions recovered some of their mid-century splendor. In 2012, President Barack Obama, a Democrat, occupied the White House—not simply any Democrat, but (for some Republicans) not even a "true" American—with a Kenyan, not a white man born in the United States, for a father; a suspicious-sounding (that is, "Muslim") first and middle name; and a birth in Hawai'i, not, for instance, in one of the 48 landlocked states, much less in one of the 13 original colonies or in the South.

The crowd that awaited Romney's acceptance of the Republican nomination on that warm August evening, then, expected a speech (and an introduction for Mitt) that would build upon the party's overwhelming victory in the 2010 elections and catapult him into the presidency. The Tea Party wing of the Grand Old Party (GOP) had taken over the House of Representatives and increased their hold upon Statehouses across the country. Its members aimed to overturn President Obama's signature Affordable Care Act; block his appointees to major governmental posts; and defund or at least slash governmental programs that benefited men, women, and children hurt by the collapse of the economy of 2008. The November 2012 election would vindicate their view of America as a God-given right of white, wealthy, "religious," and patriotic (largely) men. Who better to introduce their champion than Clint Eastwood, almost mythical representative of the iconic status of the lone gunslinger individualist in American society?

What happened then shocked not simply the viewing millions but also the planners of the convention, the consultants, and politicos who had planned—or so they thought—the so-called optics of the convention down to its last smiling child and digitally produced backdrop.

When Eastwood walked on stage, there it was, hovering above him: a larger-than-life, orange-tinted Josey Wales, a gun in each hand, with half of his face obscured by shadow. Below the image, the actor and director himself smiled graciously and bit bashfully. After the star quieted the crowd and provided a short introduction to his comments, he gestured to an empty stool that had been placed beside his podium and said: "I've got Mr. Obama sitting here, and . . . I just was gonna ask him a couple of questions."

And ask he did. In a performance that Mark Halperin and John Heilemann call "partly an homage to Bob Newhart and 100 perfect dada dinner theater" (Halperin and Heilemann 2013, 374), Eastwood asked the invisible president about closing the prison at Guantánamo Bay, the staggering amount of unemployment that followed the crises of 2008, Obama's broken promises, and Afghanistan. In between the items, Eastwood cracked jokes with his imaginary Obama, made a few salutary comments about Romney, and, 11 minutes after beginning, and at the prompting of a woman screaming in the audience, he finished by saying, "Go ahead . . . " and allowed the crowd to finish the quotation in unison, "make my day!"

The speech was not a vintage "Republican" speech, but it was *quintessentially* Eastwood. His primary critiques of the president—his policies on Guantánamo Bay and the war in Afghanistan—were minor planks in the Republican platform that actually emerged as policy during the last (Republican) administration. His digression on why lawyers make bad presidents—they are too measured, they are "always taught to weigh everything"—seemed to apply equally to the famously meticulous Mitt Romney. Eastwood delivered uncomfortable truths, primarily about the costs of waging war in Afghanistan and the persistence of mass unemployment, but the truths did not serve the Republican cause.

And then there's the larger-than-life backdrop, supposedly a fittingly glamorous introduction to the RNC's larger-than-life keynote speaker. Ah! Before the now-mortified convention planners decided to invite Eastwood to speak, they should have watched *The Outlaw Josey Wales* again, or at least watched the last half, the part that follows the Gatling Gun massacre. The movie turns a revenge drama—the triumph of a lone and embittered man of violence with his legendary six-gun (and Gatling) facility—into a story about peace and the building of a multi-generational, multicultural family.

If the planners had examined the film, the character, and the man who created both, then, they would have realized that over Eastwood's long career he has upended genre conventions (including expectations for a "convention speech") far more than he has fit himself and his art into them. The iconic image of *The Outlaw Josey Wales* that hovered above Eastwood and an empty chair far exceeds its surface interpretation as glorifying a vigilante gunslinger.

Eastwood, too, exceeds the images often ascribed to him. Even limiting our scope to his life as an artist and public figure, the person is far more complex than the identities associated with him. The man who escorted Angelina Jolie at the Cannes Film Festival in 2009 evokes the associations, some of them hard to shake. A five-disk boxed set of *Dirty Harry* movies was issued in 2008 and 2010 and a 35-disk set of Eastwood movies, "Clint Eastwood: 35 Films, 35 Years at Warner Bros.," a boxed set of 35 films, appeared in 2010. *The Good, the Bad, and the Ugly* plays regularly in cinemas all over the world, the latest one in 2012 at Music Box in Chicago as part of a series called "Epic." The seductive but misleading trailer for *Gran Torino* played heavily upon the Dirty Harry persona.

Other attachments to "Clint Eastwood," personality and actor, however, belong to a movie director far removed from Hollywood's tidy plots and easy answers. Eastwood across his long career has taken pains to mark out the differences between heavily marketed "product" and the movies he wants to make no matter what return he makes on his investment. He has directed small, idiosyncratic films like *Bronco Billy* (1980) and *Honkytonk Man* (1982) and unlikely romances such as *Blood Work* and *The Bridges of Madison County*. Movies like *Bird*, *Unforgiven*, *Mystic River*, and *Million Dollar Baby* present a stinging indictment of injustice that flies in the face of *Rambo*, the *Terminator* franchise, *Pearl Harbor* (2001), *Transformers*, and the Iron Man movies (2008), *Argo* (2012), and any other popular movie that reenforces the myth of American superiority. Then we have Eastwood's Westerns, which "display an unusually expressive feeling for landscape," as the British Film Institute (BFI) introduction to Eastwood's movies notes— the emotional landscape as well as the natural terrain (BFI Southbank London notes for August 2008 retrospective, www.movingimagesource .us/events/clint-eastwood-20080801).

To confound matters further, in 2006 Eastwood—long a master at capturing a sense of place, the look, sounds, and feel of American spaces—directed two politically charged movies not so much antiwar as deeply humanistic and compassionate testaments to the tragic waste of young lives in wartime. Could this be Clint Eastwood, onetime mayor of Carmel, California (where he shot his first film, *Play Misty for Me*), who directed *Flags of Our Fathers*, an exposé of racism and government propaganda during World War II? Is this the hard-bitten patriot of *Heartbreak Ridge* who directed *Letters from Iwo Jima*, a war movie in Japanese set on a Japanese island that sympathetically portrays Japanese characters, played by Japanese actors? Why did the RNC privilege Josey Wales, as opposed to his more recent films? Why, for that matter, didn't Romney, well-known meritocrat that he is, choose an image from Eastwood's greatest commercial success, the comedy *Every Which Way But Loose*, in which his costar was a beer-swigging orangutan?

But no one idea of "Clint Eastwood" withstands even a casual examination. From the beginning of his career as a movie director, Eastwood confronted major social issues such as the futility of war that place that famous iconic identity of rugged American masculinity in tension with a broader vision of individual and social wholeness. Clint Eastwood demonstrates what William Beard calls a "persistence of double vision," in which his iconic persona, on the one hand, "represents probably the single strongest icon of heroic masculinity in popular cinema over the past quarter century," but on the other, is "continuously, almost systematically, hedged round by reflexive and deconstructive elements whose actions undercuts its [the iconic persona's] stature": a paradox which results in what Beard calls an "ironic shadow" (Beard 2000, ix) to the heroic persona with which Eastwood is most regularly associated. The shadow is not an accident but rather a result of specific choices made by Eastwood and his collaborators over half a century or more.

Eastwood as a director may play with many variations on these iconic figures, but his personal films engage enduring questions about human life and the social order. How should we live together? How do we define the "good"? What is family? What does it mean to be human? And who belongs to "the human family"? He displays emotional as well as artistic empathy with the people he portrays—outcasts and pariahs and all the marginalized men, women, and children who have been left outside the gates of paradise they had so passionately longed to enter.

Eastwood unspools tales of endless journeys across America's magnificent landscape in the South and the Far West, undertaken by pioneers and slaves or their descendants who pushed west or south after the Civil War or by those who migrated to the cities in a quest for employment, identity, or peace. Movies like *Josey Wales*, *The Gauntlet*, *Pale Rider*, *Unforgiven*, *A Perfect World*, *The Bridges of Madison County*, and *Million Dollar Baby* present equally poignant tales of forgotten men and women.

Eastwood's directorial work in films like *Letters from Iwo Jima* and *Million Dollar Baby* plays neither to the iconic masculinity that characterizes his earlier roles, nor can we find the ironic subversion that Beard sees. In the great final films, irony is absent. The postmodern winking or wry quotation that the spectator sees in Eastwood's roles in *Fistful of Dollars* or in the action hero playacting of *The Eiger Sanction* has been replaced by characters whose suffering fills the screen. The late films, many of which I will discuss later in the book, seem timeless. They enable viewers to have empathic relationships with the characters, a degree of empathy that ironic, distanced portrayals of characters do not typically allow.

How are we to explain the radical disjunction, not between masculinity and its "ironic shadow" but rather between the image of violent machismo often (but not always) integral to his screen presence and the critical sensitivity evident in many portrayals? On the one hand, Eastwood embodies maybe more than any other actor the iconic force of the vengeful American killer, machismo at its most remorseless and violent. On the other hand, we have Eastwood's cinematic direction with its focus on forgotten lives, storytelling marked by eloquence and compassion.

The split naturally invites the question of how Eastwood used his early experiences not only to populate his artistic worlds, as novelists John Steinbeck in *Cannery Row* (1945) or Harper Lee in *To Kill a Mockingbird* (1960) did, for instance, but also to shape works with a distinctly ethical edge that mark him as a revolutionary thinker— even though that is a role usually not assigned to him in the public imagination.

The false impression is due in part to his own statements, in which he sometimes portrays himself as an anti-intellectual. As a close look at his iconic movies shows, however, he reads widely and commands a broad knowledge of films from outside the American movie industry. His mastery of literary and cinematic genres allows him to use their templates, mix them up, or counter them whenever possible. What is Clint Eastwood's own story, and how has it influenced his remarkable artistic output?

EASTWOOD'S LIFE STORY

Eastwood drew upon his own memories of living on the edges of mainstream American society to create movies populated by inhabitants with distinctive personalities, quirks, and back stories, with far more nuance than the image of Josey Wales's unhinged gunslinger would suggest. Richard Schickel's *Clint Eastwood: A Biography* (1996), Robert

E. Kapsis and Kathie Coblentz's *Clint Eastwood Interviews* (1999), and other profiles and interviews describe his early life during the grim years of the Depression. It was the beginning of a life that would both make him an icon and make him resistant to the trappings of being one.

Clinton Eastwood Jr.—always "Clint Eastwood" or just "Clint"—was born on May 31, 1930. A little older than my husband, a generation younger than my parents, he lived through the Great Depression that began in 1929 and continued for the next devastating decade. He was always fed, but sometimes he was tucked away in the mountains with his grandma. The family was always moving, moving, moving in that Pontiac he often speaks of, as his mother and dad looked for permanent work up and down the west coast of a massive country laid low by economic collapse. Schickel, the biographer most attuned to Eastwood's self-image, says that "there was never any panic or desperation in these moves. The elder Eastwood always had a job lined up before his family began packing" (Schickel 1997, 22). Other versions make the family seem even more well-off.

Does it matter? Clint and his family did move a lot. He was a child of the Great Depression, even if his family's particular economic circumstances were better than many. "The Great Depression" takes different turns in Eastwood's stories about this rootless childhood as a precursor to his stardom. He may have cultivated a myth that his family was poor—perhaps as dirt-poor as the Oklahoma farmers he eulogizes in *Honkytonk Man*, seduced as they were by the quintessential rags-to-riches stories of 19th-century author Horatio Alger and the dominant images of the "American Dream." The degree of poverty is a contentious subject for biographers—the poorer his early days, the more dramatic his rise to fame could seem. The poorer his family, the more he could talk of his father's hard work, with the spoken or unspoken message that anyone could become successful if he was.

His father, he told interviewer Paul Nelson in 1979, had been a "big time high school football player" (Avery 2011, 15) who dropped out of college after a few years, married early, and started to work. Times were tough, but the family always had food on the table. By the middle of World War II, his father held a steady job. "It wasn't *The Grapes of Wrath*, but it wasn't uptown either" (Cahill 1985). Clint Sr. had to give up the good job he had as a jewelry salesman to join the defense industry to avoid the draft, which he did during the war. In his formative years, the young Clint slouched his way through high school—he felt more at home in a jazz club than a classroom—and graduated in 1949.

I have always read Eastwood's life story (mythologized as it has become) as common to all Americans after the banks closed, money and jobs disappeared, countless people killed themselves in desperation or disgrace, and the world teetered on the edge of disaster. The majority of Americans were severely affected by the Great Depression that began with the stock market crash of October 1929 (Clint's dad, too, was crushed by the collapse). Back in the early thirties, when Clint and his sister were young, mothers and fathers were desperate to feed their children—one of the intents of the New Deal: "Relief for the unemployed and poor." In those days, my mother and father told me, their friends all talked about a shared national commitment to survival.

Hitler assumed power in Germany; the Japanese military took control of the East; and Jewish men, women, and children all over Europe began to disappear. Clint Sr., Ruth, little sister Jeanne, and the quickly growing boy mostly stuck together. Mother sang. Grandma had an old record player and lots of 78s. Once in Piedmont, he went to Havens Elementary and then Piedmont Junior High School. The teenager attended two high schools, Piedmont High and Oakland Technical High School, excelling in neither but far happier among the economic and racial diversity of Oakland, rather than in the posh and homogenous Piedmont (Schickel 1997, 38).

For two years after he graduated from high school at 19, Eastwood worked, as he often claims, at a dizzying number of jobs that simultaneously gave him an appreciation for the hard work of ordinary people and established (in the mythology of Eastwood as a masculine type) his ethic of "hard work." Judy Fayard, writing in *Life* in 1971, describes him "in and out of a dozen different jobs" (Fayard 1971, 48), and lists logger, gas station attendant, and steelworker. Another account says that Eastwood "cut timber, baled hay, fought forest fires, and labored more than a year as a lumberjack in Oregon. He has worked a blast furnace for the Bethlehem Steel Company in Texas, worked for Boeing in Seattle" (Grenier 1984, 62). For good measure, Grenier adds that Eastwood worked part-time as a stevedore. This is a comically long list of stereotypically masculine jobs, almost certainly more than he could have held in a mere few years—unless they overlapped: perhaps he fought fires during his time as a lumberjack, say.

Accuracy is not the point. The mythmakers are looking for some secret formula for the self-made man to attract other men not born to privilege. In Grenier's essay on Clint's early popularity, the time Eastwood spent wandering, working, and wandering some more presents a central strain. The places where he worked are the places where he was popular: "everyone in the movie industry knows that Eastwood and [Burt] Reynolds have a 'regional' appeal—so-so at best in New York (where the critical community is centered), but colossal draws in the West and South" (Grenier 1984, 62). Grenier says that his observations of movie audiences led him to think that "there are virtually two nations, each easily recognizable by manners and speech. Jane Fonda draws the 'university' crowd. Eastwood draws the skilled industrial workers, farmers, men who if they no longer work with their hands come from a different America from the Vassar that produced Jane Fonda and Meryl Streep" (Grenier 1984, 62). Clint appeals to those who, like him in these years, worked hard, were unpretentious, and adhered to a certain idea of manliness.

The tension between freedom and restraint, produced sonically in Clint's beloved jazz, can be used here as a frame to analyze and understand his own life. "Basically, I'm a drifter, a bum," he said in a 1969 interview (Warga 1969). "Drifting" up to Oregon to become a lumberjack is part of this mystique—he had the freedom to do what he wanted. The jobs were never easy: they required physical fitness and hard labor that required a discipline to bring the freedom under control.

Freedom in Clint's post–high school years meant working innumerable jobs across the western United States: a lumberjack in Oregon, a steelworker in Texas, a gas station attendant in California, a baler of hay, and others—masculine, labor-filled jobs, which would serve publicity departments well later in his life. He worked hard—his work ethic became famous—but he hesitated to commit himself too readily to a single bailiwick.

The paradox of Eastwood's career begins to form during discussions of his post–high school life. His work ethic allows him to work well within the constraints of budgets and shooting schedules. Yet, he always has preserved the freedom to do the unexpected, to try something

new. This tension undergirds the stories of the young Clint's wander-
ings, switching from one thing to the other but always committing to
the job at hand when he has it.

Restraint was thrust upon Clint when he was drafted into the Korean
War whether he liked it or not. I don't remember the fear of the draft
in the fifties, although I remember my cousin John, who was deployed,
complained of an astonishing lack of planning by the generals that put
him and his boys in danger the entire time.

But the Vietnam draft—and the terrible fear of the A-1 draft notice
that meant horror, maiming, murder, lifelong nightmares, and possibly
death—marked the sixties and seventies. Clint was wise enough to fear
the Korean War and want a draft exemption. He planned to enter college,
in part to get an exemption, but the draft board, in Schickel's words, was
"in no mood to indulge young men who had wasted years finding themselves while their more prudent contemporaries had been busy securing
their college exemptions" (Schickel 1997, 47). Clint received the draft
notice, forwarded from a previous address, a mere week before he was due
to report for duty. Luck, for once, was not enough to satisfy Uncle Sam,
and his period of freedom and wandering ended in spring 1951.

Because Clint was an excellent swimmer, he was assigned to be a
swimming instructor at Fort Ord, not far from Carmel, where he would
eventually settle. "Everybody got shipped to Korea except me," he re-
called later. "My name just didn't come up. So I figured I'd make the
best of it and went up and talked to the captain. I said, 'Look, I'm only
a private, but I think I can handle this swimming pool thing' " (Knight
1974, 60). The captain agreed, and he spent the next few years at the
pool. It was a pleasant assignment, hardly the disaster he had feared
when he received the notice, and far from the combat in Korea. He
enjoyed far more freedom than most members of the armed services—
he even had time, according to Schickel, to add to his list of manly
jobs, albeit part-time ones: a sugar refinery worker and as a night club
bouncer (Schickel 1997, 57). All in all, it was a "terrific deal for being
in the Service" (Knight 1974, 60), as he put it.

In the fall of 1951, however, a harrowing plane crash provided the
Eastwood myth with fodder that served his publicists well in his early
years as a burgeoning television and film star, even though Eastwood
himself did not discuss it very much. To get back to Fort Ord from a trip

to Seattle, where his parents and a girlfriend lived, the young soldier hitched a ride on a small Navy plane, which ran into trouble during the trip. The plane lost communications and ran out of gas, and eventually the pilot had to ditch the plane into the ocean, a bit north of San Francisco. Accounts vary about what happened next. On October 1, 1951, long before Eastwood was anything more than an army private, *The Los Angeles Times* ran an Associated Press report, which said:

> Pvt. Clinton Eastwood, 21, of Seattle, a Ft. Ord soldier returning from leave, and Lt. (j.g.) F.C. Anderson of San Diego, the pilot, reached separate points on the rocky Tomales Bay Point Reyes coast after paddling several hours in small rubber life rafts . . . . He [Eastwood] said breakers had tossed him off the life raft and he was caught in an undertow attempting to land, after paddling about two miles from the crash. ("Two Men Swim Ashore . . . ")

An account from 1969, when Eastwood was a huge star, portrays the journey as more harrowing: "[The pilot] had a Mae West [life jacket] and I didn't," an article by Wayne Warga quotes him as saying. "We both made it, but I had the most work to do. I didn't mind the swim, it was the five-mile hike before I found a highway" (Warga 1969).

The account of Richard Schickel, Clint's friend and approved biographer, goes into much more depth and includes evocative details like the bioluminescence of the sealife that caused the young man to wonder if, in his exhaustion, he were hallucinating (Schickel 1997, 54). In this version, however, there are neither rafts nor life vests: Eastwood swims the whole way, and it's a longer distance—three or four miles— than in the Associated Press (AP) report. Stories like this complement early profiles that portray the actor as extremely masculine and physically fit. In spite of any exaggerations, the incident was doubtless terrifying. Eastwood's late career movie *Hereafter*, the beginning of which takes place as a tsunami engulfs a small community and the movie's heroine, captures some sense of near drowning.

By the summer of 1953, Clint was out of the army and moved to Los Angeles, in part to be near his new girlfriend, model Maggie Johnson. They married in December. Using the GI Bill, he enrolled in college at the City College of Los Angeles, where he took classes while he worked more odd jobs: gas station attendant, apartment building maintenance man, swimming pool digger.

During the mid-fifties, Clint first became interested in acting. Stories of his entry into Hollywood emphasize happenstance, in keeping with the narrative of Clint as a wanderer unwilling to commit too readily to any one path. According to most accounts, including a July 5, 1959 *Boston Globe* profile, and "The Luckiest Gunslinger," a profile by Rick Du Brow that ran in the *Chicago Tribune* on December 24, 1961, the story begins with a visit to Fort Ord by an assistant director at Universal pictures. The man, who was shooting film on the base, invited Clint to look him up on the studio lot after discharge. Other aspiring actors, including David Janssen—who would eventually star in the popular television series *The Fugitive*—were also stationed at Fort Ord and may have helped pique Eastwood's interest, as did another friend, Chuck Hill.

Even though the assistant director did not work at Universal by the time Clint left the army, Clint still managed to make his way onto the lot. There, he made friends with a cinematographer, Irving Glassberg, and a director, Arthur Lubin, who became his champions. After a few false starts, Lubin convinced Universal to sign him as a contract player (Eliot 2009, 33). It was hardly his great acting talent that led Lubin to advocate for him. Rather, Eastwood was young, charming, and good-looking. Lubin is quoted as calling Clint "quite amateurish" but also "tall and slim and very handsome looking," according to Patrick McGilligan's biography (McGilligan 2002, 60). Marc Eliot writes that Lubin, a contract director with a series of unremarkable credits, may have been looking for a fruitful director–star relationship like the one shared by Douglas Sirk and Rock Hudson (Eliot 2009, 37).

Regardless, Clint's time as a contract player did not last. He appeared in a few small roles but nothing that took advantage of his particular strengths. In October 1955, his contract was not renewed by Universal. He returned to odd jobs, this time digging swimming pools. For a while, he collected unemployment (Eliot 2009, 37).

Clint was accepted as a client by the agent Irving Leonard, whom he had met at Universal. Leonard landed him a small part in *The First Traveling Saleslady* (Eliot 2009, 39). He had nearly renounced acting when *Rawhide* came along. Clint was cast (not without difficulty) as the sidekick Rowdy Yates to Eric Fleming, who played trail guide Gil Favor. *Rawhide* was the break he sought.

REFERENCES AND FURTHER READING

Alford, Matthew. 2010. *Reel Power: Hollywood Cinema and American Superiority*. London: Pluto Press.

Avery, Kevin, ed. 2011. *Conversations with Clint: Paul Nelson's Lost Interviews with Clint Eastwood, 1979–1983*. New York: Continuum.

Beard, William. 2000. *Persistence of Double Vision: Essays on Clint Eastwood*. Edmonton, Canada: University of Alberta Press.

Cahill, Tim. 1985. "Clint Eastwood's American Dream." *Rolling Stone*, July 4. http://www.rollingstone.com/movies/news/clint-eastwoods-american-dream-19850531. Accessed February 20, 2014.

"Draft Call for 'Rawhide' Star Led to Acting Career." *The Boston Globe*, July 5, 1959.

Eliot, Marc. 2009. *Clint Eastwood: American Rebel*. New York: Crown Publishing Group.

Fayard, Judy. 1971. "Who Can Stand 32,580 Seconds of Clint Eastwood?" *Life*, July 23, 44–48.

Gorman, Bill. 2012. "Republican National Convention Draws 30.3 Million, Down 8 Million from 2008." *TV by the Numbers*, August 31. http://tvbythenumbers.zap2it.com/2012/08/31/republican-national-convention-final-night-draws-30–3-million-viewers-down-8-million-from-2008/146959/. Accessed February 20, 2014.

Grenier, Richard. 1984. "The World's Favorite Movie Star." *Commentary*, April, 61–67.

Halperin, Mark, and John Heilemann. 2013. *Double Down: Game Change 2012*. New York: Penguin Press.

Kapsis, Robert E., and Kathie Coblentz, eds. 1999. *Clint Eastwood: Interviews*. Jackson: University Press of Mississippi.

Knight, Arthur. 1974. "*Playboy* Interview: Clint Eastwood." *Playboy*, February, 57–72, 170–72.

McGilligan, Patrick. 2002. *Clint: The Life and Legend*. New York: St. Martin's Press.

Schickel, Richard. 1997. *Clint Eastwood: A Biography*. New York: Vintage.

"Two Men Swim Ashore After Naval Plane Crash." *The Los Angeles Times*, October 1, 1951.

Warga, Wayne. 1969. "Clint Eastwood: He Drifted Into Stardom." *The Los Angeles Times*, June 22.

Chapter 2

CLINT: FROM *RAWHIDE* TO THE SPAGHETTI WESTERNS

Rawhide, which aired on CBS from January 1959 to January 1966, tells the story of a cattle drive led by trail boss Gil Favor (Eric Fleming) and his right-hand man, the incomparably named Rowdy Yates, played by Clint Eastwood. It played for 217 episodes over eight seasons, including 13 with Eastwood as top-billed. The big break, however, almost did not happen. The studio shot the pilot episode of the series in February 1958 and after it was picked up, the first 10 episodes were shot from June to September. As John Fink put it at the time, "Scheduled to start on TV Sept. 29, the series suddenly was withdrawn—forever, as far as its cast knew. It finally found its way to TV in January" (Fink 1959), almost a year after the pilot was shot. The article notes that the uncertainty was particularly hard for Eastwood. "The anxiety was terrific," Eastwood explains in the article. Using his history of odd jobs and hard work, he continues:

When I first got out of the service I went to the Los Angeles State college [sic] during the day and studied at night. I managed an apartment house and worked nights as a mechanic [another job for the list!], and then I'd come home and listen to the complaints of the tenants, all their little problems, and I got pretty sick of it. (Fink 1959)

Rawhide, the article concludes, "ended what Eastwood calls a year of acute frustration." And when it premiered, it was a hit.

Looking back from 2014, it is difficult to imagine how popular Westerns were on television around the time of *Rawhide*'s premiere. Eliot notes that in 1958 "a little less than one-third of all prime-time network TV shows (30/108) were westerns" (Eliot 2009, 49). Airwaves of the late-1950s were flooded with shows like *Maverick, Sugarfoot, Gunsmoke, The Virginian, The Rifleman, Lawman, Have Gun, Will Travel, Colt.45*, and many, many more. The shows were formulaic throwbacks to the B-movie Westerns of the early Hollywood studio system, often produced by the same studios, like Warner Brothers, that produced those earlier films.

Rawhide was neither the most successful, nor the least. It was a bit of a late arrival but was among the longest lasting of the Westerns, and for four of its seasons, it was in the top 25 programs on the air (Brooks and Marsh 1981, 924–25). I watched the program nearly every Friday evening with my dad, a professor of American History and a specialist in the post–Civil War period in which the show takes place. In college, young men and women my age preferred *The Huntley-Brinkley Report*, believe it or not, a news program that aired every weeknight. We crowded the dormitory lounges to follow the election news (Kennedy vs. Nixon); threats from Red China, the Soviet Union, and a hardly chastened postwar Germany; and the dramatic events in Cuba.

But back home during vacations, I sandwiched *Rawhide* in between dates; papers on topics such as Gray's "Elegy in a Country Churchyard"; or studying textbooks for courses I wanted to avoid by taking the final exams before the class started. Or movies like *Carousel* or *Vertigo* (1956 and 1958, respectively) that played at the nearby one-screen movie house that once dotted every main street in America. *Rawhide* ended in January 1966, but like most long-running serials, it had a healthy afterlife as syndicated reruns. My dad and I swung right back into those heady days whenever I came home to visit, adding reruns of *Bonanza, Gunsmoke*, and *Have Gun, Will Travel*—all popular shows from the same period.

Clint's sweet role in the TV hit Rawhide *prepared audiences for the release of the brilliantly scripted Spaghetti Westerns, which made him an international star and an icon. (AP Photo/DFS)*

The show was envisioned as Eric Fleming's, but as anyone who watches the first season knows, Clint stands out. The show of course had many appeals—not the least of which was the theme song, insanely catchy and written by Oscar-winning composer Dmitri Tiomkin. It was mesmerizing, unforgettable, like the theme to *Chariots of Fire* or *Star Wars*. Composer Dmitri Tiomkin won two Oscars for the music to the hit movie *High Noon* in 1952, which starred Gary Cooper, with whom the young Clint Eastwood was frequently compared. Clint was bit shorter and much slimmer than Fleming, with a sweet if slightly kooky comic manner and a tendency, befitting of the name Rowdy, to get in trouble whenever he went into town along the long trail from San Antonio to Sedalia, MO. While Fleming had the deep-bass-voice-seriousness of Brace Beemer in *The Lone Ranger* (a popular radio show, with 2,956 episodes that played from 1933 to 1954), Rowdy's voice and manner pleased viewers with its slight lilt and frequent humorous asides. His hairstyle and face reminded teens and older teens (say up to age 70 and beyond, males and females) of other stars like James Dean and Marlon Brando. Gil Favor was the straight (very straight) man to Rowdy's slightly off-kilter playfulness.

Clint Eastwood may have possessed the manly demeanor of these stars, and he was certainly a screen idol like them (albeit on a smaller screen), but his acting style differed from theirs. The rigors of the method acting style did not suit his preference for improvisation and intuitiveness, better fitted to the fast pace of a television series and grounded in an artistic sensibility long immersed in jazz.

A television show provided Clint a paycheck and popularity, but creative freedom—the ability to choose roles, direct, be in movies, or just relax—eluded him. In a 1959 article by Ron Tepper, Eastwood alludes to the rigors of that drive, noting that he works "six days a week and eight to 10 hours a day" (Tepper 1959). This is almost certainly less than the reality, since network or studio publicists would not have wanted him or other actors describing poor working conditions. The network also exercised tight control over his personal appearances and hiatus roles. Eliot relays that the network would not let Clint take any movie roles or guest appearances in non-cowboy clothes (Eliot 2009, 54–55), and he had an undoubtedly full schedule being a screen idol. In one publicity blurb he is seen modeling the latest lawn equipment with his wife. Freida Zylstra talks about his cooking prowess in another publicity piece that ran in the *Chicago Tribune* on July 6, 1962, under the headline "Rawhide Ramrod at Home on the Kitchen Range." Eastwood even provides a (publicist approved, one presumes) recipe for barley and bone marrow soup. Universal hired him out with Paul Brinegar and Sheb Wooley to do rodeo performances: they performed by "singing, dancing, fake rope twirling" (Eliot 2009, 55). The experience on the road endlessly rehearsing the rituals and myths of the West influenced Eastwood's later, deeply personal film *Bronco Billy* (1980). The established trajectory of young television stars meant that Clint had to cut a record of two popular songs of the period, whether he wanted to or not. "Bobby-Sox Idol Made it the Hard Way," reads the headline of a James Bacon article from November 26, 1961, in the *Baltimore Sun*. Bacon proclaims wryly: "He can carry a tune—and that's not commercial anymore. But we recorded him anyhow" (Bacon 1961). Clint's refusal to follow the time's musical trends probably thrilled him. He eventually recorded a full album, *Rawhide's Clint Eastwood Sings Cowboy Favorites*. All of this was in addition to the grueling production schedule of an hour-long television program. Surely the low point of his *Rawhide* days was his appearance on *Mister Ed:* "Clint Eastwood meets Mr. Ed."

Over the course of the series, the drive encounters bandits, Native Americans, corrupt towns, and many, many women. One of the many publicity items written on Eastwood once *Rawhide* began airing calls it a "never-ending cattle drive" (Tepper 1959). Clint says in the article: "I don't know if we'll ever finish our cattle drive but if we do we can always pick up another herd and head back to Texas" (Tepper 1959). Watching the show, the cattle drive does seem never ending, with an infinite supply of conventional Western tropes like ghost towns, corrupt lawmen, "fallen" women, and mysterious strangers. A small band of regulars includes a Mexican named Jesus and listed in the credits as "Hey Soos," and the comic cook Wishbone, a ubiquitous figure in narratives about men on journeys, whether on horses or ships, played by Paul Brinegar. After Fleming left the series, producers added Raymond St. Jacques, the first African American actor to appear in a regular role on a Western series.

A review of the premiere in the industry magazine *Variety* trashes the show with gleeful abandon:

> To discuss the premiere story on CBS-TV's latest commercial entry, "Rawhide," in detail would be to give it too much credit. But the initial hour, modeled somewhat after the frame-story format of the much better "Wagon Train," was absolutely—to the point of near incredibility—loaded with every well known cliché in hoss [Western] opera-dom, put together with random thoughtlessness. (Art. 1959)

Later reviews from the magazine are kinder, though they still focus on the clichés that dominate the storytelling and the padding necessary to stretch the show to an hour. Most Westerns were half an hour (Jose 1960). Reviews did not seem to matter, though; one critic noted with accuracy that "For the fans, Eric Fleming as the trail boss, and Clint Eastwood, as his stalwart young sidekick, probably can do no wrong" (Horowitz 1962). It was the winning cast—and Clint was the most winning of all—that led to the show's popularity.

We can peek behind the phony sets, prosaic camera angles, and thin characterizations to find not only the basis for Eastwood's stardom as an actor but also the raw materials for many of Eastwood's later directorial efforts. In a late episode, "Encounter at Boot Hill," Rowdy and his gang come across a town whose corrupt sheriff is protecting the men who killed one of Rowdy's crew—a plot that resonates with Eastwood's 1992 masterpiece, *Unforgiven*. Rowdy's relationship with his father recalls an early Western that Eastwood admired, *The Oxbow Incident* (William A. Wellman, 1943), which in 1968 was to inspire Malpaso's first film, *Hang 'Em High*, in which Clint starred but did not direct.

The festering post–Civil War animus between North and South is common to *Rawhide* and to Eastwood's revisionist effort *The Outlaw Josey Wales*. The war's trauma also runs like a polluted river underneath *The Searchers*, John Ford's landmark Western, one of the first along with Ford's later film *The Man Who Shot Liberty Valance* that sought to rework and undermine the conventions of the Western genre.

An active process of demystification drives *The Searchers*, as the Western genre, constructed in part by Ford himself in earlier films like *Stagecoach*, suddenly collapsed under the moral weight of westward colonialism and violence toward Native Americans. *The Searchers* has everything: violence, forbidden love, an uncharacteristically complex portrayal by Ford of Native Americans, and John Wayne as a Civil War veteran with an evil past, who, after the war, roams the country robbing Union pay stations. He is a vehement racist, and spends years—the bulk of the movie—searching for his niece who was abducted by the Comanche. In *The Searchers*, the fate of the Western hero is bitterly clear: he becomes extraneous to American civilization's progress, a wanderer not by choice, but rather because the domesticated world he helped make possible through his violence has no room for him.

In a few years, Clint Eastwood would join a late-career John Wayne on lists of the country's top box office draws, with films that revisit and revise the Western myth, much like *The Searchers* does. But *Rawhide* also resonates with *The Searchers*. The sense of justice that transcends political or legal bureaucracies appears in *Rawhide* episodes like "Incident of the Thirteenth Man," in which Rowdy is placed on a jury for a trial against a town's most prominent citizen (synopsis based on Tim Booher's summary from the *Rawhide* site by Debra Hamel). The guilty defendant, with the help of an informant and yet another corrupt sheriff, intimidates the jury into an acquittal, and only the cook

Wishbone's, and then Rowdy's, sense of justice prevents the acquittal from succeeding. The idea of an individual sense of honor that stands as a bulwark against the corruption of a bureaucratic justice system recurs in several Eastwood films, including the wildly successful *Dirty Harry* series. *Rawhide* was the first step in Eastwood's long history with the Western and the first step toward his superstardom. Its success paled, however, before the sensation that followed.

It might not seem like it in 2014, but the 1950s and 1960s were a time of crisis for the movie industry. At the same time that top television programs routinely had 30 million viewers or more (more than any single TV show now receives, besides a few football games and awards shows), the film industry was flailing. The Hollywood studio system, in which studios controlled production, distribution, and exhibition of films, was deemed monopolistic in 1948, which forced studios to sell their lucrative theater chains. Television's ascendancy also drew audiences away from movie theaters. It was not until the late 1960s that the "New Hollywood Cinema" appeared, instigated by the successes of *Bonnie and Clyde* and *The Graduate* and then with the blockbuster business model (fewer films but with larger budgets) that began with *Jaws*. The 1960s were a time when those who could make films often took risks, because the studios had little to lose. It was also a time when foreign films—Michelangelo Antonioni, Jean-Luc Godard—started to gain real traction.

A television star who wanted to break into movies had few options. CBS imposed restrictions on the kinds of roles he could take, and the movie industry did not seem to welcome television actors. Thus, in 1964, during *Rawhide*'s summer hiatus, Eastwood decided to shoot a film in Europe, a decision that would catapult him to fame beyond anything he had achieved before. *Rawhide*'s ratings had slid since its peak in 1960–1961 (Brooks and Marsh 1981, 925), and Clint's attempts to direct episodes of the program were consistently rebuffed, to his chagrin. Only in later tellings, including the more-or-less authorized account in Schickel, does the tumult in his personal life emerge as another contributing factor in his decision to leave the country. He was on rocky ground with his wife; his relationship with Roxanne Tunis, who sometimes appeared in *Rawhide*, produced his first daughter, Kimber (Schickel 1997, 127–28).

He would also tell *Rolling Stone*, "Sergio [Leone] had only directed one other picture, but they told me he had a good sense of humor, and I liked the way he interpreted the *Yojimbo* script. And I had nothing to lose, because I had the series to go back to as soon as the hiatus was over. So I felt, 'Why not?' I'd never been to Europe. That was reason enough to go" (Cahill 1985). The decision to take a chance on the young director Sergio Leone and a low budget was more luck than wile. Eastwood agreed to star in *The Magnificent Stranger*, to be shot at a breakneck speed in Spain (Frayling 2000). He was paid $15,000, a small sum for a movie, but more than he could have made digging swimming pools. He was well prepared for the quick pace and shoddy sets from his time on *Rawhide*, but Leone's directorial vision was new: he had style, and lots of it.

The film, *A Fistful of Dollars*, as it was subsequently renamed, was an unauthorized but instantly recognizable Western remake of Akira Kurosawa's 1961 Samurai film, *Yojimbo*. Eliot notes that Clint loved Kurosawa films and "had often shown them during his projectionist stint at Fort Ord" (Eliot 2009, 59), another addition to his list of odd jobs. In addition to *Yojimbo*, Leone's film was influenced by the 1929 Dashiell Hammett novel *Red Harvest* (Paul Nelson quoted in Avery 2011, 30) and the 18th-century Italian farce by Carlo Goldoni, *Servant of Two Masters*, still performed by theater troupes and recently adapted into the Tony Award–winning play *One Man, Two Guvnors*. More than anything, however, *Fistful* was a capital-W Western—part of a group of movies named Spaghetti Westerns because the majority (among a cohort of over 300) were Italian-language productions.

Clint starred as the Man with No Name (a "ronin," a man with no master), who, dressed in a serape and often shot in dramatic extreme close-ups, rides into a Mexican border town and rids it of two corrupt and warring factions, all while opportunistically making money for himself. Unsurprisingly, Quentin Tarantino loves the Eastwood/Leone collaborations: the trilogy was Western in the way that *Pulp Fiction* is a crime film or *Inglourious Basterds* is a war film: the genre is embraced, exaggerated, and subverted simultaneously. With the *Dollars Trilogy*, the sunlight was brighter, the violence more graphic than in any other Western. The score by Ennio Morricone instantly conjured gunfights and cowboys on horseback. The theme of *The Good, The Bad, and the*

Ugly—doo-da-loo-da-loo . . . Wah wahhh wahhhh—along with the one from *Rawhide*, quickly passed into screen music history.

And Eastwood was the Western hero or antihero *par excellence*. He immediately commands the screen even in a distance shot (the opening of *A Fistful of Dollars*), imaged by a pair of worn boots (a trope from *For a Few Dollars More* that reappears at the opening of *The Gauntlet* when Clint's character Gus and his empty whiskey bottle tumble out of a car), or whispering through his cigar to the consternation and terror of the bad guy in front of him (*The Good, the Bad, and the Ugly*). He told interviewer Tim Cahill that much of the Man with No Name's laconic demeanor was due to his own reworking of the script: "The script was very expository, yeah. It was an outrageous story, and I thought there should be much more mystery to the person. . . . In the script he [the Man with No Name] just goes on forever. He talks about his mother, all kinds of subplots that come out of no-where, and it goes on and on and on. I thought that was not essential, so I just rewrote the scene the night before we shot it" (Cahill 1985).

Clint finished the shoot with a crew that worked in three languages: English, Spanish, and Italian (Eliot 2009, 66). By the way, when the star introduced Morricone's lifetime achievement award at the Oscars in 2009, he spoke in flawless Italian. Certainly he could have memorized the lines, but with his overall talents and musicality, he might well have learned Italian on the shoots in the sixties and maintained it. He often masks his intellectual side, an imagined anti-intellectual identity that conservatives are happy to promote. (A good lesson to learn from Clint's engagement with the Spaghetti Westerns: If someone ever suggests that you go abroad and hang out with people who speak a lot of different languages, just go. Maybe you'll get lucky.)

Soon Eastwood was back on *Rawhide*. He was certain that if the Leone movies were a bust, it would be a bust an ocean away; his reputation, such as it was in the sixties, was hardly at stake. During *Rawhide*'s six-day workweeks, he did not think about it much at all. In one dramatic and funny telling:

[Eastwood] would have forgotten the whole thing, except for a trade paper blurb. It seems that some new film in Rome was making money hand over fist. Its title, appropriately, was "Fistful of

Dollars." With astonishment Clint read one day that its star was an American player named Clint Eastwood. (Adams 1969)

Without realizing it, because he was not aware of the title change, Clint Eastwood had become a major international star. As he recounted later: "It became just a *huge* sensation all over the country [Italy]. Then they sold it to Spain—Spain was co producer on it—and Germany. It was doing real well in all those places, but they couldn't release it over here [in the U.S.] due to all the litigation on *Yojimbo*" (Avery 2011, 29).

A Fistful of Dollars led to two more Spaghetti Westerns, as the Italian-made films were known, that featured the collaboration between Leone and Eastwood: 1965's *For a Few Dollars More* and 1966's *The Good, The Bad, and The Ugly*. Each was an international sensation, and Clint's salary skyrocketed from a puny $15,000 for the first film to $50,000 for the sequel and $250,000 plus a percentage of the grosses for the third (Crowther 1966).

One problem remained, however: Clint, Leone, and United Artists still needed to get the *Dollars Trilogy*, as it was known, into American theaters. Although the films were extremely violent by the tame standards of American studio film, restrictions on violent content loosened quickly in the wake of 1967's *Bonnie and Clyde*, with its famously ultraviolent finale. *Yojimbo*'s copyright holders caused more pressing legal trouble. Leone had asked Kurosawa for the right to adapt *Yojimbo* but did not have the $10,000 Kurosawa demanded. Kurosawa refused the deal.

The three films were finally released in the United States during 1967. Clint as the Man with No Name supplanted Clint as *Rawhide*'s Rowdy Yates in the American imagination. Ironic, irreverent, and episodic replaced sweet, goofy, and formulaic.

American critics did not quite know what to make of the *Trilogy*. It arrived from Europe around the same time as art house classics like *Blow Up*, *Week End*, and *Persona* (by Antonioni, Godard, and Ingmar Bergman, respectively), but the Spaghetti Westerns were far from art house. They bordered on exploitation. Most critics at the time agreed that they were not good—always a touchy word in film criticism—although some critics embarrassingly seemed to enjoy them anyway.

Regardless, they are now considered classics, elevated through decades of fan love, including from latter-day filmmakers like Quentin

Tarantino. In 1971, Rex Reed called them "camp institutions" (Reed 1971). Crowther refers to Leone as an "avant-garde John Ford" (Crowther 1966). Later, in Crowther's review of A *Fistful of Dollars* for the *New York Times*, he expresses his bewilderment at what he saw when he watched: "Cowboy camp of an order that no one has dared in American films since, gosh. Gary Cooper's 'The Virginian' (which is prototypical) is flung on the screen with shameless candor in the European-made, English-dubbed, Mexican-localized Western, 'A Fistful of Dollars'" (Crowther 1967). He calls Clint a "cool-cat bandit," and "simply another fabrication of a personality, half cowboy and half gangster, going through the ritualistic postures and exercises of each." His distinction, Crowther continues, "is that he succeeds in being ruthless without seeming cruel, fascinating without being realistic. He is a morbid, amusing, campy fraud" (Crowther 1967). Schickel, Eastwood's biographer, describes other critical responses: many thought it was sadistic or just bad (Schickel 1997, 179). By the time of the release of *For a Few Dollars More*, Crowther had reached "full moral outrage" at the film's violence, according to the assessment by Schickel (1997, 181).

Rawhide made Clint a star, but the Spaghetti Westerns made him an icon. Clint's Man with No Name has an indelible stare. In Leone's extreme, wide-screen close-ups, Eastwood's steely eyes, squinting in the bright sun, quickly became a signature image. A cigarillo stuck out of his mouth; it does not often appear lit, but the viewer has the impression that he does not care (Clint himself does not smoke). His face was weathered, his gait was insouciant, his speech, when he did speak, dripped with wry disdain. The word for the Man with No Name was "cool." He was comic, but not in an obvious way. It never seemed as if he were working too hard, whether it was to rid a town of corruption or to gain an audience's approval. The minimalism of Eastwood's acting suddenly seemed an asset—the nonchalance arising not from lack of affect but rather from lack of what we might call moral outrage. Journalist Ken Michaels put it this way:

How did Clint happen and what does it mean? The Western-looking guy with the hard Western name who rides in coolly and shoots up the town. That's the image. You don't mess with him.

His eyes say it. His face. His whole demeanor. Cool. Controled
[sic] . . . the coolly controlled man of violence. (Michaels 1970)

Eastwood's persona was integral to the success of the *Dollars* trilogy just
as the trilogy became a vital component in his meteoric rise.

With such massive successes, however, came the ambivalent role
of "icon," to return to our discussion of Clint's appearance before the
RNC in 2012. When American moviegoers imagine Clint Eastwood,
they imagine the steely glare, the cigar, and the serape (unwashed over
the three movies) and associate him with particular now-indelible
markers of the Western antihero.

Or, after *Dirty Harry*, some Americans (whether they have seen Eastwood's early movies or not) associate him with shooting punks and a
disregard for legal bureaucracies. Or, after *The Outlaw Josey Wales*, they
(or at least spectators who do not examine the movie closely) associate
him with a furious snarl and a pistol in each hand. Clint Eastwood's
status as an icon—thoroughly masculine, thoroughly American, drip-
ping with 1970s disenchantment—began with these films. The iconic
image, embellished over four decades, embodies his wild successes but
also constrains him. He cannot speak as Clint Eastwood, the man (or
even as an ironic stand-up comic named Clint Eastwood) without fall-
out. With that massive image of *The Outlaw Josey Wales*, detached from
context, beamed onto the wall behind his Tampa lectern, he fell prey
to well-worn forces of deification or demonization after his infamous
RNC convention appearance.

REFERENCES AND FURTHER READING

Adams, Marjory. 1969. "Clint Eastwood's Credo: Say It with Action,
Not Words." *Boston Globe*, March 16.
Art. [no further name given]. 1959. "*Rawhide* Review." *Variety*, Janu-
ary 14, 39.
Avery, Kevin, ed. 2011. *Conversations with Clint: Paul Nelson's Lost
Interviews with Clint Eastwood, 1979–1983*. New York: Con-
tinuum.
Bacon, James. 1961. "Bobby-Sox Idol Made It the Hard Way." *The
Baltimore Sun*, November 26.

Brooks, Tim, and Earle Marsh. 1981. *The Complete Directory to Prime Time Network TV Shows, 1946-Present*. 2nd ed. New York: Ballantine Books.

Cahill, Tim. 1985. "Clint Eastwood's American Dream." *Rolling Stone*, July 4. http://www.rollingstone.com/movies/news/clint-eastwoods-american-dream-19850531. Accessed February 20, 2014.

Crowther, Bosley. 1966. "U.S. Actor Heads 'Em Off at Piazza." *The New York Times*, May 30.

Crowther, Bosley. 1967. "Screen: 'A Fistful of Dollars' Opens." *The New York Times*, February 2.

Eliot, Marc. 2009. *Clint Eastwood: American Rebel*. New York: Crown Publishing Group.

Fink, John. 1959. "Actor in a Void: What Does He Do, Waiting for a Break? He Sweats It Out." *The Chicago Tribune*, March 7.

Frayling, Christopher. 2000. *Sergio Leone: Something to Do with Death*. New York: Faber and Faber.

Hamel, Debra. *Rawhide* website. http://www.rawhide.ws/. Accessed February 21, 2014.

Horowitz, Murray. 1962. "*Rawhide* Review." *Variety*, September 26, 30.

Jose. [no further name given]. 1960. "*Rawhide* Review." *Variety*, October 5, 37.

Michaels, Ken. 1970. "Fugitive from a Spaghetti Factory." *The Chicago Tribune*, Nov 15.

Reed, Rex. 1971. "Despite His Spaghetti Westerns, Clint's Head, Heart Not Tied to a Tumbleweed." *The Chicago Tribune*, April 4.

Schickel, Richard. 1997. *Clint Eastwood: A Biography*. New York: Vintage.

"Spring Roundup of New Garden Tools." *The Los Angeles Times*, May 20, 1962.

Tepper, Ron. 1959. "First Big Break: Clint Eastwood Thrives on Never-Ending Cattle Drive." *The Los Angeles Times*, April 26.

Zylstra, Freida. 1962. "Rawhide Ramrod at Home on the Kitchen Range." *The Chicago Tribune*, July 6.

Chapter 3

CLINT TAKES CHARGE: MALPASO

By the end of the sixties, Clint Eastwood was four years out of a successful television series and two years past the American release of the final film in the *Dollars Trilogy*. Things should have been going well. Clint still was not satisfied, however, because he wanted to direct. His attempts to direct episodes of *Rawhide* had been refused. The critical establishment did not take him seriously as an artist, and opportunities did not appear. As tough as it was—and still is—for television actors to become major movie stars, it was—and still is—at least as difficult for a movie actor to successfully transition to directing, as George Clooney, Ben Affleck, and Jodie Foster could attest.

Clint's bundle of dollars (the infamous "fistful") allowed him to form his independent company, Malpaso—his first step to directing. True to Leone's satirical style, the word "malpaso"—the name for a creek near his home—means "bad step" in Spanish. In addition to the creek, the name gestures toward the riskiness of the proposition. Clint loved the dual meaning (Warga 1973). He did not have absolute freedom from having his own production company. For instance, he did not have the clout to diverge too heavily from the Westerns on which his name was built. At least he was not locked into a contract like the movie stars of old, or like he had been when making *Rawhide*. In 1968, he made *Hang 'Em High* and *Coogan's Bluff*, his first Malpaso productions.

While he was making *Coogan's Bluff*, Clint entered into fruitful collaboration with the second of his major, firsthand directorial influences, Don Siegel. Siegel was best known for his 1956 version of *Invasion of the Body Snatchers*, a brilliant science fiction movie shot in black and white that speaks to the atmosphere of paranoia prevalent in the 1950s, much like the fears spread by the Tea Party and right-wing radio today and very like a French movie from the forties, *Le Corbeau*, and a Danish one from 2012, *The Hunt*. A small-town doctor suspects that his patients' bodies are being taken over by aliens. *Invasion* so perfectly distilled the American political moment of the 1950s that we can hardly imagine that lightning would strike twice with *Dirty Harry*, Siegel's equally and perfectly of-its-time portrait of 1970s cynicism that followed the idealistic 1960s. A number of factors influenced Clint's development as a director, including his appreciation of classical Hollywood directors like Hawkes and Ford and his time on a fast-paced television show. But Leone, from whom Clint was estranged for at least 20 years, and Don Siegel informed so many facets of the young director's development.

Siegel and Eastwood shoot films efficiently, on time and under budget. Eastwood is famous for this, and at times (depending on the interviewer and publication, of course) he disparages directors whose obsession with formal flourishes, retakes, and obsessive planning get in the way of the production of a decent film (Avery 2011; Bates 1979). Some of the directors, who often use self-conscious and allusive visual styles, are considered the paragons of "New Hollywood." They absorbed classical film history as well as recent trends in art cinema like the French New Wave and saved the film industry—so the story goes—after the collapse of the studio system.

When I think of New Hollywood directors, the so-called movie brats come to mind: Francis Ford Coppola, Martin Scorsese, Roman Polanski, Robert Altman, Terrence Malick, and Sam Peckinpah, among others. I am not sure why they are at the top of the 1970s New Hollywood canon whereas others like Bob Fosse, Elaine May, and Clint Eastwood are relegated to the second breath. But in Eastwood's case, the economy of his direction may separate him from those with more flash. He never seems to be showing off, which may have garnered him critical derision early on but which also gave him a sense of nonchalant cool—what the Italian Leone would have called *sprezzatura*—that propelled his career. "I feel that, to call yourself a director, you've got to direct on the set," Clint told his friend Paul Nelson (Avery 2011, 39). The actual time spent among crew and with actors has to be more important than the storyboards and the editing and the obsessive planning. But at the same time, as Eastwood's preference for first takes is well known—when it comes to it, efficiency and economy were the greatest assets for him, at least in his early efforts. "I do have a fierce sense of economy," he told an interviewer in 1973 (Shales 1973). That sense allowed him to pursue projects for which the budgets may have been out of reach otherwise.

Siegel's and Eastwood's second collaboration produced *Two Mules for Sister Sara*, a Mexico-set Western in which Clint played opposite Shirley Maclaine (who currently co-stars in *Downton Abbey* as Lady Cora's American mother) as a prostitute posing as a nun. Clint also acted in *Paint Your Wagon*, yet another Western, a Lerner and Loewe musical loosely adapted by acclaimed writer Paddy Chayevsky and revised yet again by Lerner himself. (Clint sings.)

Where Eagles Dare, an action film set during World War II, made on location in Salzburg, and starring Richard Burton alongside Eastwood, exposed the contradictions of Clint's life even this early in his career. When asked why Richard Burton would make a wartime action movie, Burton apparently replied, "Because Clint's doing it" (Schickel 1997, 205). Eastwood thought the opposite—he wanted to work with Burton. Richard Burton was a movie star of the highest order, and during the *Where Eagles Dare* shoot, he was well into his first marriage to Elizabeth Taylor. The couple was the Kimye or Brangelina of their time, or perhaps the Beyoncé and Jay-Z, only bigger than all three. Eastwood would join the couple for drinks during the shoot—Burton throwing back far more than Clint, who stuck to beer (Schickel 1997, 204).

The two men's star images contrasted starkly. Instead of posing for or escaping the paparazzi with his even-more-famous wife, as Burton did, Clint kept his personal life private. At the beginning of the Austrian-set production, Clint had one daughter, though not with his wife. By the end of the filming, which went far beyond schedule, he and Maggie had a son, Kyle. Because of the production delays, he was unable to be present for the baby's birth. But did reporters follow him around, desperate for the latest scoop on his personal life? Not really, especially when compared to the swarms that followed Burton and Taylor. Clint Eastwood was a different kind of star. He was already an icon, to be sure, but so far associated with the Man with No Name, rather than with a lavish, diamond-studded private life or private jets in the Taylor–Burton style.

The films—*Two Mules for Sister Sara, Paint Your Wagon, Where Eagles Dare*—ran the gamut of minor hit to minor disaster, but 1971 established the next major turning point in Clint's career. Only huge hits and epic disasters followed over the ensuing 40 years, although which film was which depends upon perspective. He starred as a Union soldier in a Southern gothic drama; acquired his most iconic persona in *Dirty Harry*; and directed his first film, *Play Misty for Me*. The 1970s—Eastwood in his 40s—would be Clint's decade.

In the summer, Clint appeared in the Southern Gothic film, a third film for Siegel called *The Beguiled*. Clint described it as "our [Siegel's and his] version of an antiwar movie, and how people's lives are affected being even on the periphery of a war and how adversely it affects the civilian population" (Avery 2011, 57). Clint found himself

Clint in a scene from Two Mules for Sister Sara. *(AP Photo)*

opposite the legendary Geraldine Page, alongside a cast of young female actresses playing the students at the school. The film's narrative
of an injured Northern soldier taking refuge in a girl's school in Loui-
siana is heavy with atmosphere and Freudian symbolism: it was more
visually distinctive than Siegel's other films. It is also a racy film, full
of sex and violence, but so steeped in myth and symbolism that it does
not come across as excessive—it seems so atmospheric that it's hard to
believe the characters are real people rather than avatars telling some
deep, mythic story. Ken Michaels, who visited the set of the film for
an article in the *Chicago Tribune*, explains the content of the film in
a different way: "It's all matter-of-fact here: for nude scenes, obscenity
and all manner of violence the only operative judgment is pragmatic: if
something works, you do it. Responsibility, morality, taste—you don't
even talk about them" (Michaels 1970).

Present-day audiences, including—or perhaps *especially*—those who
do not enjoy Clint Eastwood movies in general, treasure *The Beguiled* as
a disturbing, weird, sexy, masterwork, but at the time, it was an unmiti-
gated flop. About a decade later, he would tell Paul Nelson:

> I've been accused of falling back to action-oriented films because
> of the failure commercially of that picture [*The Beguiled*], but that
> isn't the truth at all. . . . Don [Siegel] feels that the studio deserted
> on us. We had offers to take it to the Cannes Film Festival, for in-
> stance. I think we would've won it. The studio wouldn't do that.
> (Avery 2011, 59)

Indeed, the film *might* have taken home Cannes's highest prize, the
Palme d'Or. The French, including French critics and academics, began
to appreciate Eastwood's talents early on, far earlier than the American
critical establishment did.

Furthermore, in hindsight, the film complicates any predictable
narrative of Clint's career—that he is a bad actor who lucked into
roles because of looks. Once he achieves success as a director, it became easy for critics to pigeonhole Eastwood as a mediocre actor who
is also a great director. *The Beguiled*, along with the various other
small, quirky roles in which he cast himself (or, less frequently, was
cast by others), shows that Eastwood's interest in acting did not wane

with his directorial successes. If anything, his success as a director gave him the freedom to choose meatier roles and direct odder films than ever—*Bronco Billy* and *Honkytonk Man* (1982), unpretentious movies that he loved and that I love, too.

In 1971, however, American audiences greeted *The Beguiled* with a shrug. Without the film festival cachet, it failed as an art film, and since it did not seem to fit the typical Eastwood mold, it bombed commercially. Clint need not have worried, however, because 1971 also led to his directorial debut, a film packed with some of the problematic themes as *The Beguiled*: weaponized sexuality, emotional manipulation, and duplicity between the sexes. *Play Misty for Me* is a small film, a proto-*Fatal Attraction* about a disc jockey whose brief affair with a mentally disturbed listener—she always requests the titular song "Misty"—leads to terror and violence. Clint shot it economically, and to save money, worked for the minimum wage permitted by the acting and directing guilds (Schickel 1997, 248). Jessica Walter, known to contemporary audiences for her roles as Lucille Bluth on *Arrested Development* and Mallory Archer on *Archer*, played the female lead. As a side note, Clint could have lodged a plagiarism suit when *Fatal Attraction*, which starred Michael Douglas and Glenn Close, was released in theaters to great acclaim, but he just laughed.

During pre-production for *Misty*, Clint's father died suddenly of a heart attack, a devastating loss that caused the young man to commit even more to physical fitness. Tensions built between Clint and his studio Universal, which partnered with Malpaso on the latter's productions (Eliot 2009, 128). And yet, *Misty* was not a particularly difficult shoot, either. Clint's first film as a director featured a DJ literate in jazz—a perfect choice for someone whose artistic identify blossomed under the wings of the greats like Charlie Parker. It was a period of freedom for him: once again (as with *The Beguiled*) he was playing against type; he was able to make a film that interested him; and he could play with his own image as a masculine idol in intriguing ways. If the film has moments of self-indulgence, we must forgive them, for these diversions are *de rigeur* among first-time directors.

Consider another actor-turned-director, George Clooney, whose directorial debut *Confessions of a Dangerous Mind* is also overstuffed with stylistic flourishes, as though he wanted to fit in every idea he had in case he never got to make another film. The same went for Clint: he may have filmed *Play Misty for Me* on the cheap, but if he wanted to include a lengthy scene set to Roberta Flack's weepy ballad, "The First Time Ever I Saw Your Face," he was going to include it. In later films, he would establish a directorial style to match his minimalist acting and efficient shooting schedules, but even in this first directing effort, we can spot signs of what would become his signature style—especially the use of low-key lighting schemes, sometimes with only a single light source (credit Leone there, too).

Play Misty for Me did decent business in spite of a poor publicity campaign from Universal but was not received kindly by critics. As with *The Beguiled*, its reputation has since improved. Also like *The Beguiled*, some academics object to the film's portrayal of women. In interviews, Clint is not nearly as defensive about criticisms of his skill as an actor as he is about his skill as a director, and *Play Misty* brought him his first reviews as a director. Now that Clint Eastwood the director is wildly beloved by everyone, we cannot imagine how passionately some American critics disliked his films in the 1970s. His greatest critical foil was Pauline Kael at *The New Yorker*, whose brutal pans of his films are almost sardonically negative, but she was far from the only critic to dismiss his work. At times, as in his "lost" interviews with Paul Nelson from the late 1970s, finally published in 2011, he speaks as though the critics have a personal vendetta against him: "I remember I showed [*Play Misty for Me*] to John Cassavetes and he said, 'God, if they put Hitchcock's name on this, everybody'd rave'" (Avery 2011, 63). Cassavetes thought that critics were biased against Eastwood. Clint himself sometimes seemed to think so. The gulf between the negative critical response to *Misty* and its box office success widened with *Dirty Harry*, amazingly also released in 1971. Siegel directed it, but Clint himself took the reins when Siegel was not on set (Fayard 1971, 46). It became one of the highest-grossing films of the year and a hugely profitable franchise for Eastwood and his company. "Dirty" Harry Callahan is a San Francisco inspector pitted against a sadistic serial killer loosely based upon the Zodiac Killer in northern California of the late sixties and early seventies. Harry finds the killer—here called "Scorpio"—too late to save the little girl Scorpio had raped, buried alive, and left to die. Because Callahan searches Scorpio's apartment without a warrant, the police are forced to release the killer. When Scorpio strikes again, Callahan takes matters into his own hands and kills Scorpio himself.

Dirty Harry proved one of the most divisive films of the 1970s, with such wildly polarized responses that it seems to portend the contemporary political divide between left and right in 2014. Regardless of a spectator's individual political views, it is difficult to see *Dirty Harry* as anything other than an indictment of 1960s leftist idealism. That decade, epitomized by Bay Area student movements and hippie culture, led to a 1970s saturated with ineffective bureaucracy and political correctness run amuck, at least as *Dirty Harry* and Harry himself sees it. Played by Andy Robinson, Scorpio is a doughy sociopath, "a blank-faced embodiment of evil who personifies all that the American tough mentality despises: long-haired, pacifistic, whiny, effeminate," as one critic puts it (Epps 1972). He seems especially effete when compared to Callahan's cool, masculine angularity, further sculpting Clint Eastwood the actor into the icon inseparable from the image of his face. The conservative journal *Human Events* lavished praise on the film precisely because it seems to espouse a right-wing ideology about the role of police power. Verdon Cummings, writing in the journal, says that "In *Dirty Harry* we may have the first right-wing melodrama" (Cummings 1972, 12). He continues:

> *Dirty Harry* is more than an action film. It is social commentary, the kind of thing we received in the '60s with . . . films that told us that the right wing is going to take over the country. Only this time the roles are reversed. It is the *liberal* who is the villain. . . . It is the false compassion of liberals that is to blame for the punk's [Scorpio's] terrorist acts. (Cummings 1972, 12)

Critics on the left agreed, though unlike Cummings, they hated the film for this reason. Garrett Epps, whose column in his college newspaper *The Harvard Crimson* was reprinted in the *New York Times*, calls it "the vilest of the bunch" of similar films that include *Straw Dogs* and *The French Connection* (Epps 1972). "Its message," Epps continues, "is a frontal assault on the concept of law" (Epps 1972). "Fascist" is a descriptor often bandied about in discussions of *Dirty Harry*. Conservatives would probably reject this label, but as Eastwood's appearance at the Republican National Convention (during which he led the audience in a recitation of one of the character's most famous lines, "Go ahead, make my day") makes clear, many Republicans still embrace Harry Callahan and the values he embodies.

Clint, however, repeatedly denies that *Dirty Harry* or its sequels have any political content at all. He insists that the film is only a story. In a 1974 interview for *Playboy* with film scholar Arthur Knight, he says, "I don't think *Dirty Harry* was a fascist picture at all. It's just the story of one frustrated police officer in a frustrating situation on one particular case" (Knight 1974, 68). To Paul Nelson: "A lot of people tried to label *Dirty Harry* as a politically-oriented film. It wasn't that at all" (Avery 2011, 69). In *Life*, to Judy Fayard during the filming of *Dirty Harry*: "A lot of actors have gotten too involved with trying to make message pictures" (Fayard 1971, 48). In a 1992 interview with *Rolling Stone*:

> I remember when Dirty Harry was offered to me. It was offered by an executive who said that Paul Newman had told him about it and had said it's a great script, but he couldn't do it, because of political implications. It disagreed with certain feelings of his. Well, I read it, and I said, "I'll do it." . . . Both Don Siegel and I had a great time doing Dirty Harry in 1971—we were both pro victim's rights, but we weren't anti accused rights. We just thought: "Here's a story that talks about the victim's rights. Okay, we'll do this story." Now, if there was a great story about the rights of the accused who had been railroaded into prison, it would have been just as exciting to play that. (Breskin 1992)

Eastwood's disclaimers are both preposterous and perfectly in character: his whole life he has resisted being slotted into categories; he denies that his films might apply outside their specific stories and thus avoids being labeled as an advocate for one political position or another. He refuses to believe that *Dirty Harry*, or any of his films, might be generalized to make a statement about society as a whole.

Nonetheless, the success of films like those in the Dirty Harry franchise arises partly in the ways they resonate with real-world issues. He does not see the story of Harry Callahan as a symbol of anything outside its own narrative. Yet Eastwood's skyrocketing appeal then and now is based in part upon his appearance in films like *Dirty Harry*. Witness the hysterical adulation with which the RNC audience finished his signature 1983 *Sudden Impact* quote: "Go ahead, make my day," also one of the top 100 movie quotes in the 2005 American Film Institute poll and a favorite movie quote of President Ronald Reagan.

Despite controversies, the banner year 1971 opened doors for Clint. His directorial debut was a modest commercial success, and *Dirty Harry* turned him into one of the world's top movie stars. Before *Dirty Harry*, he was second only to Paul Newman (Fayard). Through much of the 1970s he was at or near number one on lists of box office stars, and in 1978 *Esquire* called him "Hollywood's richest actor" and cites unnamed Hollywood sources that claim that he could make up to $10 million for a single film—equivalent to $36 million in 2013 (Vallely 1978, 43).

The next year, Alison, his daughter with Maggie, was born—his second daughter and first with Maggie. He also starred in a mediocre Western, *Joe Kidd*, though he did not direct it. (The director was John Sturges, who, like Leone, had adapted a Kurosawa film as a Western—he made *The Magnificent Seven*, a remake of Kurosawa's *Seven Samurai*.) Starring in Westerns helped burnish Eastwood's star image—stoic, angular, wry. In hindsight, it seems inevitable that he would eventually turn, as a director and not for the last time, to the Western genre, with which he is indelibly associated. With his Westerns, Eastwood asserted himself as a major directorial voice. He was still making untold heaps of money from the sequels to *Dirty Harry*, and his personal life may have been rife with problems (about which there were only whispers until much later), but Clint Eastwood was also quickly maturing as an artist.

Eastwood's artistic identity asserted itself in 1973 with *High Plains Drifter*, a film that pondered major philosophical questions. What would you do if you could start all over—escape your past, choose your friends, and select a spot of natural beauty to create a perfect world in which you would become happy and wealthy? The debate over "happiness" has not died down despite the horrors of modern totalitarian systems in the 20th century—Nazi and Communist programs, for instance—or the failure of utopian communities through urban "renewal" schemes in 19th- and 20th-century America. The millions of people who poured out of Europe into the New World in the 17th through

19th centuries literally banked upon a vision of happiness to be found in an actual physical paradise and a new life. The land companies sold to those who had money. Individuals with none sold themselves or a child into servitude. Land grants made during the Revolutionary War ironically allowed communities to stake out territory where they could live together in harmony, free from war. The great uncharted West beckoned with its promise of wide open lands.

The United States government periodically opened up its purchases to summon restless and hopeful men and women to stake out their bit of paradise—a perfect, or at least a better, life than they had known back across the ocean. The Homestead Acts of the 19th century allowed enterprising, hopeful, or just desperate men and women to claim federal lands in the Western states, converting a literal "no man's land" (or no white man's land, at least) into parcels for cultivation. The homesteaders who took advantage of the Acts gave the Western genre an endless, mythic backdrop against which the genres conflicts, between wilderness and civilization, the individual and the collective, could play out. Nearly all Westerns engage the subject.

For his third personal movie, then, Eastwood chose a story that not only encompassed America's dawning history but also expanded the moral and social judgments of *Hang 'Em High* (an innocent man unjustly condemned) to western expansion more broadly. *High Plains Drifter* (1973) evokes several *Rawhide* story lines: the moral intensity of *The Oxbow Incident* or *The Hunt*, a Danish film from 2012 with an innocent man betrayed by his own community. Amplified color and sound, as in a Spaghetti Western, intensify the satire of commerce.

We cannot brush off *High Plains Drifter* as popcorn entertainment. Eastwood's high plains drifter rides down from the mountaintops into an oddly static town freshly built alongside a vast body of water, all fluid motion set against the townspeople's icy stares. Opening with a wide shot, the camera cuts across the horizon and exposes the eerie newness of a small settlement—Lago, an anagram for "goal" (but also the word for "lake" in both Spanish and Italian)—perched along the edge of a vast lake scooped out of endless desert and settles upon the immobile face of the rider in a series of complex shots that cement the viewer into the unfolding action even though no shots include a frontal close up to establish the lead character's point of view.

The town's peculiar location and construction emphasize its falsity, an allegorical theatrical set located between its false paradise magazine-perfect externals and its internal hell. By 1973, when *Drifter* was released, Eastwood was already an international star; *Dirty Harry* was in the air, and serial Westerns such as *Gunsmoke* still played almost nonstop on television. The Paris Peace Accords had been signed. American troops were pulling out of Vietnam, and United States citizens could begin to fantasize once more about peace, equality, and justice.

High Plains Drifter, like its follow-up *Pale Rider*, offers a reflection on justice that reimagines *Shane* and *High Noon*, "without the arty self-importance of those earlier films," as filmmaker Alex Schwarm told me in 2009. The movie, written by Ernest Tidyman of *French Connection* fame, was shot in the Sierras at Mono Lake, California, with some shots done in Inyo Forest, California. The town was built from scratch and burned for real. Note the image of the rider shimmers as though he arose from the heat of hell. Eastwood's cinematographer creates the illusion of heat by holding a flame under the camera, as Chicago filmmaker Mike Smith conveyed in a 2009 e-mail.

In Eastwood's version, the sheriff is dead; the deceased is resurrected and mad as hell; the prosperous new town is burned down; and redemption is scarcely whispered. In several interviews, Eastwood notes that this is a "what if" film: What might have happened if the Gary Cooper character in *High Noon*, a sheriff who single-handedly stands up against his town's apathy, were killed (Kapsis and Coblentz 1999, 99–100)? As he put it, "*High Plains Drifter* was great fun because I liked the irony of it; I like the irony of doing a stylised version what happens if the sheriff in *High Noon* is killed, and symbolically comes back as some avenging angel or something—and I think that's far more hip than doing just a straight Western. . . . I like stories you can't guess the endings of. Most Westerns, you can guess the ending" (Wilson 2007, 134–35).

"What-if?" cannot convey the horror of the film's two flashback sequences, in which we watch in drawn-out detail the excruciating pain of a young man as he is whipped to death. The interpolated sections function the same way Raskolnikov's dream of the little nag, a weak horse, functions in *Crime and Punishment*: as the torture death of an innocent, even to the whip lashes across the victim's eyes. As

Dostoyevsky described Raskolnikov's dream, the animal serves as displaced human sacrifice (again, like *The Hunt* from 2012).

> He runs past the horse, runs ahead of her, sees how they are lashing her on the eyes, right on the eyes! He is crying. Heart is in his throat, the tears are flowing. One of the whips grazes his face, he does not feel it. . . . But the poor boy is beside himself. With a shout he tears through the crowd to the gray horse, throws his arms around her dead, bleeding muzzle, and kisses her eyes and mouth. (Dostoyevsky 1992, 57)

The spectator does not need the novel's commentary that the nag's owner or the murderer of the young marshal is "no Christian," nor does the plot require the little child's intervention. The camera tells all in the two flashbacks. In the movie, the stranger comes as his own ghost and avenges the death of the defenseless man. Dostoyevsky's intensity permeates all of Eastwood's best films, despite the director's various throwaway comments in interviews that he and his team were just having fun playing with a story.

Some critics and fans see in *High Plains Drifter* and other Westerns that Eastwood directed a focus on violence as an end outside of moral questions, but such an interpretation misreads his accomplishment. Eastwood does not abandon moral questions—in spite of what he himself might claim in interviews, his films deeply engage with history, morality, and politics. He does, however, abandon the false certainty of easy answers and Manichean distinctions. Hence, Eastwood's Westerns lay out the precarious position of "the community." In *High Plains Drifter*, however, the community is as likely to be a source of evil as of goodness. Further, as the film is shot from the point of view of the stranger, the viewer becomes invested not only in the character's actions but also in his moral judgments.

REFERENCES AND FURTHER READING

Avery, Kevin, ed. 2011. *Conversations with Clint: Paul Nelson's Lost Interviews with Clint Eastwood, 1979–1983*. New York: Continuum.

Bates, William. 1979. "Clint Eastwood: Is Less More?" *The New York Times*, June 17.

Breskin, David. 1992. "Clint Eastwood" (Interview). *Rolling Stone*, September 17, 66ff.

Cummings, Vernon. 1972. "Is Dirty Harry a Right-Wing Melodrama?" *Human Events*, April 1, 12.

Dostoyevsky, Fyodor. 1992. *Crime and Punishment*. Translated by Richard Pevear and Larissa Volokhonsky. New York: Vintage Classics.

Eliot, Marc. 2009. *Clint Eastwood: American Rebel*. New York: Crown Publishing Group.

Epps, Garrett. 1972. "Does Popeye Doyle Teach Us How to be Fascist?" *The New York Times*, May 21.

Fayard, Judy. 1971. "Who Can Stand 32,580 Seconds of Clint Eastwood?" *Life*, July 23, 44–48.

Kapsis, Robert E., and Kathie Coblentz, eds. 1999. *Clint Eastwood: Interviews*. Jackson: University Press of Mississippi.

Knight, Arthur. 1974. "*Playboy* Interview: Clint Eastwood." *Playboy*, February, 57–72, 170–72.

Michaels, Ken. 1970. "Fugitive from a Spaghetti Factory." *The Chicago Tribune*, November 15.

Schickel, Richard. 1997. *Clint Eastwood: A Biography*. New York: Vintage.

Shales, Tom. 1973. "Cool Clint Eastwood: The Millionaire Drifter." *Boston Globe*, May 27.

Vallely, Jean. 1978. "Pumping Gold with Clint Eastwood, Hollywood's Richest Actor." *Esquire*, March 14, 38–45.

Vallely, Jean. 1978. "Pumping Gold with Clint Eastwood, Hollywood's Richest Actor." *Esquire*, March 14, 38–45.

Warga, Wayne. 1973. "Eastwood a Pussycat behind Camera." *The Los Angeles Times*, January 2.

Wilson, Michael Henry. 2007. *Clint Eastwood: Entretiens avec Michael Henry Wilson* (Interviews with Eastwood). Paris: Cahiers du Cinéma.

Chapter 4

THE ICON AND HIS LEGEND, CONTINUED:
THE OUTLAW JOSEY WALES

Violence, vengeance, and the conflict between the individual and the collective undergird Eastwood's second iconic Western as a director. His personal life, still complicated, became increasingly more so during the seventies; his wealth increased exponentially; and critics still generally dismissed him. Yet, he crafted a stunningly beautiful, philosophically profound movie in *The Outlaw Josey Wales* that prepared the way for *Unforgiven* in 1992 and the flood of art films that began with *Mystic River* in 2003.

Josey Wales, a young Missouri farmer content with himself, his family, and the land, turns over the sod on a late spring afternoon in the early 1860s, his smiling face turned toward his little son. The setting sun filters through the trees and over the stream, laid out in hues of soft brown. After the scorching inferno of *High Plains Drifter*, we are soothed by the stream's soft ripple; the image of mother, father, and child; and Jerry Fielding's music on the soundtrack. The father wears a hat of soft brown felt: the gear of a farmer, not a warrior.

Any young family might have hoped for such a paradise at the beginning of a terrible decade: a place of lush fertility and spiritual tranquility far from the crowded Eastern cities or the foul mines of Wales. Battles raged as early as 1854 along the Kansas–Missouri border. Some feel that the Missouri wars over slavery and land precipitated the Civil War (Faust 2008). For the moment, in this movie, Josey seems safe from bloody conflicts.

The astute watcher of Westerns expects change—the sound of hoof beats, an arrow in the shoulder, the high-pitched whoops of an invading force. Even seasoned viewers, though, could not have predicted the cinematic cataclysm about to engulf them. Color and sound suddenly shift, as mother, child, and homestead are ravaged in economical strokes: a wisp of smoke, the flash of horse hooves glimpsed through the brush, blonde hair streaming over a woman's partially stripped body, bright flames devouring a sturdy farmhouse. In a series of shots that recall the warriors' rush into action in Akira Kurosawa's *The Seven Samurai* (1954), we follow the young man's panicked dash as he cuts through the saplings toward his home. The camera immediately plunges the spectator

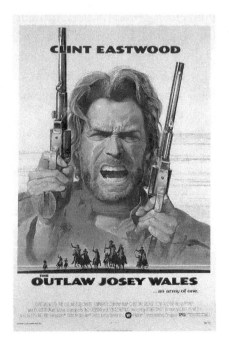

Clint considered The Outlaw Josey Wales *as significant a movie as his later* Unforgiven *(1992). Despite the violent poster image, the movie constructs a society of peace and reconciliation among warring peoples. (Warner Brothers/Photofest)*

into the unfolding death scene, as we experience the horror through Josey's eyes.

The cartoon-like torching of the corrupt town in *Drifter* takes on hellish urgency here, for *Josey Wales* is anchored in the earthy substance of real lives, not in archetype, parable, or myth. The homage to Kurosawa's masterpiece signals that Eastwood plans to depart from the terrain of the B-Western to capture the desperation and beauty of ordinary, not mythically or heroically glamorous, lives—a film wholly attuned to his interest in lived experience. In the second scene, the camera hovers near a mounting pile of earth in ghastly replay of the earlier pastoral shots. As Josey drags a body bag toward the fresh grave, a little hand pops out of the seam. The father tenderly replaces it inside its burlap winding sheet, as historian Elizabeth Lewis Pardoe has noted in conversation.

High Plains Drifter sizzles with apocalyptic fury. *Josey Wales* begins rather with grief and sorrow, as the young father marks the grave of wife and child with a cross and a fir tree. The camera shows his farmer's hands digging a gun and holster out of the rubble. The subsequent shots intercut between target practice and a series of warmly lit single shots of what the young man must now leave. The gun and the clean hits are sharply in focus, but Josey's face and body are obscured. (A similar sequence appears in *Unforgiven* when Will Munny prepares to go on a bounty hunt. That film is saturated with references to the physical act of killing itself. Will's face and body, clearly visualized as inseparable from his deadly actions, are witnessed by his incredulous and judging children.)

We see the ruins of Josey's homestead, the grave, a small fir tree, his donkey, and the rich brown soil he so recently coaxed into fertility. Anchored firmly to the earth and to Josey's life story, these images will float timelessly in the memory of a man with no surviving past except suffering, no name except legend, and no future except wandering.

When the Missouri Bushwackers, sympathetic to the Confederacy, appear over the horizon, they offer Josey an irresistible proposition. Revenge yourself on the Union slayers. It's time to inflict a Kansas bloodbath. As spectators, we ask: will Josey become another figure not simply of legend (Jesse James; Billy the Kid; Will Munny) but also of American literature—the American soul defined by D.H. Lawrence as "hard, isolate, stoic and a killer" (Lawrence 2003, 65)? Well, to paraphrase Dirty Harry, will he?

Now that Josey's backstory has been laid out in the movie and he has signed on to pursue vengeance, credits begin to roll over images of thousands of corpses. Lest the fetching fife and drum music that runs under the shots seduce the spectator, the images are shot in muted and distancing blue tones like the early glass photographs of the period, with burnings, hangings, and beheadings obscured by the fog of war. Two years before *Josey Wales*, the celebrated French director Robert Bresson opened his movie *Lancelot du Lac* (1974) with a similar montage: knights ride in quest of the Holy Grail but burn, torch, lynch, and behead. Their lances sweep across holy altars in desecration of the spiritual symbols the men seek to validate. The killers in both movies are shot from a distance and appear nearly faceless, the Knights of the Round Table shrouded in armor, the guerrillas nearly invisible behind the legs of hanging bodies or the smoke of burning barns.

Lancelot and *Josey Wales* deal with the quest for revenge increasingly cut off from an original fault. The Bushwackers, exhausted at war's end and willing to surrender, are betrayed, the oldest of human vices, according to Eastwood in a 1984 interview with Michael Henry Wilson. Josey, a lone holdout from postwar amnesty, sees their slaughter from afar and rides in to avenge his friends' deaths in a horrific, immediate burst of matching Gatling-gunfire that should satisfy the fans of superhero comic fare everywhere. Josey finds himself pursued by Union law enforcement, or rather by the renegade Redlegs, who insinuated themselves into the Union army at the end of the war, like Civil War Blackwater contractors (Wilson 2007, 39). Josey turns his legendary killing skills toward survival.

But this is survival of a different kind from your average *Fugitive* story line, like the long-running television show (1963–1967) that starred Eastwood's friend David Janssen, the Harrison Ford movie by the same name, or any prison break movie. It resembles Eastwood's own prison break movie *A Perfect World* (1993), where the hero is on the run, but danger and escape make up only a small part of what unfolds during the film.

Josey Wales is a far richer film thematically and visually than a plot summary indicates. Eastwood himself said in an interview that given different circumstances, the movie could have been as successful commercially and critically as *Unforgiven*. He considered it an equally revolutionary take on American history and his own persona crafted from the Spaghettis and *Dirty Harry*. The transfer of violence from civil war and solitary revenge to commerce occurs in *Unforgiven* only at the end, as the framing narrative helpfully leaps from the point of view and judgment of the heroine's mother to the cool, detached, and thoroughly unreliable impersonal narrator. In the scrolled material in the closing frame story, we read, "It is said that Will Munny moved to California and succeeded in dry goods." Commerce threads through the movie and leads us to this moment: the main characters' names all refer in some way to currency, as Patrick McGee helpfully observes (McGee 2007, 195).

The dark monetary undercurrents in *Unforgiven* had their precursors in *Josey Wales*. As Josey flees farther and farther south and as the episodes with assorted fools become stranger and stranger, the movie increasingly diverges along two distinct narrative paths: the pursuit of money, which subsumes even the desire for vengeance; and the haphazard and completely free acquisition of "worthless" cast-offs from the great American Dream. If a human being is only "worth" what he or she can bring in cash or horses, what can we say about the costuming of Lone Watie (Chief Dan George) once he burns his black tie getup and top hat, Grandma Sarah (Paula Trueman) and Laura Lee (Sondra Locke) wearing tattered remnants of their elegant dresses, or the patchwork duds of the rest of the gang Josey picks up once he gets to Texas? The characters defy stereotypes with their mobile faces, growing affection for each other, and disregard for social boundaries.

The buyers and sellers of human flesh are sharply drawn: figures of dark comedy closely allied with the mercenaries who pursue Josey. The antiphonal structure of the movie is carefully constructed, with the two-faced boatman paired with the charitable old woman on the one shore and the white-suited carpetbagger peddling false goods as his metaphorical mate ferried to the other. The initial betrayal of Josey's leader Fletcher, who sold his own friends for a bag of gold, becomes a chorus of nascent capitalists: the backwoodsmen who crow "I got me the Josey Wales," to the two "pilgrims" and Zukie in the trading post who wheedle "I saw him first," to the carpetbagger and the dry goods salesman who would be "glad to share in any award." The two bounty hunters recall the scams of Blondie and Tuco in *The Good, the Bad, and the Ugly* even as they anticipate *Unforgiven*'s Will Munny and Ned: "A man's gotta do somethin' to make a living"—especially when the war is over and Will's pig farm fails.

It would be easy to dismiss the episodes that follow as comic relief along the desperate vengeance trail followed by the picaresque fugitive Wales. The Missouri Boat Ride incident, after all, introduces all kinds of charlatans and fools who look just a bit too over-the-top for a well-dressed middle-class audience. Instead of escaping on his swift steed, Josey drags along a mortally wounded child soldier, Jamie. To reach the Indian nations and safety, the fugitives have to cross the river (the Missouri or the Mississippi, whichever lies between them and the South), watched over by the afore-mentioned two-faced ferryman reminiscent of Charon and the river Styx—a character more like the slippery trickster Tuco in *The Good, the Bad, and the Ugly* than a savior.

The fugitives depend upon the charity of Granny Hawkins, an old crone watching over supplies. Framed by low-hanging vegetation at river's edge, she takes pity on the wounded boy Jamie and his protector and gives them food and bandages for free. The white-suited carpetbagger's sleazy, florid speech and grubbing for profit will be mirrored in the figure of the television announcer in *Invictus* (2009). Always shot in white, harsh light, the squat little man oozes the false face of evil, like Herman Melville's *Confidence Man*—the opposite of Granny Hawkins's plain speech and penetrating assessment of Josey's character. Her truth-telling honesty will reappear in the characters of Sue and the Hmong shaman in *Gran Torino* (2008).

Western expectation hovers as the ferryman, harshly lit, his features distorted by a raffish grin, abandons the fugitives and hastens to deliver Josey to his pursuers. The camera pulls away as Josey refuses to slaughter the approaching soldiers, spotting his victims through the branches of his sheltering tree and shooting out the ferry rope instead (yet another reference to *The Good, the Bad, and the Ugly*).

In Leone's great antiwar masterpiece, Blondie ("the Good," played by Eastwood) remains aloof, disdainful, and generally unaffected by what he sees around him. The disparity between his low affect and the chaotic bloodletting around him underscores his comment about war's enormous waste of human lives for nothing. Not so with *The Outlaw Josey Wales*. Josey may seem detached, almost paralyzed by "what he has seen, what he has done," a phrase to be echoed by the war-damaged men in *Flags of Our Fathers* and *Gran Torino*.

But the movie *The Outlaw Josey Wales* is anything but detached. It presents one furious critique of war and greed after another. The double-dealing ferry boatman may be a figure of comedy, but like the white-suited charlatan, his duplicitous nature bottom-feeds off the Civil War's bloodshed and the dregs of postwar violence. The entire movie takes place during the years when millions of citizens, North and South, were teetering on the edge of extinction—this added to the deliberate destruction of its Indian tribes and the return to virtual slavery of its newly "freed" black citizens. Even though (again, adapting the source novel) the movie appears to demonize the North and praise the South, Eastwood the director spreads the judgment. Loss was not the property of the "victimized" South; every family in the vast expanse of our country suffered the loss of a husband, father, or breadwinner.

How does a movie that initially celebrates vengeance become a movie about peace and reconciliation? When you have been grievously wronged, when you have lost all that you cherish, as Josey Wales has, in what ways should you respond? How do you learn to lay hold of the past's corrosive memories and move into the future? Here is where the Angel of Death agenda established in the early sequences of the film yields to the powerful narrative pull of the Angel of Mercy.

The regenerative path of the movie was already well under way when Josey rescued Jamie, his war companion (Sam Bottoms). It continues appropriately enough with a sewing story. Josey has carefully shepherded the wounded Jamie, despite the boy's weakened state and the threat to his own life. There's nothing crisply square-jawed and hyper-masculine about a hero wandering around with a bleeding, singing adolescent who blathers about his daddy embroidering linsey-woolsey shirts for him. Any notion of a monolithic masculine model (how Eastwood was already described in the press) is completely undone by the appeal of the image: the father, in Jamie's fevered memory, sits and sews as he sings "Rose of Alabamy" to his motherless child. Word and image are duplicated for our eyes and ears as Jamie now sings the old ditty to Josey.

The older man quietly assumes the role of father and caregiver to his simple charge, just as early in the movie he smiled down at his own little boy. The viewer who looks back at the 1976 movie's understated tenderness after seeing *Gran Torino* must consider the rich embellishment of the father–son theme between then and 2009. Josey acquires a son to cherish after his own little boy has been burned alive, but he is already accepted as kin. Walt Kowalski, having reared two despised sons who want to file him away in a retirement home, is also given a second chance to become a father—not with a kid who resembles him in looks, history, or life experience, but one—Thao—who has been thrust into an alien culture without a guide. Walt becomes a careful and loving guide through gardening, woodworking, and a dubious but hilarious education in what it means to be an (American) man. The movie radically recasts sonship to supersede violence as part of masculinity—a model that redefines kinship in human, rather than ethnic, terms.

With Jamie's death, Josey pronounces words of parting free of the husks of ritual that attended the deaths of his wife and child—a reference to an absent God as disturbing as the bedside sermon of the pastor in Ingmar Bergman's *Cries and Whispers* (1972). For the orphan Jamie, he speaks simply of loyalty to kin and friend, unknowingly taking a step toward the family he will form during the remainder of the film.

The reconciliation strand of the narrative strengthens with each episode that follows. The instances of crass commercialism multiply with endless variations, but the strength of weakness becomes ever more prominent. What Karli Lukas calls the shift in the film from "Eastwood as weak" to "Eastwood as star" makes a catchy theory, but in the overall plan of the movie, the "weakness" in the eyes of the powerful (an armed, commercially driven, postwar society) becomes redefined as strength (Lukas 2004). What matters is not power or money—a glimpse of the Texas town full of regulators and amputees tells what became of the men caught in postwar scrambling for power and gun-running wealth—but rather shelter for the displaced, cheated, violated, dispossessed, and homeless.

And Lone Watie, odd even by the untutored Jamie's example, enters Josey's world almost as a classic illustration of the movie's embrace of the dispossessed. If Jamie's speech rhythms seemed almost too unsophisticated to be true, if his anecdotes seem to slow the swiftly paced pursuit narrative, Lone Watie's tales take a seemingly random, alternate narrative pattern even further. As Josey snores away, the aging chief treats the audience to a much-needed history lesson on the human costs of land acquisition—a story largely omitted from textbooks in American classrooms until recent decades. It's a story that needs to be told to give historical background and context for the rest of the movie. Here's another man whose monumental losses—wife, sons, home, culture, place in the natural world—would surely demand violent revenge. He's an older version of Ten Bears (Will Sampson), the Comanche chief who dominates the reconciliation plot toward the end of the movie.

Lone Watie's role in *The Outlaw Josey Wales* switches quickly from sidekick and occasional protector to reborn man who falls in love. Will Josey similarly open his life to love and rebirth? The scene at the Trading Post probes that question even as it explores Josey's conflicted selves through lighting and music. It further embellishes the postwar robbery motif—here identified with adulterated goods and rape—and introduces the "imperiled woman" theme even as it displays Josey's wildly theatrical killing skills.

This is not just any showdown scene between the hero and the bad guys. It takes place not in a saloon but in a trading post, supposedly one site (like a 19th-century lunch counter) where human beings should be able to purchase food and supplies free of discrimination. (Eastwood was to elaborate on such cruelty in *Bridges of Madison County*.) Shot almost devoid of natural light, the intimacy of the enclosure allows the cinematographer to manipulate the space and emphasize Josey's emerging darkness. As Josey and Lone Watie approach the post to buy a horse, we see the building from Josey's point of view, a tiny speck at the bottom of a valley. Its owner, Zukie (shorthand perhaps for Zuckerman, the trader shot in the back by John Wayne's character Ethan Edwards in *The Searchers*) cheats the two Indians who want to sell pelts. He beats his Navaho assistant Little Moonlight (Geraldine Keams) for breaking a bottle, then allows the two roughnecks to rape her for money.

Suddenly Josey enters, silhouetted in the doorway—again, a reference to John Wayne's character in *The Searchers*. For the rest of the scene, only a strong edge light outlines his form and part of his face, as filmmaker Matt Mckenna has written. The silhouette and darkness cloak Josey "in an element of mystery and danger," a "moving force of darkness, a violent shade of a man."

Yet the compassion that Josey showed the dying Jamie resurfaces, as he and the young woman exchange glances. Josey takes over from there, and the pilgrims are history. Once the liberated Little Moonlight catches up with Josey and Lone Watie, she weaves her way into their male friendship and into Lone Watie's heart.

More evidence of Josey's dual nature appears with the rescue of the Kansas women; the superhuman defeat of their captors, the savage Comancheros; and the shooting of the bounty hunter even as he adds five new family members, survivors of another new American commercial venture, a silver mine. The past is being left behind, slowly, as the soundtrack underscores the arrival of the ragtag family at their new Texas home, an abandoned ranch.

Significantly, the former owner of the ranch, Tom, died in a skirmish along the Kansas–Missouri border. But the tragic past is forgotten as the little group rounds a bend and enters the grove where the house lies. An extreme long shot unites the voyagers visually as a group as one by one, they spot the small house. The camera darts around looking for reactions: is this really the paradise that Grandma Sarah had predicted? Joy bursts from the "birth of the new collective," as Hayley Schilling has written.

The music that accompanies their entrance, "The Sweet Bye and Bye," will be repeated in the service of thanksgiving that follows their first settlement. For now, there's work to be done and gender roles to be overturned. Grandma bustles around inside the house to bring order and prepare to feed everyone; the men begin to repair the fences.

But what of Josey in this domestic scene? When he tries to enter the doorway, he's framed for a moment by light in another echo of the opening and closing shots of The Searchers (1956). The camera cuts to an over-the-shoulder shot that for a moment makes Josey and Grandma appear the same height, signaling "the shift in power" from Josey the trailblazer and protector to the older woman as the organizer.

One of the most powerful scenes in the movie occurs later that night. It begins with an intimate conversation between Lone Watie and Josey that will be echoed in tone with Scrap and Frankie Dunn in Million Dollar Baby. As Lone Watie assures Josey, you have your home with us. In response, Eastwood places a meditative Josey above the bustling homestead as the rest of the family repairs, reshapes, rebuilds. The movie has yet to work out its tensions—vengeance or reconciliation? New love and new life, or a future forever observed from a distance, Josey's body blacked out in shadows against a cloudy sky as he is here and as he will be when he finally corners Terrill, the pursuer and murderer?

Josey falls in love again, not with a kind-hearted prostitute or a schoolteacher as in the classic western *High Noon*, but rather with Laura Lee, a fellow sojourner given to otherworldly flights of fancy. Both lovers have been marked by heart-stopping loss, but how refreshingly she begs the sorrowing giant to dance and how generously he smiles and stumbles as he joins in the family's celebration. The colors are bright, as each of the family members expresses a differing dance style. The sequence is drawn out for pleasure. We detect hints that "come spring," Josey's sweetheart might add a baby to the little family of outcasts, and so she did in the source novella. No cowboy celibacy, a common trope in the Western, for Josey! Combined with the prostitute Rose, a saloonkeeper, two Mexican workers, and a fiddler, Josey's world is now complete. And the world of the film is complete, too.

The composition of Josey's family group overtakes the destructive vengeance of the Abel and Cain drama in the rest of the movie, vicious reprisals against men and women not too different from you. The Man with No Name finally has a name and a home—even if at the end of the film, when he rides out of town, the spectator is not sure if Josey returns to his little family in Texas or if the new all-embracing social model we see at the end of the movie (a commune with ethnic, gender, and economic parity in peace with the neighboring Comanche) ever spread to other parts of America.

Even if Josey ever did return, could he ever forget the war traumas that engulfed him? Eastwood's later war movies—at least *Flags of Our Fathers* and *Gran Torino*—suggest that war's injuries endure far beyond the media flurry that reports or distorts them. Eastwood deliberately left the ending ambiguous, as he told interviewer Michael Henry Wilson. Even more outrageously, *The Outlaw Josey Wales* dares to model peace, bane of the traditional Western and enemy of an American imperialism inherent in endless land grabs and exterminations of native peoples. In a magnificent set piece framed against a glorious blue sky, Josey offers the chief of the Comanche, Ten Bears, life rather than death. They cement their bond in blood. Josey promises to supply food for the Comanche journeys.

The peace pact startles the more because of the antiphonal structure that marks many Eastwood films, the oppositions of Kansas and Missouri, North and South, brother against brother. In *Josey Wales,* Eastwood highlights not only the ways that Josey releases the demons of wrong done him by his own people but rather: How will survivors of the Civil War embrace the peoples both sides had excluded from the American family for centuries—Indian tribes, former slaves, women, and the poor?

Josey Wales rejects the culture of death—including the ravages of capitalism—in favor of new life, human dignity, and expanded definitions of family. He must find a way to bring the paradise of the little homestead back out to the wider world, but for now, this beautiful movie looks vengeance in the eye and turns toward the sun.

REFERENCES AND FURTHER READING

Carter, Forrest. 1989. *Josey Wales: Two Westerns (Gone to Texas/The Vengeance Trail of Josey Wales).* Albuquerque: University of New Mexico Press.

Faust, Drew Gilpin. 2008. *The Republic of Suffering: Death and the American Civil War.* New York: Knopf.

Lawrence, D. H. 2003. *Studies in Classic American Literature.* Edited by Ezra Greenspan, Lindeth Vasey, and John Worthen. Cambridge, UK: Cambridge University Press.

Lukas, Karli. 2004. "On Hell's Hero Coming to Breakfast: Clint Eastwood and *The Outlaw Josey Wales.*" *Senses of Cinema* 31 (April). http://sensesofcinema.com/2004/cteq/outlaw_josey_wales/. Accessed February 23, 2014.

Melville, Herman. 1991. *The Confidence-Man.* Edited by Stephen Matterson. New York: Penguin Classics.

Wilson, Michael Henry. 2007. *Clint Eastwood: Entretiens avec Michael Henry Wilson* (Interviews with Eastwood). Paris: Cahiers du Cinéma.

Chapter 5

CLINT EASTWOOD: SUPERSTAR

The Outlaw Josey Wales marked a major leap forward for Eastwood's artistic production, but initially, it was not even his film. The movie was to be directed by Philip Kaufman, though as a Malpaso production, and Eastwood would exert considerable influence. Costar Sondra Locke (who would figure so prominently in his private life over the next decade) described the conflict between Kaufman and Eastwood. "Kaufman has an *entirely* different approach than Clint to making a film. He is very meticulous and thoughtful and layered about each shot—an intellectual as well as a visual approach. Clint is all guts and instinct" (Locke 1997, 140). Kaufman's directing style might resemble that of Kubrick or Coppola, whose obsessive planning Eastwood scorned, than Eastwood himself.

Clint fired the director and put himself in the director's chair. In his own telling, Clint calls it "the worst moment of [his] life" (Thompson and Hunter 1978, 31). He praises Kaufman's work on the script but portrays Kaufman as too inexperienced to work on the film's large scale. The Directors Guild, which represents film directors, protested mightily, since Eastwood's actions undercut the authority of a director, and the Guild ever since has expressly forbidden the replacement of a fired director with someone who to that point had been in-volved at all with the film. It did little to endear him to Hollywood, though the quality of the final film quickly cast these concerns aside. (Kaufman, for his part, went on to a successful directing career him-self, including the excellent 1978 remake of Don Siegel's classic, *Invasion of the Body Snatchers*.)

In general, though, Eastwood shielded himself remarkably well from public view during the years when he was arguably the world's greatest movie star. His wife Maggie and their children Kyle and Alison lived in Carmel, away from the hubbub and prying cameras of Hollywood. Only rarely did he let the public see Clint Eastwood the family man, doubt-less at the urging of studio publicists. The publicity machine simply saw a quiet family man. Judy Fayard in *Life* writes that "he lives simply, for a rich man, in a big-but-ordinary house in Carmel, with his wife of 17 years, his 3-year-old son Kyle, and a basset hound named Symphony Sid" (Fayard 1971, 48) Add his daughter Alison, and adjust the ages of his children and the number of years he has been married, and this sentence could come out of any of the few "Clint at home" profiles until the late 1970s: nothing too dramatic is given away, and the family seems ordinary, even boring. "Privacy is another part of his ethic," she notes (Fayard 1971, 48).

Clint has since spoken more openly about his private life, and it appears that he had many affairs while married to Maggie—how many depends upon which biography one reads. Maggie would ask his friends questions but would either project an air of naïveté, or else was in le-gitimate denial. Throughout most of the 1970s, however, few people knew that his marriage was anything but happy.

Whenever he spoke about his wife, Clint did so affectionately. In his 1974 *Playboy* interview, Clint speaks about marriage and lavishes praise on Maggie. When asked why his marriage had lasted as long as it has (20 years at that point), he adopts an "aww shucks" demeanor: "Gee. I don't know. I'd better not say too much; I'm liable to jinx it. . . . I guess people grow away from each other. . . . I don't think that's happened in our case" (Knight 1974, 60). Later, the interviewer Knight asks, "do you have a fairly open relationship yourself, with Mag?" although the specific inflection of the question is not clear. Regardless, Eastwood re-plies, "Sure. Oh, yeah, we've always had—I'd hate to say I'm a pioneer with women's lib or whatever, but we've always had an agreement that she could enter into any kind of business she wanted to" (Knight 1974, 70). It does not appear that he is saying that she expressly approved of his affairs, although he does add, "I'm not shooting orders to her on where she's supposed to be every five minutes, and I don't expect her to shoot them at me." Regardless, no one can say what Maggie knew about Eastwood's extramarital affairs, but by 1979, the couple formalized the slow deterioration of their relationship in a legal separation.

The relative tabloid indifference toward Eastwood's private life is particularly notable in light of an unbelievable popularity that I cannot overstate. The mid- to late 1970s, from the period right before *The Outlaw Josey Wales* up to *Any Which Way You Can* (1980), Clint Eastwood's star was at its peak. In the 1990s and throughout the 2000s, critical opinion of him would soar, but only in the 1970s would he appear shirtless and bench-pressing on the cover of *Esquire* under the headline "Pumping Gold with Clint Eastwood, Hollywood's Richest Actor" (Vallely 1978). His relationship with Sondra Locke eventually thrust his personal life into the public realm, but it also affirmed the sense that he was finally a "movie star" in the way that Richard Burton was a decade earlier when the two teamed on *Where Eagles Dare*.

During the 1970s, Clint starred in *The Eiger Sanction*, an action film *par excellence* in which he is an undercover assassin tracking evildoers through the Swiss Alps. Scenes of mountain-climbing and other derring-do abound, and the location shoot (on the Eiger in Switzerland) proved hazardous. Clint was drawn to the production not because of the story—a warmed-over James Bond-style espionage tale—but because of the limits a location shoot in the Alps would impose on the crew: "Nothing could be more to his liking than shooting a film's crucial sequences on a remote mountaintop in Switzerland, which would perforce limit cast and crew to a daring handful" (Schickel 1997, 313). It was an ideal challenge for him: physical fitness and efficient filming. After throwing himself headlong into training, he and his skeleton crew trekked to the Eiger, considered among the more dangerous mountains to climb on earth.

The mountain lived up to its reputation: on the second day, a climber hired to assist in the shoot was struck by a falling rock and died (McGilligan 2002, 246–47). Eastwood's confidence in the project was justifiably shaken, especially since he was committed to complete the stunts himself. The treachery of the environment required a degree of planning that conflicted with his "shoot first, ask questions later" philosophy. But he and the crew persevered. Patrick McGilligan, later to write a biography of Eastwood but at the time a critic for the *Boston Globe*, calls the film's portrayal of the Alps "breathtakingly picturesque" and praises the cinematography and Eastwood's stunt work (McGilligan 1975). The plot, though, was preposterous at best and incoherent at worst. Vincent Canby similarly wrote that "What is more important than mystery is the spectacle of the climb, which looks difficult and very beautiful" (Canby 1975). It seemed that the climbing sequences, which cost a life and caused such strife for the crew, were the film's greatest assets. The reviews also express a self-conscious pleasure about Eastwood's movies, as though the critics were embarrassed to have enjoyed them, as when Canby calls *Eiger* "long" and "foolish" but then adds, almost bashfully, that it is "never boring" (Canby 1975).

After *The Outlaw Josey Wales* came *The Enforcer*, the third *Dirty Harry* film, directed by first-time filmmaker James Fargo. Critics were never fond of the *Dirty Harry* films, but the movies made money anyway. The franchise was far from over, as the 1980s would produce two more *Harry* titles, including *Sudden Impact* (1983), whose famous catchphrase, "Go ahead, make my day" joined "Do you feel lucky?" as Harry's (and Clint's) most iconic one-liner.

In *The Gauntlet*, Eastwood's first directorial effort since the triumph of *Josey Wales*, his character does not display the ruthless confidence of Harry Callahan. Rather, Ben Shockley, a dysfunctional and alcoholic cop, must transport a prostitute from Las Vegas to Phoenix to testify against mobsters. Clint undersold the film, more complex than it appears on the surface, by saying "*The Gauntlet* cop is, of course, much less secure with himself, never been in the big bust. Dirty Harry's been in on all the big busts" (Avery 2011, 115).

Curiously, *The Gauntlet*, but not *Bird*, was featured in the Museum of Modern Art (MoMA) movie festival in Spring 2008, honored for its jazz score (Seitz 2008). The opening of the film juxtaposes the rich riffs of a jazz score against a barren urban concrete cityscape (the movie is mostly set in Phoenix). Electronic music or rap might have better suited any part of this opening, from the hazy polluted sunrise to the shady nightclub from which the hero emerges to the broken asphalt and sterile geometry of the city's empty buildings. *The Gauntlet*, a tale of police corruption and personal redemption, is set in the post-Eden, post–Gold Rush, post–Depression Southwest, with its massive governmental attempts at social restitution.

Jazz creeps in and around the cultural markers of wasted lives and deserted buildings like trailing roses, blooming when you least expect it. Jazz soaks up suppressed passions, absorbs and transforms pain, erases race and class and gender, and paves the way for a love story. Only the power of the film's opening jazz score and its haunting, hopeful lyrics could sustain an assault on two lovers, Ben (Eastwood) and Gus (Sondra Locke), as they try to make it to the courthouse to testify at a trial. Eight hundred armored policemen with assault rifles line the road to the courthouse as their bullet-ridden bus drives right to the front door. The couple's dream of a small cottage far away from urban corruption reappears in *Million Dollar Baby* and *American Hustle* (2013), the contribution to the possibility of personal redemption for the least likely characters.

Sondra Locke had auditioned for a role in Eastwood's small 1973 effort *Breezy*, and, although she was not cast, Eastwood remembered her and hired her for *Josey Wales*, even though the film was scheduled to be directed by Philip Kaufman. As she tells it in her barnburner of an autobiography, their affair began on the second night of shooting. Press stories like the one that appeared on the cover of *People* magazine in 1978 likely accelerated Maggie's decision to separate formally from Clint. The magazine published a cover story shortly after the release of *The Gauntlet* that described rumors surrounding Eastwood and Locke, the film's stars. "Clint Eastwood & Sondra Locke: He and his new star ride out Gauntlet of gossip," the cover declared (Armstrong 1978). Their relationship soon became public, and that year, they collaborated in *Every Which Way But Loose*.

With *Loose*, Clint doubled down on the strategy to trouble his iconic cool tough-guy persona by choosing roles that undermined it. Directed by Fargo, the movie was a surprise smash, becoming Eastwood's most commercially successful film then and perhaps ever. In an interview with Paul Nelson, Clint relays that his lawyer and agent advised him against taking the project: "[They] said, 'Don't' do that. That isn't the kind of thing you want" (Avery 2011, 119). They were particularly nervous that Clint's character would not end up happily ever after with his love interest, played by Locke. Warnings of another "bad step" were once again for naught.

With a supporting cast that includes famed actress Ruth Gordon and an orangutan, the screwball comedy evokes the classics of Preston Sturges and Howard Hawkes. Eastwood proved to be an adept comic actor, a facility that has remained vastly undertapped over his career. Further, he uses his established screen persona to great effect. His character, Phil, gets into more than his share of fist fights, which would not be out of place in any Eastwood films. Phil, however, hopelessly smitten, is prone to deliver long, existential monologues to his simian sidekick.

Clint's characters in the films that followed—*Escape from Alcatraz* (his final collaboration with Siegel), *Bronco Billy* (Eastwood), the *Loose* sequel *Any Which Way You Can* (directed by Eastwood's longtime stunt coordinator Buddy Van Horn), *Firefox* (Eastwood) and *Honkytonk Man* (Eastwood) would oscillate between the masculine hero and the vulnerable romantic. His iconic screen persona was so well known and long established that it could be used as a tool in his filmmaking and acting—as a standard to be subverted, a baseline against which he could play against type and upend expectations or play to them, as he did in *Gran Torino* (2008).

In the 1980s, Eastwood's career and public life took several strange turns. For instance *Firefox* (1982) is a silly espionage film about an attempt to steal Soviet weapons and fighter-jet technology. The film was roundly criticized, and, although, in the neoconservative journal *Commentary*, Richard Grenier calls it "the most resolutely anti-Soviet film to be made in this country in a very long time" (he is paying the film a compliment), yet he also calls it "not a very good move; in fact . . . a wildly implausible and rather awful movie" (Grenier 1982, 66). Critic Andrew Sarris notes that Clint "has always looked ill at ease in uniforms and organizations" (quoted in Schickel 1997, 378), and it is true that there is something incongruous about Eastwood, who chafed against military discipline even when he was in the military, playing a former air force pilot.

Eastwood, of course, would deny that the movie is political at all, but rather would insist that it is simply a stand-alone story. *Honkytonk Man* and then *Sudden Impact*, another Dirty Harry movie, a strange thriller *Tightrope*, and an awful film *City Heat* (not directed by Eastwood, but costarring Burt Reynolds with whom he was often compared) followed. The personal ones that resonated with critics (like *Honkytonk Man*) had trouble finding audiences, and the popular ones were rehashing the same Dirty Harry themes, over and over. It took until *Pale Rider* (1985) for Eastwood to again marry commercial success with artistic ambition.

Around this time, Eastwood involved himself in one of the few emphatically political undertakings of his life. After the Vietnam War, rumors circulated that American soldiers officially listed as missing in action were alive, being held as prisoners. (The possibility of live prisoners was a major impediment to the normalization of relations between the United States and Vietnam. Normalization did not occur until 1995.) A Vietnam War veteran, Bo Gritz, one of the many Americans who believed that Americans were being held prisoner, began to solicit support in the early 1980s for a mission to sneak into Laos and search for American prisoners. Gritz planned to stage a film shoot in Thailand as a diversion to allow him and his men to cross over into Laos undetected.

Gritz eventually garnered Eastwood's support—$30,000 worth. When he gave the money, Eastwood likely did not see the mission as political: in an interview with Nelson, he remembers thinking, "I wouldn't be able to sleep at night if I thought there was *one* person over there" (Avery 2011, 191). "Eastwood Told Reagan of Planned POW Raid," announced a headline in the *Los Angeles Times* (Meyer and Gladstone 1983), although Clint himself disputes that he discussed the matter with the president (Avery 2011, 193). The *Times* article says that national security advisers told the president that Gritz was "not somebody we ought to be involved with" (Meyer and Gladstone), advice that Eastwood himself would have been smart to take, because the mission was a fiasco. One of Gritz's associates discussed plans for the mission in a magazine for mercenaries, *Soldier of Fortune*, in exchange for money—the publicity undermined whatever thread of legitimacy and credibility the group had (Branigin). As a whole, those involved in the mission, particularly the leader, seemed more invested in garnering publicity for themselves and for various far-right groups than they were in locating prisoners. No prisoners were found, but over the course of two missions (in late 1982 and early 1983), two Laotian guerillas working with Gritz died, and several Americans spent time in Thai jail. "They seemed to have gone public with the thing without any consultation with me or anything," Eastwood recalls (Avery 2011, 192). Gritz fell deeper and deeper into paranoid, far-conservative lunacy. Clint's brief association with him was uncharacteristic for a man so resistant to political parties and causes.

Then he slipped briefly into *electoral* politics, albeit of the nonpartisan kind. In 1986, Clint ran for mayor of Carmel, the seaside California village he called home for well over a decade. His most plausible opponent was the incumbent, a retired librarian. The campaign garnered attention nationwide, far more so than was otherwise warranted by a municipal election in a sleepy seaside town: people just seemed interested, and rightly so, in Clint's candidacy, because, as one article put it, he "has made a career portraying steely existentialist heroes for whom the only law was their own personal sense of right and wrong" (Stein 1986). How would Clint Eastwood, whose films he steadfastly refuses to deem "political," govern in a political office, even a low-stakes one?

With his common-sense practicality, Clint could hardly have run for a more appropriate position because Carmel had the reputation as a town with excessive government interference. It was undoubtedly picturesque, but critics were grumbling that the cost of preserving its charming atmosphere was too high: zoning rules were very strict. Eastwood was less of a hardliner when it came to zoning ordinances. The incumbent administration also proposed to ban homeowners from building second kitchens to rent them as vacation homes. Other hard-hitting issues, according to press accounts at the time, included prohibitions against playing Frisbee in parks, and ordinances preventing fast-food restaurants and take-out ice cream stands (Stein 1986, 1986b).

Behind these zoning rules, and undergirding what Schickel rosily calls "one of the most tasteful campaigns in the history of modern American politics" (Schickel 1997, 416) was Clint's anger at a perceived personal affront. When he announced his candidacy, he spoke fondly of Carmel, but the press also noted that he had "considerable enmity for its elected leaders" (Stein 1986). The article continues:

> Eastwood, his former wife and another partner sued the style-conscious city last year when it blocked their plans to build a two-story commercial building next to the actor's popular restaurant, the Hog's Breath Inn. The city sniffed that the building would sit too close to the sidewalk and that its exterior contained too much glass and not enough wood. In their suit, Eastwood and his partners complained that city regulations on the subject were "vague, subjective, ambiguous, unintelligible, and obscure." (Stein 1986)

Eastwood settled with Carmel out of court, but the episode left him angry. It is easy to imagine why—Eastwood, so impatient with bureaucratic inefficiencies, here was cast into what for him must have been a Kafkaesque nightmare, albeit on a small scale. Luckily for him, he was handily able to convert his anger into a well-received populism. When the votes were counted, he received 2,166, 72 percent of the total cast, and handily ousted the incumbent (Stein 1986b).

His mayoralty was less interesting than the campaign. "He made the streets safe for ice cream. He made it somewhat easier to build or to renovate property. He got a tourist parking lot constructed" (Schickel 1997, 418). During Pope John Paul II's 1987 visit to the United States, he visited Carmel, where Catholic priest Junipero Serra ran a mission in the late 1700s (Eliot 2009, 236). This was a major victory for Eastwood, but the minutiae of small-town governance soon wore on him, and, having accomplished what he set out to do, he did not run for reelection.

Through the campaign and brief time in office, *Heartbreak Ridge* or the latest Dirty Harry film alternated with more complex, personal ones. *Pale Rider* (1985), for instance, is another Western, but a strange one, with Eastwood playing a ghostly preacher who rides into town like Shane in the 1953 movie by the same name. Eastwood's Preacher arrives to rid a small California town of a corrupt mining firm and its brutal owners, but the entire film is ambiguous. The Preacher himself seems part corporeal, part apparition.

Do we see him or not? The camera may be tricking us. Is he dead or alive? Or is he the living dead, like the stranger in *High Plains Drifter*, a refugee from a horror film? Naturalistically low-lit sequences emphasize his physical substance. The display of a hearty appetite at his first meal with Megan's family, for instance, alternates with sudden appearances or disappearances, like his apparitional vanishing at the train station when the main mining villain comes to town. Even more disorienting, his presence on screen is accompanied by Bible texts riddled with death, not life. "His name is death" and "And hell followed with him" cue his first appearance in the mining camp. The scars from seven bullet holes in his back are displayed for the spectator but are surprisingly ignored by Hull, the miners' leader, who may not only wish but also expect his preacher-rescuer to walk the thin line between this world and the netherworld.

Regardless of the Preacher's identity, apocalyptic judgment hangs in the air from the film's opening. But who judges? And what exactly is at stake? What apocalypse does Eastwood the director want us to consider—the murderous henchmen and the rapacious mining company, the complete destruction of the small community, or the evil marshal and his six hit men? The three disasters require at least three separate responses.

First, there comes the thundering unthinking herd, the mounted robocalls who intend to instill fear. Mighty on their powerful steeds, they boldly kill a calf and a little pet dog, knock over the miners' shacks, rip up laundry lines, and terrify women and children—all signs of the domestic life which threaten the all-male corporate structure. This narrative line is situated solidly in the realm of (possible) history, as the opening so thoroughly shows the specific identities and multiple ethnicities of the small miners. The henchmen expose the little settlement's vulnerability and the fragility of its social structure—to make us care about the fate of the individuals whose faces the camera caresses and whose voices we hear throughout the movie.

Second, the threat to a community posed by an outside force is Western fare—*High Noon*, for instance, or *The Man Who Shot Liberty Valance*. Fearsome as they appear initially, the henchmen are only minor players in a larger and long-term destruction of the earth. Ecological disaster was hastened by destructive hydraulic mining, a practice that began in California around 1853, resumed in earnest in the mid-1860s, and stopped only in 1884 after decades of protest from farmers whose land downstream was ruined by the companies' dumping. Greed unleashed massive destruction. Usually Westerns ignored the devastation of the land the homesteaders, cattle barons, and cowboys roamed. *The Searchers* and Jim Jarmusch's *Dead Man* (1995) are outstanding exceptions.

Regard for the land may comprise the larger agenda that holds all the movie's parts together, greater far than the personal revenge angle or even the survival of the small mining community. Eastwood told Michael Henry Wilson what he found when he scouted locations for the film.

> My grandmother lived at Angels Camp, in the heart of the gold country, in fact very near to one of the places where we filmed. I also had filmed certain episodes of *Rawhide* there, and it's there, at Sonora, that I shot the sequence of the train. During the course of scouting, I traveled to the North, in Idaho, where many mining exploitations had used hydraulic means. One still finds the vestiges of their machines, but we finished by reconstituting everything ourselves. Happily, this proceeding was forbidden in California shortly after the period evoked in the film because that ruined the earth. (Wilson 2007, 58)

Perhaps, then, the larger backstory of environmental degradation unites all the plot threads. The small apocalypse figured in the shots of hydraulic mining at work might lead to a larger disaster shortly afterward—the destruction of the fresh waterways and forests in that area, for instance, and the poisoning of the rich farmlands downstream.

In *Pale Rider*, then, the extensive attention given to hydraulic mining itself—not simply to the greedy men who run the company and hound the little community—argues that science and technology are not value-free. The land becomes an "industrial commodity." The near-rape of the young character Megan references the byproducts of unfettered power: human tragedy is unleashed beyond the power of its possessors to contain it, like Frankenstein or Prometheus or the Golem-like creature in *No Country for Old Men*. The creators cannot control their creatures.

Despite the horror movie music that rumbles whenever the Preacher appears, his near-silence and shadowy lighting when he is with the miners, and the operatic orchestration of discordant music and drumbeats during the final showdown, the most striking visuals and sounds during the movie swirl around corporate mining operations. The link between the near-rape of Megan by LaHood's son and the rape of the land is established by the extensive screen time given to sights of hydraulic machines at work. Eastwood dwells on the details: majestic trees torn up by their roots and felled, the chasm dug into the earth, foul slush washed into the stream. The scene begins with a shot of a deforested mountainside, with giant trees toppling off its edge and the denuded land separated only by a fragile line of firs and water pipes in foreground.

Shockingly, in the middle of a sequence of brutal destruction, the shot turns grey. Two men are silhouetted for seven long seconds against the cascades of water. One bears the outline of the cowboys who run this operation. The other, dressed like a Chinese worker, alludes to the role played by the hundreds of thousands of Chinese who built the railroads that in turn fueled increasing American prosperity. The men stand precariously on a sterile wasteland devoid of color and life in almost eerie anticipation of the barren rock that becomes the tomb of Japanese soldiers in *Letters from Iwo Jima* (2007). The subject of the Chinese workforce, yet another terrible injustice that stains the story of America's progress, is brought up and almost passed over in *Unforgiven*, with English Bob's offhand remark about shooting Chinese. The film *3:10 to Yuma* also images this, as it does torture. *Tombstone* (George P. Cosmatos 1993) contains a throwaway line by one of the characters that refers to the "Anti-Chinese Society" of *Tombstone*. The cinematography in *Pale Rider* creates an image of the earth after life has been extinguished: the terrain of *Children of Men* (2006), for instance, or *Apocalypse Now* (Francis Ford Coppola, 1979).

Whatever archetypal Western sheen *Pale Rider* possesses (the Preacher trades his collar for a gun belt), like that of *The Outlaw Josey*

Wales, the fabric of *Pale Rider* is woven from dozens of small moments of connection that taken together present a fresh vision of human community, a new "family" or "neighborhood" that expresses the righteousness of living together in wholeness. If justice is interpreted only as vengeance, then it fails as the basis for human interactions. *Pale Rider* does contain slick gunfighter and savior elements, but community wins out thanks to the breathtaking, life-affirming visual compositions and repeated undercutting of Preacher by horror music, silence, and backlighting.

Not all of Eastwood's films in the late-1970s and 1980s were as thought-provoking. Overall, the eighties, a strange period for Eastwood, coincided with his equally strange relationship with Locke. None of the films between *The Outlaw Josey Wales* and *Unforgiven* resonated like Dirty Harry, Josey Wales, and the Man with No Name. He also found himself in the news more than usual, not always in a flattering light. We cannot know the influence of his relationship with Locke on Eastwood's film output (he cast her in five films), though apart from the provocative *Pale Rider*, his art retreated.

During Clint's relationship with Locke, he fathered two more children, neither with Locke and neither acknowledged publicly when they were born. The children's mother was a former flight attendant, Jacelyn Reeves, who lived in Carmel (Schickel 1997, 409). Further, in 1988, while he was still involved with Locke, he began an affair with Frances Fisher, who appeared in *Pink Cadillac* and whom Eastwood cast in *Unforgiven* and *True Crime*.

For a man whose public persona relies to such a large degree on limiting access to information about his private life, the public nature of his breakup with Locke surely rankled. Competing stories about their breakup circulated, but regardless, it was far from Clint's finest moment. The two had drifted apart for years; events exploded in 1989. Locks were changed, accusations hurled. The specifics of the breakup differ depending on the account read, but regardless, Clint took a drubbing in the press, and suddenly his private life was public. His strong, masculine persona—still alive and well—contributed to an image of him as an aggressor and her as a victim.

Locke filed for palimony, and though the case was settled (albeit years later), another lawsuit followed that involved the terms of the first suit's settlement—for instance, a deal to develop pictures at Warner Brothers, Malpaso's studio. The suit dragged on through much of the 1990s. Eastwood testified at the trial. As it became clear that he might to lose, he settled out of court before the court could rule against him. Through the waning days of his relationship with Locke and through the first years of litigation, Eastwood rededicated himself to making powerful, brilliant films: in particular *Bird* in 1988 and *Unforgiven* in 1992. *Bird* marked an artistic triumph. In 1992, press accounts saw *Unforgiven* as a career renaissance and valedictory, but little-seen and little-known *Bird* revealed that Clint Eastwood's ambitions and artistry continued to flourish even earlier.

REFERENCES AND FURTHER READING

Armstrong, Lois. 1978. "Taking Up the Gauntlet." *People*, February 13, 56.

Avery, Kevin, ed. 2011. *Conversations with Clint: Paul Nelson's Lost Interviews with Clint Eastwood, 1979–1983*. New York: Continuum.

Bingham, Dennis. 1990. "Men with No Names: Clint Eastwood's 'The Stranger' Persona, Identification, and the Impenetrable Gaze." *Journal of Film and Video* 42, no. 4: 33–48.

Branigin, William. 1983. "American Who Sought POWs Surrenders to Police in Thailand." *The Washington Post*, March 1.

Canby, Vincent. 1975. "'Eiger Sanction,' Film of Climbing Spies." *The New York Times*, May 22.

Eliot, Marc. 2009. *Clint Eastwood: American Rebel*. New York: Crown Publishing Group.

Fayard, Judy. 1971. "Who Can Stand 32,580 Seconds of Clint Eastwood?" *Life*, July 23, 44–48.

Grenier, Richard. 1982. "Summertime Visions." *Commentary*, August 1, 65–70.

Knight, Arthur. 1974. "*Playboy* Interview: Clint Eastwood." *Playboy*, February, 57–72, 170–72.

Locke, Sondra. 1997. *The Good, the Bad, and the Very Ugly: A Hollywood Journey*. New York: William Morrow and Company.

McGilligan, Patrick. 1975. "'Eiger Sanction' a Pleaser for Eastwood Fans." *The Boston Globe*, May 26.

McGilligan, Patrick. 2002. *Clint: The Life and Legend*. New York: St. Martin's Press.

Meyer, Richard, and Mark Gladstone. 1983. "Eastwood Told Reagan of Planned POW Raid." *The Los Angeles Times*, February 2.

Schickel, Richard. 1997. *Clint Eastwood: A Biography*. New York: Vintage.

Seitz, Matt Zoller. 2008. "Jazz on Screen: The Sparks Are Electric." *The New York Times*, April 13.

Stein, Mark. 1986. "Eastwood Asks Carmel to Make His Day, Elect Him as Mayor." *The Los Angeles Times*, Jan 31.

Stein, Mark. 1986b. "Eastwood Scores Easy Win in Carmel Mayor's Election." *The Los Angeles Times*, April 9.

Thompson, Richard, and Tim Hunter. 1978. "Clint Eastwood, Auteur." *Film Comment* 14, no. 1: 24–32.

Vallely, Jean. 1978. "Pumping Gold with Clint Eastwood, Hollywood's Richest Actor." *Esquire*, March 14, 38–45.

Wilson, Michael Henry. 2007. *Clint Eastwood: Entretiens avec Michael Henry Wilson* (Interviews with Eastwood). Paris: Cahiers du Cinéma.

Chapter 6

JAZZ, NOT VIOLENCE: *BIRD*

Let's start with what Clint's beloved film project *Bird* is not. Eastwood did not create a hagiography—a saint's life—of jazz musician Charlie "Bird" Parker. The movie is far from a traditional biopic, either, a "soupy Hollywood good black musician," as Laurence Knapp puts it in his discussion of the film (Knapp 1996, 133–37). The miserable state of race relations in mid-century America—especially job and education opportunities–denied America's own citizens—could have consumed Eastwood's entire movie on the life and music of Parker, and yet as a director, lifelong jazz lover, and accomplished performer, he had the good fortune (and perhaps the personal grace) to develop his own artistic gifts in the racially open atmosphere around Los Angeles. He shaped the movie *Bird* with Charlie Parker the artist, the man, and his music at the center. Is it a cautionary tale about drug use, as we might think in the light of Philip Seymour Hoffman's tragic death this year (2014).

The drugs cannot be forgotten. They fueled Bird's wild self-destructiveness and derailed his career, just as in February 2014 Philip Seymour Hoffman succumbed to the sickness that afflicted him from his early years. From Bird's high in the late forties and early fifties, he slipped with greater frequency into the chaos that pursued him since his teen years. The sight of a young man dead from an overdose reappears in Bird's nightmares. And yet, it is not a preachy antidrug tale either. The movie is something entirely different. But what?

Bird (which stars Forest Whitaker as Parker and Diane Venora as Chan, his partner) marks a culmination in Eastwood's decades-long love of jazz music. Charlie Parker's own playing (though digitally enhanced), taken from Chan's old recordings and separated from the backing tracks, infuses almost every scene until the last half hour of the movie. (It takes a second viewing, or hearing, to realize how distinctive the sound is.) Despite some objections, to hear Bird's performance isolated, cleaned, and accompanied by new instrumentalists is better than listening to almost any other jazz musician and far better than keeping those old recordings locked up in a closet.

Eastwood had always paid particular attention to the scores of his films, even composing a few himself before *Bird*. He had come far since Dee Barton's score for *High Plains Drifter*, with its eerie whistles and guitars in the style of Ennio Morricone, the composer for the Spaghetti Westerns. The wind and horror orchestration spook the viewer, who fears retribution for sins not yet committed. How far Eastwood had come from Jerry Fielding's lush country and Western-flavored score for the wide open spaces of *The Outlaw Josey Wales*, with its inset of "The Rose of Alabamy," a southern adaptation with roots in minstrel or at least in black or Mexican culture! Only three years before *Bird*, Lennie Niehaus, the jazz artist with whom Eastwood worked for decades, had written original music for *Pale Rider*.

Providing a precedent for *Bird*'s nonstop jazz, *The Gauntlet* (1977) opens and closes with the jazz spiritual "Just a Closer Walk with Thee," a song woven into the fabric of Jerry Fielding's score. Neither *Bird* nor *The Gauntlet* is alone in the world of jazz-infused films, however. Henry Mancini scored *Touch of Evil* (Orson Welles, 1958); Miles Davis provided a lush score for Louis Malles's *Elevator to the Gallows* (1957), with a young Jeanne Moreau; and Jean-Pierre Melville used jazz scores almost exclusively in the mid-fifties to early sixties, as with *Bob le Flambeur* (*Bob the Gambler*) and *Le Samourai* (1967).

Increasingly, Eastwood composes more of his own material, but takes his time writing the music. Although he is famous for scouting, setting up, and shooting in record time, he is deliberate when it comes to music. For *Mystic River*, for instance, it took as long as four months to compose the music. And while his music when it appears interlaces closely with the events on screen, his overall approach seems to be the one he established with *Bird*: music is a character, an equal player, not a throwaway score mass-produced to encourage complacency.

Bernard Herrmann's "distinctive sound universe" (he scored Alfred Hitchcock's *Vertigo*, for instance) applies to *Bird*. Parker's jazz and bebop are played both diegetically (within the story world), when he is seen onstage, and non-diegetically (outside the story world) as mood or statement. Bird soars like his song when he plays, and at the film's ending, his funeral, "Kansas City" reminds the audience of the opening sequence that showed Parker's childhood but also of his dazzling stage performances.

An article in the *New York Times* noted the "complex, somewhat wary interaction [of jazz] with cinema"—one that fundamentally differs from the "alliance between film and its longtime go-to music source, classical" (Seitz 2008). Significantly, the cinema and jazz exposition to which the article referred highlighted *The Gauntlet*, not *Bird*. In *The Gauntlet*, the dominant jazz performance sets up call and response between the spiritual comfort of its lyrics and the sordid reality of the interior story, which anticipates the cleansing of a soiled prostitute and an alcoholic cop and baptizes their new love. The jazz pieces sometimes surround the images and sometimes comprise inset "performances" fueled by speed and desire. With *Bird*, the faster the scenes move as they flip in and out of time and space, the higher the spectator's spirit soars with the music. The viewer becomes part of the (jazz) performance.

Though *Bird's* genius centers primarily on the sounds of jazz, the visuals and narrative structure are equally striking. They mimic a jazz-like structure (theme, variation, riff, spin-off, spin-off the riff until the theme returns), which doesn't allow for tidy analysis. Each sequence vibrates with its own musicality, repeating not only the cautionary side of drug use, but also the threat of early death, as ineffective a measure as using the death penalty to deter crime. The threat of incarceration is embodied in the spectral white cop who trails Bird for 10 years and later sends Red to prison. The threat of the loss of his livelihood—or worse, his gifts—still cannot stop his downward spiral into destitution.

He loses his license, the clubs on 52nd Street turn into brothels, and he plays little after his daughter's death and the family's eviction from their Central Street apartment. Worse: as his daughter lies dying, then lies in a casket, he sits immobilized in another city with his mistress, able only to write endless telegrams to his wife but never able to board a plane home.

But what a deliriously rich film with its set pieces, in sound and off screen, its thousand shades of darkness, its quirky dialogue and the sense of life on the streets during the great days of jazz. What did aspiring jazz players such as Parker and his friends do? They played at clubs if they were lucky, but if not, they played at Jewish weddings. Then they tour through the South, skirting racial madness by billing Red Rodney, a white trumpeter playing with a black band, as "Albino Red." As a white man, Red runs into stores to fetch the groceries, then hops into the band's getaway car and zips down the road, leaving the store owners furious. (A version of this scene, the denial of food, appears in *A Perfect World* a few years later.) Posing as an albino, Red sees first-hand the roach-infested motel beds where blacks are consigned when on road trips.

Laurence Knapp calls the film "an expressionistic labyrinth, a circular and elliptical journey into a tortured musician's soul" (1996, 133–37). Knapp comes close to capturing the almost avant-garde approach of *Bird* by noting its call for the spectator to participate in what we see and hear, where "backlighting and intimate framing, subterranean lighting and transmutable montage" create a "nocturnal, underground film." The film is filled with moving shots to emphasize his flight (like a bird, Knapp writes)—"arc pans and camera tracks," camera actions unusual in Eastwood.

Critic Jonathan Rosenbaum objects to the film's too-easy treatment of interracial romance, preferring the raw in-your-face emotions of John Cassavetes's *Shadows* (1959), also structured like a jazz composition. But Eastwood is a different kind of filmmaker from the edgy Cassavetes—always treading carefully between the worlds of popular cinema and audience demands and the artier, more philosophically inflected films he preferred to make (*Josey Wales* and now *Bird*; and then with *Unforgiven* until 2011, a career full of highly personal art movies). *Shadows* is a towering achievement, shot on the streets of New York

City rather than in studios, spun out with a lot of improvisation rather than a script, fragments, extreme close-ups, and terrible betrayal and desertion as impossible to watch as it is to experience.

Eastwood had something different in mind with *Bird* nearly 30 years after *Shadows* appeared—a film that would add another register to Cassavetes's jazz-image-improvisation combination. The mythical aspects of *Bird* ennoble the terrible reality we see on screen. If the relationship between Bird and Chan (Diane Venora) seems too quirky, too close, too loving to be real, that is entirely in keeping with Eastwood's habit of removing the sermon from "race."

Few American movies show black and white relationships at all. In *Bird*, Eastwood considers the couple's attraction as one person to another, and their problems as human, not bizarre. Chan's white daughter calls Bird "Daddy," naturally; the doctor who wants to commit him to the state asylum doesn't locate his decision to administer electric shock in "race" but rather practices bad medicine, as Chan pointedly comments. (Electric shock was the preferred therapy in the late twenties when Christine Collins was incarcerated, in the forties, and still in the early sixties, when I reluctantly assisted in such "treatment" at the hospital where I interned.) Chan is a part of the club scene, and the audiences Eastwood shows in the postwar jazz boom are largely black mixed with white, and black navy men and white women.[1] The white Red Rodney (Michael Zelniker) is accepted into Bird's ensemble because of his talent, not because of or despite his color.

Eastwood, fervently opposed to racial prejudice, makes his points about injustice and intolerance in other ways. After Bird comes to fetch Chan, his love, at her apartment in New York, they go dancing at a club to the tune of "Moonlight Becomes You." A crane shot establishes the club's clientele and the couple's position in the space. Whites at three different tables turn their censorious faces toward the dance floor, obviously scandalized by the presence of an interracial couple. A riot could have broken out and Bird and Chan thrown out,

---

[1] Harry Truman begins efforts to desegregate the armed forces in 1945. Only the high casualties in the Korean War forced the issue, and the three branches were almost fully integrated by the end of 1951.

but instead, Eastwood turns the camera toward one of the band members, who cries out, "Look! It's Charlie Parker!" effectively defusing a potential spectacle and emphasizing Bird's name, not his color, the paradigmatically Eastwood gesture of privileging the individual over the category, lived experience over abstraction.

More famously, though, Bird and his band need to devise ways to survive during their gig through the South. In rapid succession, they market Red as an albino and their star; send him as a white man into a grocery store to get food (blacks would not be allowed to enter); and sneak him into motels, where he gets a firsthand look at "separate but equal" living accommodations. Bird's troubles with the law come from his drug use, not from his color (although the courtroom scene takes place in New York, not the Deep South, where he never would have been allowed to plead his case). Throughout the sequences in the South, comedy leavens the approaching tragedy to relieve tension and open the subject of racial discrimination without sterilizing it.

So many stunningly shot scenes appear in *Bird* that the spectator comes away dumbfounded with the film's virtuosity. The opening three scenes establish themes, visuals, relationships, and musical devices that will reappear throughout the film. As opening credits roll, we meet Bird as a young boy playing the flute while he rides on a pony, which anticipates the later sequence of Bird as a young man "rescuing" Chan on a white horse. Significantly, the opening shot of the Warner Brothers logo appears on screen in black and white, perhaps signaling that this film, like some of Eastwood's later ones (*Mystic River*; *Letters From Iwo Jima*), has been shot in color as though it were a black and white movie. The opening fragment of the sequence is shot in brown tones like *Beguiled*, then cuts to black screen before the title *Bird* flashes on screen: one word, alone, as if to anticipate the loneliness of Charlie Parker the man, addict, and musical genius whose life story we are about to witness.

The young boy presumed to be the young Charlie Parker continues to play under the actors' names until the fragment segues into an adolescent Charlie practicing "O Christmas Tree" on a sax. The camera pans along a long wooden porch inhabited by men smoking weed. The sound fades into music from a nightclub and more credits. The minute we hear Parker begin to play, the credit "Music by Lennie Niehaus," known by name, not by race, appears on screen.

The camera circles around Bird as a spotlight beams like a star on a man so dark that only the front of his face and the back of his suit are lit. As he plays, the restless camera moves around him to focus on his fingers and face, although we still can barely see them. Cuts begin to accelerate, viewing the charismatic player from multiple angles as he deploys call and response with his clapping audience spellbound in ritual admiration, murmuring like birds. Dizzy Gillespie (Samuel E. Wright), who appears in the film as a character counterpoint, applauds and cheers him on. Other than the smoky darkness of the sequence, we could be watching a documentary like *Jazz on a Summer's Day* (Aran Avakian and Bert Stern, 1960). The virtuoso performance fades out with Bird's face in the left corner of the shot, displaced in a dissolve by a flying cymbal that cuts across a blue ground the color of Bird's suit. Before any kind of story line can be laid down, the spectator has glimpsed Parker's childhood home and the male models that surrounded him, scented a life-shaping humiliation not from whites but rather from men he admired, and witnessed his awesome career in full bloom—triumphant years slashed like the cymbal slashes the blue ground (symbolic of the fabric of his life).

The third scene of the film establishes more background for the genesis and development of Bird's music. We see the tortured relationship between Bird and Chan; the recent death of their child; Bird's return to drug use; and his suicide attempt, which we will learn later in the movie is not his first attack on himself. Underneath some of the shots we hear Bird's music again, dipping and soaring. Sequences four through 11 spin various levels of backstory through shifting time periods. We learn that Bird has few contracts (his recent suicide attempt is due in part to the recent decline of his career, the admitting doctor intones); his drug use has escalated; and his lack of professional confidence somehow relates to a thrown cymbal (public humiliation some eight years before).

Eastwood now shifts the movie's focus from Bird to Chan, his wife. Her sassy, no-nonsense sparring with Bird and the doctor who wants to lock him in an institution reminds me of Strawberry Alice in *Unforgiven* or Sue in *Gran Torino* or even the prostitute Gus Malley in *The Gauntlet*, women with no illusions about life who are every bit a man's equal. As the sequence opens, Chan has just called the dismissive doctor's bluff. Positioned in his office, standing over the seated wife, he intones magisterially: "If your husband were my brother, believe me, I'd commit him." Chan snaps back, in control: "Oh really? What's your brother's name?" In response, the doctor has to admit, "I don't have a brother," defusing the potential confrontation between a man used to dispensing orders and a woman who is as strong as he is. The scene prepares us to absorb the unfolding drama of years of fruitful collaboration between husband of wife that sours but never ends.

The camera now moves in on Chan's face, the screen darkens, and a lap dissolve carries us back in time to a younger Chan emerging from her brownstone with a light step and a big smile. The jazz starts up in the middle of the sequence in dialogue with shots of neon club signs, period cars gaudy in their boxy pretension, and the streets full of young cats and beautiful women. Once Chan has disappeared into the 18 Club, the all-seeing camera pans right to left to follow the hawking doorman around cars, past clubs, through the crowds along jazz-hopping 52nd Street, and finally back to the 18, where he meets Buster Franklin (Keith David). Then, cut, cut as Buster attempts to explode the myth of the "new man on the scene," Charlie Parker. A reprise of Bird's early failure feeds into the near-present of Bird's wild success and Chan's rapturous love. Suspense and progression build, as in a music composition.

Chan refuses to have Bird committed (for now we return to the present of this extended sequence) or subjected to electric shock, treatment certain to kill the heart of his creativity. (Eastwood displaces Chan's spirited defense of an innocent in Changeling, where an illegally incarcerated Christine Collins has been strapped to the shock table with only crusading preacher John Malkovich to rescue her. Like everything else in his career, Eastwood nibbles on the same themes repeatedly, building on one as he tackles the subject—perhaps justice or confession—from a new perspective.)

The rescue in Bird will not play out in this crazily nonlinear narrative line. Time flips back to the courtship, then to a magnificent early Bird performance; winter of 1946, with the sinister apparition of a drug dealer on the street; a rapturous performance with Dizzy Gillespie as "bebop invades the West"; the first of Bird's encounters with other white women; and more rescues and returns. After the dizzying trips through time and space, the image of a drunken Bird staggering behind a garbage-infested building opens up into the beginnings of Birdland and Bird's acclaim in Paris, one of the film's most graceful moments. It's slightly more than halfway through the movie, with Bird's band yet to move through the South, Red to get hooked on drugs, Bird and Chan to move into their new apartment, spectators to experience the death of their little girl, and the couple yet to move to the countryside to seek peace.

Before the last half-hour of the film begins, the sights and sounds of Bird in performance in real time (the Jewish wedding; the club in the South) or in memory (his various club appearances shown in the movie) fade. Bird walks down a rain-slicked street in the dark with no music to sustain him. More brief shots of his life will follow before movie's end, but the music has disappeared on screen and off, only to resurface in the oddly distanced funeral—the camera fixing its roving "bird's eye" on Bird's lifeless body. The final sequence begins with the cymbal's final fall, its circular shape mirrored in the dozens of umbrella tops we see from the camera's high perch above Adam Powell's Harlem church. "Come with me if you wanna go to Kansas City," croons the soundtrack ("Parker's Mood," recorded in 1947), as the funeral goers pack a partly visible coffin into the hearse and slowly process into the distance. It's now 1955, a time when white people would not even have considered this man's story worth telling. The shell of Charlie Parker's devastated 34-year-old body moves away from the viewer, leaving only his still-soaring spirit among us.

Bird, released soon after Eastwood's time as mayor and produced during his term, did not resonate with audiences in the United States. It was successful in Europe, however, and like many of his films, was particularly beloved in France. Still, its brilliance did not stop the whispers that the nearly 60-year-old Eastwood was on the decline. Part of this, of course, was because he was mayor of Carmel for some of this time, and was beginning his long breakup drama with Sondra Locke, but part was simply that his commercial films such as *Sudden Impact, The Dead Pool,* and *The Rookie* failed to resonate with audiences as much as they did in the decade prior, and the personal films such as *Bird* and *White Hunter, Black Heart* failed to find passionate champions besides a few lone reviewers.

After *Bird*'s triumphant reception in Paris, Clint acted in *The Dead Pool*, the fifth Dirty Harry (directed by Buddy Van Horn). As a director, he had long alternated small, personal films with blockbusters intended for wide audiences, but what a reversal for Clint the actor this time: from a labor-of-love biopic, *Bird*, to the final gasp of a long-in-the-tooth crime franchise. *The Dead Pool* was the least commercially successful of any of the Dirty Harry films (Schickel 1997, 432). Worse, it is boring.

In 1989, Eastwood fared no better: the same year that he broke with Locke, the same year that their acrimonious split spilled into bitter

Forest Whitaker, awarded Best Actor at the 41st Cannes Film Festival for his role as jazz great Charlie Parker in Eastwood's Bird. *(AP Photo/Pierre Gleizes/Gilbert Tourte)*

court filings, he slipped into *Pink Cadillac*. The movie, also directed by *The Dead Pool*'s Buddy Van Horn, ranks with *The Rookie* as a real mistake. Critic Tom Matthews puts it as though it were entirely obvious, "Eastwood, of course, called the shots on both films" (Matthews 1989, 102). It was another slight road film notable chiefly for the appearance of Bernadette Peters and for some hints of homoeroticism. The villains included a group of white supremacists. A trade journal article from the time praises Eastwood's studio, Warner Brothers, for its 1989 releases of the smash hits *Batman* and *Lethal Weapon*, but laments that *Pink Cadillac* was Eastwood's "poorest showing ever with a commercial vehicle (*Honkytonk Man* aside), indicating that some career retooling is in order" (Meisel 1990, 20). Matthews was even more dismissive:

One sure couldn't tell it from the Hollywood media mill, which continues to refer to Clint Eastwood as a certified box-office giant, but old Squintin' Clint hasn't been a major ticket-seller for some time now. Although his fall from popularity has not been as severe as his one-time rival Burt Reynolds, it appears that Eastwood's long reign at the theatres is fading fast. (Matthews 1989)

Clint's star was falling.

Next came *White Hunter, Black Heart*, like *Bird* and *Pale Rider*, an official, in-competition entry into the Cannes Film Festival. Clint's primary contribution to the evergreen "movies about moviemaking" genre, *White Hunter, Black Heart* is a roman à clef (or rather, film à clef), about legendary director John Huston's attempt to shoot his 1951 film *The African Queen* on location in Africa, at a time when few films were shot off studio lots. Eastwood's film is thinly fictionalized—the novel it is based on was written by *The African Queen*'s screenwriter. It had, and continues to have, its defenders, and its selection to compete in Cannes testified to the consistently high esteem in which the French hold him. Commercially, however, it was not a success, grossing even less than *Bird* did (Schickel 1997, 450).

If *Pink Cadillac* had its rare quirky charms and *White Hunter, Black Heart* betrayed a laudable sense of artistic ambition, *The Rookie* pandered to commercial tastes, even though it failed to capture that market. *The Rookie* is a bundle of clichés: Clint Eastwood as the grizzled veteran cop, Charlie Sheen as the hotshot rookie. Generational clashes and car chases ensue.

The Rookie, an unbearably bad film, does anticipate a few themes in Eastwood's follow-up, *Unforgiven*. In *The Rookie*, the star plays a version of the Harry Callahan "type," a tough guy facing the encroachment of age. Whether he intended to or not, he brought his previous performances as Dirty Harry to his role in *The Rookie*, all the better to cultivate the contrast between his character and Sheen's young rival/partner. In *Unforgiven*, Eastwood similarly builds upon his previous roles, this time in Westerns. Unlike in *The Rookie*, however, he does so with an artistic maturity unseen in Eastwood's best films until then and rarely in the American cinema at all in recent years. Sixty-two years old or not, he remained a powerful force among movie makers and within American popular culture.

REFERENCES AND FURTHER READING

Knapp, Laurence. 1996. *Directed by Clint Eastwood: Eighteen Films Analyzed*. Jefferson, ND: McFarland and Company.

Matthews, Tom. 1989. "*Pink Cadillac* Review." *Box Office*, August 1, 102.

Meisel, Myron. 1990. "'89 Box Office Hits Record $5.02 Billion." *The Film Journal*, February 1, 20.

Seitz, Matt Zoller. 2008. "Jazz on Screen: The Sparks Are Electric." *The New York Times*, April 13.

Smith, Paul. 1993. *Clint Eastwood: A Cultural Production*. Minneapolis: University of Minnesota Press.

Chapter 7

AN AMERICAN CLASSIC: *UNFORGIVEN*

In 1992, Clint Eastwood's Western *Unforgiven* opened to critical praise and audience amazement. A film of mesmerizing visual and narrative power, it dared to tackle the complexities and ambiguities of American history. We are, after all, a society born of violence, drenched in blood, and perpetuated by aggression that nonetheless struggles to fold into its body politic democratic ideals of freedom, peacemaking, and tolerance. How do we tackle such a conflicting and explosive heritage? We usually forget and move on, continually recreating our national image according to the various templates provided by the rhetoric of our two main political parties, and with the help of penny novels, tabloids, pulp fiction, movies, TV shows, and other media that have sought to harness memory and create a semblance of a "national" (and unified) history, as Benedict Anderson shows (*Imagined Communities*, 2007).

Even so foundational a transitional passage as the Civil War rarely has surfaced as a conceptual arena to explore the origins of our current problems (e.g., gang activity, ethnic divisions, affirmative action and its detractors, and anti-immigrant sentiment). We rarely visit our own history—except briefly as part of the 40th death anniversary of Martin Luther King Jr., and recently, with the election of Barack Obama, the

50th anniversary of the passage of the Civil Rights Bill and the 50th anniversary of the summer of 1964, "Freedom Summer," and the 2013 shocker, *12 Years a Slave* (Steve McQueen). How many citizens know about the Trail of Tears or realize how many soldiers died as a result of the Civil War and its aftermath? How many know the number of men, women, and children sold into slavery or are aware of the brutal abuse and murders of blacks that extended long after the signing of the Emancipation Proclamation?

Unforgiven, then, explores history and history's meaning. It simultaneously testifies to the vitality of the Western genre and mercilessly dissects it. As Kent Jones has written,

> With *Unforgiven*, Clint Eastwood's urge (or perhaps desire) to explore the reality of violence bloomed like a hearty desert flower, and it came as a genuine shock. *Unforgiven* took violence, broke it down, and patiently laid out the distinctions between intent, action, and aftermath, a rarity in American movies. Eastwood wasn't merely commenting on his own past, he was speaking to a country whose national profile had been tainted by the righteous postures of self-defense and hubristic bullying and whose commercial images were brimming over with violence. (Jones 2007, 182)

Eastwood is acutely aware not only of the particulars in the tradition, but also of the power of the myth to express the longings and the tensions of a people on the move. The film offers an ethical vision, not by any tidiness in its plot structure (e.g., an uncomplicated bloodbath or total conversion) but rather by the accumulation of images that convey the fragility of the human condition.

The movie engages two concerns fundamental to Eastwood's long career: the fashioning of mythic figures, especially in the Western, and the consequences of violence. The film simultaneously tells a story (Will Munny's return to gunfighting and its consequences) and presents a story about stories (replays of the myth of strong, glorious heroes embodied in Westerns). Will Munny, the protagonist, is drawn neither as a blameless hero nor as a seamless villain. He is a deeply conflicted person who struggles to carry his religious convictions into his

Director/actor/composer Eastwood in Unforgiven, *the end of glamorized violence. (Photofest)*

everyday worlds of work and family. At the movie's start, not only does he believe that he has been forgiven for robbery and murder, but he also realizes that he needs to continue to ask for forgiveness. The movie's plot recounts the testing of that forgiveness, radical by any measure. Even if his wife, whose grave he is digging in the prologue, had lived, Will could not have been cordoned off from the violence that suffused American society in the postwar years or shielded from the corrosive effects of extreme poverty. By movie's end, he rides off into a dark and merciless downpour which simultaneously signals despair over his return to violence and a hope that he might once more reclaim new life.

Fantasies of American dominance can be and are exploited by moviemakers and marketed through comic book figures. *Unforgiven* does not fit into the category of glamorous, even if restorative, violence, however. Regard the actual cinematic text of *Unforgiven*. Does this specific film glorify killing? Does it crown a savior who rides in on a white horse or in a government-issue cop car who rides into town with guns blazing? The answer is a resounding "No."

The confusion arises in part from the movie's own attitude toward the production of myths: the ways it exposes the gulf between myths that may turn violence into something positive, and the traumatic lived reality of violence, which cannot be cleansed through a narrative of redemption or progress. According to David Breskin, Eastwood commented that "it could be that the guy has all these violent images portrayed on the screen, and here comes along a piece of material that allows him to do something he's never been able to do in the past—which is to show where it all leads to. To philosophize about what is the value of it all" (1992). Elsewhere, Eastwood reflected upon the difference between "violence in movies" as "entertainment" in a 1993 interview with James Verniere. "As you get older, you tend to get more concerned about the moral values of society. . . . I wasn't doing any penance for the mayhem in my other films . . . it's just a time in my life, and maybe a time in history, when violence shouldn't be so lighthearted or glamorous. Maybe there are consequences to violence, for both the perpetrator and the victim, that are important to address" (Verniere 1993, 8–9).

The well-defined frame story encloses the turbulent, confusing, and tragic tale of William Munny's attempt to start anew. The prologue sets the stage for all that follows. Its images, music, and scrolling text place the events to come through the eyes of a horrified mother whose daughter married a (supposed) murderer and died young, not at his hands but from smallpox. Note that the text sets the stage for the spectator to believe that Will was actually a murderer, an allegation never proven in a court of law or demonstrated by evidence other than hearsay and his own "confessions." By the time the epilogue arrives to scroll down the screen, the question has become "why" the daughter had married a man "known" as a thief and murderer, "a man of "notoriously vicious and intemperate disposition." Note too that the text comes from the mother's perspective, not through a male voice-over (as in *Million Dollar Baby*; *Bob le Flambeur*; or *L.A. Confidential*, three famous examples of effective voice-overs) or an omniscient observer, who might also be presumed male.

Most critically, the objective camera and the distancing effect of the framing device remove the inner workings of the plot from the spectator's emotional engagement. The spectator remains at a significant distance from the mythmaking that usually spins Westerns out of control with worship of violence and the "heroes" that dispense it. The opening frame engages two other perspectives: that of the audience and that of the filmmaker, who controls the order in which the specta-tor takes in information. In this case, the spectator engages with Will Munny himself only after being preprogrammed by the opening frame to dislike and fear him.

The character of the Schofield Kid enters Munny's world to spread the "knowledge" about the farmer's legendary past that will drive the narrative forward. When the Kid first appears at the farm nine minutes into the film, he summarizes (in stilted language) the myth of the West-ern hero, in case we have forgotten its details: murder without remorse; fearlessness; the fracturing of social boundaries; the killing of innocent women and children. He recounts for Will the various stories he heard from his Uncle Pete about Will's exploits, stories that Will either does not remember or has chosen to forget: "Are you the same Will Munny who. . . ." Will responds: "I ain't like that no more, kid. 'Twas whiskey done it, much as anything else. My wife, she—cured me of that. Cured me of drinkin' an' wickedness." This exchange provides us with *fabula* (story) details—except that many of the Kid's details may be exagger-ated or wrong, storytellings that satisfy the needs of the myth and fit the tellers' fantasies rather than being based in historical fact.

The Kid reflects the legends, serving up variations of old ones and introducing new ones with odd, artificial flourish, always contrasting Will's present behavior with what emotions or actions Will Munny, as a hero of a certain kind of myth, ought to display. The lines of the legend are these: Will is a cold-hearted, ruthless, fearless man who has killed without remorse or reason. "You was the meanest . . . on account of you're as cold as the snow. You don't have no weak nerve nor fear." The Kid himself tries to mold his own behavior according to these ver-sions of the Western myth. "Gon' kill a coupla no-good cowboys," he announces as the purpose of his mission, as though killing is justified if the victims are known to be evil (defined as "bounty-hunters" or "mu-tilators of women").

The figure of the Kid suggests the infamous Billy the Kid, a self-created screwball who murdered randomly until his death in 1881 at age 21. He is one of our first media stars, catching the public imagination. Billy the Kid's real name was William Bonney. Is this another "What if" situation? What if Billy the Kid had been sickened by killing after his first murder, as Edward Buscombe suggests (Buscombe 2004, 34)? What if Munny had refused to accept The Kid as his apprentice into killing, exhorting him instead to refrain from murder, as Walt Kowalski pleads with Thao in *Gran Torino?*

Another character, W. W. Beauchamp, makes a living writing and embellishing the myths of Western "heroes" for readers accustomed to accounts rife with violent exploits. English Bob's story as relayed by his chronicler Beauchamp thoroughly airs the ease with which legends are created, embellished, and perpetuated. English Bob, however, is thoroughly discredited by Little Bill's "witness," while Bill himself does seem to validate the litany of evil deeds that haunt Will: "[are you] the same William Munny who blew up the train in '69, killing women and children?" Ned also corroborates a certain number of the stories, at least the ones that haunt Will the most: the drover and the man whose name he takes.

The weight of history, turned into myth, weighs upon Munny. He repeatedly admits when sober and when drunk that he has committed at least some of the acts ascribed to him in legend. In the main portion of the film's narrative, he reflects upon those acts in the context of religious belief and the law: they were wrong. Specifically, he implicitly refuses to be considered "redeemer," "avenger," "judge," when he says (of one of his past victims), "He didn't do anything to deserve [his death at my hands]." The notion of "deserving" death carries with it the implication that someone, perhaps the Angel of Death or the Avenging Angel, judges and then exacts punishment. But judgment and execution are found wanting. Ned, who at first thought that the cowboys "deserved" to die for cutting up a woman, refuses in the end to act as an avenger.

This movement forms the first part on Eastwood's statement regarding the Western and its relation to history and violence: the disjuncture between glorifying myths and the moral weight of lived history. We suspect but do not actually know that Munny has at the very least committed some of the crimes the stories relate, but his actions do not create a mythic hero. Rather, they expose the reality of a man anguished by what he remembers of his past actions.

The second critical and related aspect of Eastwood's *Unforgiven* is its view on violence. In *Unforgiven*, Eastwood the director represents violence as abhorrent, not manly or cleansing. In the final saloon scene, for instance, the natural setting, low light, and prowling camera sniff out each man's fear of death and emphasize the senselessness of the blood-bath. Will Munny has not been endowed with superhuman qualities. He is given neither star-lighting nor image-boosting that would seduce spectators into wishing that he stain himself with these murders. Every step of the film deglamorizes such extreme acts. As Richard Locke has written, "The film's relentlessly dark style prevents it from glamorizing this sordid violence and the man who dispenses it" (Locke 2008).

Will is not a slickly marketed hero who puts on or takes off his dis-guise and emerges from the darkness shouting that he is the savior of the world (or America, or the city of Gotham). Neither is he portrayed like Batman, the Dark Knight, Iron Man, Wolverine, or Superman. The main character is a person much like everyone else who has tried to shake off a bloody past. He announces his past actions as wrong and takes the consequences of his actions, even his final, murderous ones, upon himself.

Will has been changed radically by his love for Claudia, his wife. Yet again, Eastwood has reworked a long-standing plot device in the West-ern: the transformation of a (bad) man through the love of a woman. He refuses to sentimentalize, trivialize, or romanticize the love of Will and Claudia, whose surname, "Feathers," suggests either an Indian or a dancehall ancestry. For three years after Claudia's death, Will sustained his reformed life through storytelling (the recital of her virtues and her teachings, and what that love meant to him) and relationship (his chil-dren, the land, his animals). His constant refrain "I ain't like that no more" establishes an ethical norm in the movie where "wrong" means "to kill other humans." Will is trying to develop a new identity with a new center—a restored "character" shaped by the "habit of practicing virtue," creating a new (converted) life. As the movie reveals, that's a tough task without the support of a surrounding community and under severe economic hardship.

The fragile economy of Kansas where Will and his children live was destroyed by market forces—some would say cursed by living in a land that belonged to the indigenous tribes, now dead or displaced. The dictates of the "market" also lead Beauchamp to exaggerate his tales of Western gunslingers: what will sell? Droughts and plagues of locusts descended upon the state in the 1870s, while the plague of 1874 nearly destroyed all crops. Starvation threatened the settlers. During those years, the state was flooded with millions of cattlemen and their herds seeking railway passage from Texas through Kansas and Missouri to Eastern markets. *Rawhide*, which gave Eastwood his first starring role, recounted those drives, as did *Red River* (Howard Hawks, 1948). The sickness of Will's pigs may well have come from the herds relentlessly driven from Texas along the Sedalia Trail. The herds were later quarantined.

Set in historical context, then, the Kid's proposal would appeal to a man with a family to feed. Criticisms that Will is easily seduced or is charmed by the memory of his past ignore the historical facts and the misery of his life, which the visuals in the beginning of the film make painfully clear. Will is no longer a creation of legend or a conscious maker of legend, the stories we create to keep chaos at bay when faced with life's disorder. Since Eastwood shoots with natural light and on location and rarely uses stunt doubles, Will's spills into the mud or his struggles with his horse feel natural and painful. The pace of the editing reinforces the sense of weariness: rather slow, giving time for situations (falls, bungled target practice, missed mounts) to play out their feeling of age and desperation.

The first scene in Greeley's saloon, about one-third the way into the film, underlines the tired old man's fallibility. Will does not respond to taunts with guns blazing, as the genre demands, or because he is nobly self-restraining like Shane, or because he has sworn off fighting, as Will Kane did in *High Noon*. He doesn't fight back because he is ill, his gunpowder is wet, and he remains strongly under the influence of his dead wife.

Even without the qualifiers, Will is not visualized as a macho man who angers and strikes in the continuous present. He is struggling under post-traumatic stress disorder—the profound depression that sinks a person who cannot shake off dreams, sights, and back flashes of horrific events. The night before, as the three men huddled around their dim campfire, they questioned not only whether they did what others say they did, but *whether what they did was right*. The connections between apocalyptic events and ethics are made plain. The horror of Will's memories—his confession to a receptive Ned and an uncomprehending Kid—awakens conscience. The killings were not only wrong but also disgusting, defiling, and foul. Will reflects upon killing and death in ways that depart from his formulaic rehearsals of his sins he had displayed earlier for his children ("I seen the error of my ways . . . the sins of my youth," or even his confessions to Ned, "Claudia . . . leared me o' drinkin' whiskey an' all. Just cause we're goin' on this killing, that don't mean I'm goin' to go back to being the way I was. I just need the money").

Extreme close-ups of Ned's and Will's faces allow Will's deadened delivery to convey more power than his words, as he begins what will become a refrain of recollections on the brutal facts of death, memories of what happens when a bullet rips into a skull or a chest. Teeth fly out the back of the head, brains spill out—an image that recalls a passage from Book XVI in the *Iliad*:

> His teeth were all of them knocked out and the blood came gush-
> ing in a stream from both his eyes; it also came gurgling up from
> his mouth and nostrils, and the darkness of death enfolded him
> round about. (Homer)

Of the drover, to whom Will refers in his ravings: "He didn't do any-thing to deserve to get shot." Will has abandoned whatever superiority he enjoyed as hero of a legend and is "Just a fella now . . . no different than anyone else—no more."

Will has tried to live with the consequences of his acts, but he seems doomed to recall the acts themselves—endlessly, without relief—like the protagonists of *Saving Private Ryan* (Steven Spielberg, 1998), *A Very Long Engagement* (Jean Jeunet, 2004), *Flags of our Fathers* (Eastwood, 2006) and later *Gran Torino* (2008). The narrated memories of violent deaths that he himself caused echo the constant visual reminders of Will's own mor-tality: trouble catching his hogs; repeated difficulties mounting his horse. The man in the original script was 35–40, which would fit into the post–Civil War profile. Eastwood held onto the script about 10 years to be sure that he was old enough to fit the way he conceived of the role, as Richard Schickel reports (1997, 453). He gathered around him men of around the same age: Morgan Freeman, Gene Hackman, and Richard Harris.

Will blames the failures on his earlier mistreatment of animals, but his son's shrug and sober glance at his little sister say they know well that their father's powers are failing. He can no longer sleep on the ground without discomfort and illness; he is slow, tired, and sick during most of the film. Will, Ned, English Bob, and Little Bill are all of a "certain age," *totally unlike* themselves as figures in their legend. Heroes do not age, and heroes do not reflect upon the morality of their actions. Not only do they inflate deeds and conflate versions of stories, but they also stop time—they defeat aging and death itself, freezing the hero in the endless present.

Little Bill, unlike English Bob and unlike the Kid, insists on telling the truth (or so it seems) not only about written accounts of Western history but also about the human condition. If civilization is to progress in this wild country, Bill reasons, strong men must hold absolute power and the weak must be eliminated. In *Hang 'Em High*, the "hanging judge" justifies hanging, even of adolescents, with this argument. The legendary Wyatt Earp, upon whom Bill's character is based in part, also violently enforced "no guns" in his town. In Big Whiskey, Little Bill dispenses justice with complete abandon: he is technically within the law, his law. He enforces morality, a rejection of violence, by violence. Edward Buscombe notes: "[Little Bill] Daggett is a man with a past who is trying to live it down, and no more than Munny can he lay his demons to rest. At least he has the law on his side, his brutality covered with the fig-leaf of legal authority" (2004, 37).

Richard Schickel thinks that Eastwood had the beating of Rodney King and the image of Daryl Gates, police chief of the LAPD, on his mind when he created this character. He also could have referenced the debates inside the Christian Church during and after the Civil War era. Churchmen endlessly quoted Romans 13: 1–6 to defer to authorities, as English Bob pontificates: "Men must defer to the aura of royalty." "Reality" in this version of the West is not simply what is shaped and told about the past or what is shaped and written, but also what the legends of the West themselves reveal about human nature.

The ideal community that Eastwood envisions in the film abhors violence and leans toward peace, just as Ned refuses to shoot Little Davy ("I can't, Will,") and rides away from the death squad, and just as the Kid sobs with disgust and remorse after he has shot one of the "villains" at close range. Two sequences balance death's horrors with life's regenerative power, the deathbed scene in the mountain cabin outside Big

Whiskey, and the morning when Will awakens from his near-death. As he lies dying, Will "sees" the Angel of Death and "sees" his wife—not only on the plane of spiritual reality, as Ned thinks, but at the level of phenomenon (physical reality), as her rotting corpse would appear if exhumed. The dying man's head is supported by his beloved friend as the Kid looks on, all three figures barely illuminated by a flickering fire. The tableau recalls paintings and sculptures of the Virgin Mary cradling the head of the dead Christ such as Michelangelo's "Pietà." Will lies at the point of death three days, sustained by Ned's care and by the food and water provided by the prostitutes. The shack where he lies is situated "outside the camp"—far removed from the so-called civilization of Big Whiskey, its outcasts hidden from the faces of the respectable. (Although note that we see almost no one in Big Whiskey except Little Bill and his deputies: no children, no women except the prostitutes, no school, no church.)

Notably, Sergio Leone used the iconography of the resurrection at the end of *Fistful of Dollars* when the Man with No Name comes back from death and appears in a cloud on the main street. As The Man pulls aside his poncho to reveal his secret device (an iron plate that has protected his heart), he shifts from the mystical into the rational world. Eastwood removes Leone's clever debunking of mysticism in *Unforgiven*. The dying man is sustained and brought back to life not by magic but by the care of the prostitutes and his friends. Only the ancient formula—three days in a tomb—remains the same.

The sequence that depicts Will's near-death climaxes the train of shifting postures toward death in the film. "I seen the Angel of Death. . . . He got snake eyes. . . . I'm scared of dying. I seen Claudia, too. . . . Her face was all covered with worms. I'm scared. . . . Don't tell nobody. Don't tell my kids none of the things I done, hear me?" He means: Don't poison my children's memory with the tales, real or legendary.

In the cave-like enclosure of the mountain, Eastwood captures the inexpressible experience of being near death, which he recreated 14 years later in *Letters from Iwo Jima*. His films are full of campfire scenes of confession, where characters assess their lives and deal with guilt: *The Gauntlet, Pale Rider, A Perfect World. Gran Torino* includes two confessions, a false one and a real one. In *Unforgiven*, Will attempts to silence the recurring nightmares that even religious conversion did not quell. Will's feelings upon committing his first murder have been transposed and put into the mouth of the Kid.

For death is really like Young Davey's, with blood and thirst and abandonment. Death ends the life we know and should not be glamorized, as the Kid realizes when he actually kills a living, breathing human being. When men are drunk, they kill heedlessly; when they become sober, they have to drink again to forget that they have "take[n] away all [a man's] got, and all he's ever gonna have": his breath, his earthiness (his humanity, *humus*, from the earth), and his spiritual identity.

The saloon sequence activates the film's suppressed genre elements: purification of a polluted space by searing violence. A lone gunman seeks personal vengeance. But Eastwood handles the elements with care. Paradoxically, it is impelled by love of his friend that Will appears to emerge as the quintessential hero of the myth who commits the unthinkable, killing unarmed men in the name of an enlarged conception of justice that transcends Little Bill's petty tyranny. Ned has "died for what we done," as Will says, died exactly, not symbolically as his wife had, for Will's sins.

The Will who enters Greeley's saloon the second time, gun barrel positioned approximately where it would be if the spectator were holding the gun, is a Will reborn not simply of whiskey and his own bloody past but also of Ned's sacrifice in the name of all that keeps human society from degenerating into a living embodiment of death, full of worms and snakes. Conflicting versions of a savior theme are held in tension at the end: the redeemer as cleanser, like the rain (think of *Pulp Fiction*); the redeemer as an agent of transformation who steps into a social and religious void; the redeemer as the wish-fulfillment of a passive and misled viewing public. The killings can be seen as driven by the whiskey Will consumes, alluding to the American myth of purifying justice by violence, or the opposition to killing and torture performed in the name of civilization, where the spectator experiences the hideous death act as a personal violation of human dignity.

Any one-dimensional glorification of violence, however, has been undercut by the film's rejection of violence, even as the film's dramatic structure appears to push the story to its explosive conclusion. *Unforgiven* turns ideas about justice and community upside down. Its text asks when, if ever, we need to kill; it insists that as flawed human beings we can and must be redeemed by love. Myths and legends of the Old West perpetuate our violent heritage. But *Unforgiven* recognizes, dissects, and rejects this destructive code. As Richard Locke has written about *The Man Who Shot Liberty Valance*, "the entire film is a dramatic analysis of the evolution and problematic value of heroic Western legends" (2008).

Unforgiven's ending allows multiple interpretations that can range from disgust at its gratuitous violence to violence appropriate to the context to complete rejection of violence. If you commit violence to right violence, then you are trapped. Might forgiveness offer a way out? The cut prostitute wants to forgive, but the community won't let her. Eastwood's way of treating violence is thoughtful and carefully reasoned, yet there's no resolution. Ambiguity—uncertainty about what this film "means"—remains long after the movie is finished, and so does its powerful *mise-en-scène*—the isolated cabin rimmed by distant mountains and lit in the golden sunset; the hotel, which represents the little that exists of family, communal meals, and human connection in this town; Little Bill's crooked house, a physical symbol of his desire to create a civilization with his own hands according to his own (crooked) code; and the near-death sequence in the hideout cabin. But ambiguity, as Russian philosopher Mikhail Bakhtin observed about Dostoyevsky's novels (1984), marks a great narrative.

From the perspective of 1992, Eastwood, a student of war and war films, examined two world wars, Hiroshima and Nagasaki, the firebombing of the German cities and Tokyo, the Cold War, and a string of wars America either plunged into or started. Moving to 2003, Eastwood did not support the invasion of Iraq (Palmer 2011). Seen in the broader context of devastating wars, the bloodbath of the sequence in the saloon makes sense. Through his camerawork and pacing, Eastwood comments on the endless cycle of violence that made its way into sophisticated weaponry. The poverty and diminished vision of Big Whiskey's men gives yet another signal of the price humans pay to continue their battles.

A Hollywood film would have ended with Will healed, Delilah rescued from her sordid life and married to Will, and the two friends and Delilah riding back home safely for an emotional reunion with their families. Indeed, the original script for *Unforgiven* played with the romance angle. The Kid would have had glasses made and get a job in a shoe store. Will's farm would grow sunflowers and soybeans, and his children would become lawyers. In the old Westerns such as *Stagecoach*, the hero and heroine often took off into the sunset to settle down on a farm or went to California to rear a family.

Working backwards from the final frame, we hear of a rumor that Will and the kids moved to California, where he became a successful capitalist. Ned is dead. The Kid disappears, shattered by the trauma of killing another human being at close range. Eastwood captured the young man at the moment of his first murder.

Unforgiven as a movie neither advertises nor promotes the murder of Delilah's two violators. It also distinguishes visually between the principal culprit, Mike, and his simple partner, Davey. It does not applaud the violent purging activities of Little Bill and his deputies—the brutal beating of English Bob—which ironically takes place on July 4, Independence Day, before a horrified audience, including his own deputies. The merciless near-fatal beating of Will and the whipping death of Ned add to the picture of the sheriff as a sadist. When English Bob is beaten, the camera looks at Little Bill from the ground up, emphasizing the man's 6' 4" frame and his menacing features. Will is weak and feverish when Little Bill brutalizes him. And as Ned is being whipped, we glimpse not only the man's anguished face but also his killer's delight in the victim's pain.

In *Unforgiven*, the Civil War is not mentioned, but the uncontrolled violence emerged from the prewar border wars between Missouri and Kansas and from the Civil War itself, which are referenced repeatedly in this movie as well as in *The Outlaw Josey Wales*. The Civil War developed out of centuries-long enslavement and exterminations of blacks and native peoples. Even apart from the war's backstory, survivors from both sides had been brutalized in battle or in the hideous prisons of Andersonville and Fort Douglas, had seen their friends murdered, and had lost their homes and their livelihood. They saw death all around them: not only from the war, but also from the extermination of millions of men, women, and children from the tribes and their source of food, the buffalo. Eastwood strips the veneer from war movies as well as from memories of the war itself, an ethical strategy he would later follow in 2006 with *Flags of Our Fathers* and *Letters from Iwo Jima*, in 2008 with *Gran Torino*, and in 2009 with *Invictus*.

Although the final saloon sequence in the movie may fit the structural expectations of the genre (a showdown in a saloon between an admired hero and an assortment of villains), it is heavily qualified by the cinematography of the scene and by the nearly two hours of criticism of killing that has preceded it. That is, it is not shot as though it is part of a "realistic" story world in the narrative mode of "irony" or "low mimetic" (ordinary human beings) that characterizes the rest of the movie. Rather, it slips into the "mythic" mode, an interpolated tale set in the middle of a film that for two hours has insistently criticizes the violation or killing of another human being through words, glances, editing strategies, and events—the quiet exchanges that mark Eastwood's careful and deeply human visual style.

The conversation between Ned and Will as they ponder whether or not to take on the bounty assignment takes place in a darkened, cramped cabin room surrounded by the refreshing green bounty of Ned and his wife's farm. The leisurely ride from Kansas toward Wyoming crosses lush golden fields; the men reveal the depth of their friendship not through harsh, so-called manly insults but rather through humorous exchanges (the masturbation sequence, for instance). When they finally arrive in Big Whiskey, sex again becomes funny, as Ned and the Kid barely escape death through jumping out a window with their trousers partly down.

Even the final sequence in Greeley's Saloon, which many critics view as Will's return to his old ways in joy, not sorrow, is set up as an aberration—not only for Will, who when sober wished to live in peace, but also for life on this good earth. The first and last frames of the film—golden tableaux visualizing the imagined beauty of the West—display the quiet corner of the earth where the former gunslinger had hoped to make his home.

Unforgiven was a sensation. It culminated Eastwood's nearly 35-year engagement with the Western genre and, by extension, with his own screen personae and the mythos and history of America itself. It quickly silenced the whispers from the late-1980s that suggested that his time had come and gone. The film grossed over a hundred million dollars at the box office—$167,000,000 adjusted for inflation, according to Box Office Mojo and adjusted for inflation using the Bureau of Labor Statistics calculator. This is an astounding number for a violent, R-rated film with a 62-year old lead actor. It also garnered him critical acclaim the likes of which he had never before received. Even the projects that were well reviewed prior to Unforgiven—The Outlaw Josey Wales, Bird—paled in comparison to it. It is difficult to imagine now, after his astonishing run of critically adored films in the 2000s, but for most of his career Eastwood was widely considered a commercial filmmaker and actor, unconcerned with Oscar-bait projects and prestige. Although he did alternate wildly popular action and crime films with more personal projects, even the personal films were viewed by many critics as works by a filmmaker whose commercial successes gave him the right to indulge in whatever whimsical projects he wished, rather than to shape award-winning masterpieces.

Unforgiven was different. It received nine Academy Award nominations and won four, including two for Eastwood: one for Best Director and one for Best Picture (he was its producer). He was even nominated for Best Actor, itself surely a gratifying occurrence for a man whose acting ability was widely disparaged throughout much of his career. The speech that followed his Best Director win is telling. When Barbra Streisand announces his name as winner, the audience rises to its feet. His costar Morgan Freeman beams, as does Gene Hackman, also a winner for Best Supporting Actor. After a self-effacing quip, Eastwood says to the gathered audience and to viewers on television, "This is pretty good, this is all right." He laughs to himself a bit, and then continues, reminding the audience, "I've been around for 39 years." Referencing the "year of the woman" (as 1992 was called because of the election of several women to the U.S. Senate), he thanks the actresses playing the "women of Big Whiskey," whom he calls "the gals who were really the catalysts for getting this story off the ground." He then thanks the studio, the screenwriter, his agent, all common for an awards acceptance speech. He also, however, thanks "the film critics, for discovering this film; it wasn't a highly [touted] film when it came out but they sort of stayed with it throughout the year; the French film critics who embraced some of my work very early in the game; the British Film Institute; the Museum of Modern Art; some of the people that were there long before I became fashionable."

It was striking to see Clint express gratitude to the Academy for giving him the Oscar, while he also acknowledged the earlier advocates of his work. Surely he felt validated after decades of frustration over critical dismissals. His acceptance speech for the Best Picture Oscar a short time later was brief and relaxed, made memorable by his sweet shout-out to his mother, Ruth, in the audience.

REFERENCES AND FURTHER READING

Anderson, Benedict. 2007. *Imagined Communities: Reflections on the Origin and Spread of Nationalism, Revised*. London: Verso.

Bakhtin, Mikhail. 1984. *Problems of Dostoevsky's Poetics*. Edited and Translated by Caryl Emerson. Minneapolis: University of Minnesota Press.

Blight, David W. 2001. *Race and Reunion: The Civil War in American Memory*. Cambridge, MA: The Belknap Press of Harvard University Press.

Breskin, David. 1992. "Clint Eastwood" (Interview). *Rolling Stone*, September 17, 66.

Buscombe, Edward. 2004. *Unforgiven*. London: BFI.

Homer. 1994. *The Iliad*. Translated by Samuel Butler. http://classics.mit.edu/Homer/iliad.html. Accessed February 27, 2014.

Jones, Kent. 2007. *Physical Evidence: Selected Film Criticism*. Middletown, CT: Wesleyan University Press.

Locke, Richard. 2008. "Grand Horse Opera." *The American Scholar*, Summer. http://theamericanscholar.org/grand-horse-opera/. Accessed February 24, 2014.

Palmer, Martyn. 2011. "'A School Reunion? It Would Be Pointless. There Wouldn't Be Anybody There.' Clint Eastwood at 80." *The Daily Mail*, January 17. http://www.dailymail.co.uk/home/moslive/article-1347108/Clint-Eastwood-80-A-school-reunion-There-wouldnt-anybody-there.html#ixzz259WGw3S5. Accessed February 27, 2014.

Schickel, Richard. 1997. *Clint Eastwood: A Biography*. New York: Vintage.

Verniere, James. 1993. "Clint Eastwood: Stepping Out." *Sight and Sound*, September 1, 6–10.

Chapter 8

THE POETRY OF SUFFERING: FROM *A PERFECT WORLD* TO *MYSTIC RIVER*

Eastwood's primary Westerns probed the stumbling course of earthly justice, particularly as felt by people who live on the edges of American society. The social order shown in the movies—not their "plot summaries" but their actual substance—shows not the triumph of the American dream but rather the fractured lives of its victims and the rippling effects of genocide and land theft. Richard Locke refers perceptively to the "moral, even moralistic," cast in the "two elegant, fluent, beautifully constructed" Westerns, *High Plains Drifter* and *Pale Rider* (Locke 2008).

In *Unforgiven*, moreover, the disturbing elements of its rich plot— what happened, who's to blame, what can be done—takes on a distinctive cast of innocence and guilt, blame, confession, exoneration, and forgiveness more troubling and yet more grave than the vengeance story itself. The arresting visual of Will Munny (his name comments upon the cash-focused story) in the mud with his sick pigs captures the sad fall of a man once reborn and now desperate, locked into an economic system imperiled by the postwar beef economy and disease. Once (reportedly) a man of violence, he has tried to limit the amount of damage he now brings into the world by giving up the alcohol that fueled his destructive behavior and by building a home for his family. Bad luck, the death of his wife from smallpox, is followed by the sickness of his animals—diseases with possible human or social causes, but each touched nonetheless by unfathomable mystery. The last great Western "never stoops to sentimentality or glamour (or reverse chic) and is never self-important or vain. It's an inexorable condemnation of the Western gunman as a psychotic monster" (Locke 2008).

In the Westerns and the deeply personal movies, crimes encapsule more than mysteries for the detective to solve. They beg for tears. They beg for answers. Most of all, they beg for questions: Why has this happened? Who is responsible? How do we wrap our minds around such events? Yet, we must. Eastwood is one of the few American directors to think intentionally about the problem of evil as other than as a Technicolor or digitalized subject to divert audiences and feed their thirst for distanced retributive violence.

In *Mystic River* and *Changeling*, the crimes involve frightful acts of violence that may or may not be connected with human agents—acts of violence against children. Even the accident in *Million Dollar Baby* is caused indirectly by child abuse, as we see when the movie starkly details its heroine's abusive family and observes the corrosive surroundings from which Maggie was frantic to escape.

A Perfect World provided a transition from *Unforgiven* to Eastwood's current fertile period, not only in its searching title but also in its link between child abuse and a young adult's suffering. Eastwood's Texas Ranger, Red Garnett, sends the young Butch Haynes (Kevin Costner) to prison to protect him from an abusive father who otherwise would have killed him. Yet Butch's suffering has no end. Despite his attempt to reach Alaska, the "perfect world" where he dreamed his childhood might be restored, he will never get there.

A Perfect World appeared in 1993, unheralded despite its stars (Eastwood, Kevin Costner, and Laura Dern). It would be 10 more years before Eastwood recaptured with *Mystic River* the similarly intense rhythm of an existential quest woven into an apparently simple thriller. Who murdered Katie, only child of Jimmy Markum and his beloved dead wife Maria? The murder becomes entangled with another crime, the four-day sexual abuse of Jimmy's childhood friend, a troubling event that has haunted the entire neighborhood for 25 years. Nothing can ever bring back the boy's innocence and put his world to right.

The mysteries intensified with each year's stunning output. In *Million Dollar Baby*, why is Maggie poor? Why is the wise man Scrap condemned to live in a back room in the gym where he sweeps the floors and cleans the toilets? How can the rupture between father and daughter ever be mended? And what happened to Walter Collins, the abducted son of a loving single mother? *Changeling* sets out on a multilayered quest to wrest the answer from the universe itself.

The universal questions embedded in Eastwood's Westerns (the search for justice in a puzzling and brutal world) are now set in vastly different surroundings—a poor Boston neighborhood; a seedy corner of Los Angeles; and a corrupt city that could be anywhere. They take on even greater urgency as the distance between three appealing stories, all of which also feature strong women, is brought close to our own time and the price of injustice made glaringly, heartbreakingly, human. The viewer seeks answers but finds only layers of questions woven into the films' dense, poetic textures.

The press, to a degree at Eastwood's own urging, assumed that *Unforgiven* was a kind of valedictory, a culmination not only of his engagement with the Western genre but also of his career as a whole. Around the time of *Unforgiven*'s release, Hilary de Vries wrote that:

> he is making what is probably his last Western and also the final film in which he both directs and acts. His next movie, a rare non-Warners project, Castle Rock's *In the Line of Fire*, features Eastwood as an actor . . . after that he says, he will probably just direct. His first project is a thriller starring Kevin Costner. (De Vries 1992)

Eastwood did not even last as long as that thriller, *A Perfect World*, before he resumed the delicate and taxing role of actor/director. He took second billing to Costner, a major early-1990s movie star coming off of a streak of hits that included *Dances with Wolves*, *Robin Hood: Prince of Thieves*, *JFK*, and *The Bodyguard*. At least one moment of tension surfaced on the set—perhaps bound to occur when a major movie star used to getting his own way agrees to work on a film for a

director famous for moving on after only one take. In *Esquire*, writer
Tom Junod relays an anecdote from Eastwood's cinematographer Jack
Green:

> Eastwood directed [A *Perfect World*], and didn't agree to act in
> it until Costner pushed him to—because, as he told a member
> of the crew, he wanted to have a poster featuring him and Clint
> Eastwood. But Costner was a big star who had agreed to make an
> art film while Eastwood was determined to make a Clint Movie,
> and they were at cross-purposes. Finally, Eastwood called Costner
> from his trailer for a scene, and Costner told him to wait—that he
> wasn't ready. (Junod 2012)

It did not matter to Eastwood that Costner was coming off of *The Bodyguard*—he was shooting on his schedule whether the star was ready or
not. Junod continues:

> "Find his extra," Eastwood said, "and put a shirt on him."
> He wound up shooting the scene with the extra—with the
> extra walking through a field, and the camera so close to him he
> became a blur. Then Costner emerged from his trailer and an-
> nounced that he was ready to work. "Never mind," Eastwood said,
> "we're moving on."
> "You shot the scene with my *extra?*" Costner said, in what would
> be the first of several exchanges with his director. (Junod 2012)

In an odd intersection of stars, Eastwood plays the role of a sad,
somewhat embittered Texas lawman with an uneasy conscience,
while Costner shines. To indicate Eastwood's formidable ability
to rebound, within two years Costner entered a two-decade slump
revived only this year with his new movie, *Jack Ryan: Shadow Re-
cruit* (2014), with Costner not as Jack Ryan the hero but rather as
the older, wiser CIA agent Thomas Harper. Eastwood, meanwhile,
reinvented himself as a lover in the spectacular *Bridges of Madison
County* with Meryl Streep and soon passed from "best actor" to one
of America's top living directors with the string of masterworks that
began with *Mystic River*.

A *Perfect World* was well-received. Janet Maslin, writing for the *New York Times* on November 24, 1993, called it "a deeply felt, deceptively simple film," going so far as to call it "the high point of Mr. Eastwood's directing career thus far." *In the Line of Fire*, his other 1993 release, was a major hit, one of the top 10 highest-grossing films of the year. *In the Line of Fire* and *A Perfect World* evoke a common historical trauma: the assassination of John F. Kennedy. *In the Line of Fire* has Eastwood as the last active Secret Service agent to have been assigned to Kennedy at the time of his assassination, and the character is haunted by his inability to prevent the killing decades earlier. Like *Unforgiven*, the plot engages with memory, trauma, and the onset of old age. *A Perfect World*, by contrast, is set in Texas in 1963, a period of soon-to-be-shattered optimism. The budding paternal friendship between Costner's escaped convict and good-natured eight-year-old hostage, and that friendship's unnecessarily violent conclusion, resonates with the promise and tragedy of the Kennedy years.

Yet *A Perfect World* (many times voted by my students as their favorite Eastwood film, even compared with *Unforgiven* or *Gran Torino*) is far more than a "thriller" in the *Line of Fire* mold. "Compassionate" and "humanistic" (Simsolo 2003, 192), it establishes a utopian vision with its opening shot (to be repeated at the end of the film), where in a God's-eye shot the camera catches a view of Butch lying in the middle of a field, a restful, even transcendent scene underscored by meditative music. The movie explores its characters' search for "a perfect world" as they fight for survival in a deeply flawed one. At the movie's heart lies the blossoming friendship between an escaped convict, Butch (Kevin Costner) and his hostage, Phillip. Eastwood touches many of his previous themes as their friendship unfolds: damaging vs. nurturing family bonds; escape from an unforgiving prison; bumbling and even damaging law enforcement; false patriotism; evil masked as friendliness; justice tempered by mercy.

The inner plot crosscuts between festivity (Hallowe'en) and deprivation (a Jehovah's Witness family, isolated by their refusal of mainstream social rituals) and a prison break. The escape refers not only to Don Siegel's *Escape from Alcatraz*, in which Eastwood starred, but also to Robert Bresson's *A Man Escaped* from 1956, which Siegel listed as an influence on his successful film. Two men emerge from the

tunnel: Butch (Costner) and a hated prison mate. Immediately Eastwood exposes the men's characters. Jerry, violent and abusive to women,
is also a pedophile soon dispatched by Butch. Butch, we learned in part
through a running subplot that involves Red Garnett (Eastwood) and
a court psychologist Sally Gerber (Laura Dern), was a throwaway child
born to a suicidal prostitute and homicidal father. Red wrongheadedly
sent the young Butch to the juvenile detention center for car theft,
thinking to save him from death at his father's hands. Instead (as he
should have known), the prison destroyed the boy.

The film sets out to redeem the grown man, with whom the spectator comes to sympathize. Eastwood conveys its deep humanity by leisurely exchanges of glance and acts: nuanced conversations between
the boy and Butch, his abductor; and the constant contrast between
the man's and boy's quest for paradise (framed as "Alaska," where their
series of stolen cars is headed) and the cruelly commercial social order
that lies along their way. Friendly's store, where Butch and Phillip stop
for supplies, drips with heavy Texas accents, too-friendly saleswomen,
and a falsity that shields shrieking violence beneath the surface of
townspeople.

The movie's slow, gentle conversations as Butch and Phillip speed
along the Texas back roads lulls us into forgetting that Butch is fleeing
for his life as well as seeking freedom. They talk about love and Alaska,
cotton candy and freedom to do what you want in America. They
exchange a few words about their fathers, about sex and love, about
self-image. The two nighttime shots in the car's interior anticipate the
interior shots between Maggie and Frankie in *Million Dollar Baby*.

Twice in the movie Butch kills offscreen: once, we surmise that he
killed the prison guard at the gate; we see him later wearing the man's
shirt. Once, we guess (and find out shortly when the police roll in) that
he shot his escape partner, who was attempting to molest Phillip. The
incidents signal a shift in the film's attitude toward crime: murder can
be justified for a greater good (to escape to freedom; to protect a child).
Theft, too, can be excused if you need something badly (like Phillip's
theft of the Hallowe'en costume). The cardinal sin in this moral system, though, is child abuse.

Two times Butch and Phillip are rescued. Two times a "nice" family
hides abusive relationships: the white mother in the station wagon; the

black family in the farmhouse. Eastwood sets us up for a Hollywood ending: after the black grandfather welcomes Butch and Phillip with a bed and tasty breakfast, Butch and the grandmother dance to "Big Fran's Baby," played on the Victrola. What could be more comforting? But the grandfather hits his little boy, and Butch goes crazy.

When I saw this movie again, I found the split between comic and ironic figures and Butch's decency and Phillip's innocence all the more striking. Eastwood chose to film a timely topic again: Texas, with the highest rate of executions in the United States, is riddled with abuse in the prison system, particularly in juvenile detention centers. "Tough love" camps to break kids of drugs, where sometimes kids die, were slowly being exposed at the time of the movie. As an actor, Eastwood took a back seat to his superstar and his young protégé. As a director, he added to his résumé of powerful, multilayered humanistic but un-sentimental dramas.

1995 brought yet another change of pace—a full-blown romance in *The Bridges of Madison County,* in which Eastwood plays a pho-tographer who embarks on a brief, passionate affair with an Italian-born housewife played by Meryl Streep. Eastwood's characters often have love interests—though they are sometimes dead (*Dirty Harry; Unforgiven; Gran Torino*) or estranged (*True Crime*). Often they find themselves in danger (*Josey Wales*), which allows Clint's characters to come to the rescue. In terms of unabashed romantic drama, however, removed from the context of the crime film or the thriller, this was a first. Commentators were curious about the working relationship be-tween Clint Eastwood, intuitive actor, efficient director, economical producer, and his costar Streep, whose acting is an epitome of the studied, deliberate, some may say mannered, approach. As Maureen Dowd put it, "She was groomed at Yale Drama School and in Shake-spearean drama. After a stint as a lumberjack and some time in the Army, he was discovered hanging around the coffee wagon at CBS" (Dowd 1995).

Yet the two actors complemented each other. Streep, for her own part, effusively praised her director and costar: "I know a score of ac-tors who would avoid exposing their emotions the way he does in this movie. . . . He was very raw. I was shocked. I think he's just reached a point in his life where he doesn't give a damn" (Dowd 1995). Streep may be underselling his savvy, since *The Bridges of Madison County* is the type of film audiences adore: surprising, romantic, mature. It was almost universally praised as a vast improvement over the treacley, offensively patronizing book upon which it was based. Streep garnered an Oscar nomination for her performance.

Between *The Bridges of Madison County* and *Mystic River* (2003), Eastwood's artistic output slowed. His personal life also settled considerably. After the protracted litigation relating to his breakup with Locke, his more civil split with Frances Fisher must have been a relief. True to form, Eastwood began drifting away from Fisher long before they split publicly, just as with Maggie when he started seeing Locke and with Locke herself. In 1993, he and Frances had a daughter, Francesca Ruth Fisher-Eastwood, now a model and actress.

Maureen Dowd's column asserted that he and Fisher were still living together in 1995, which may have been true technically, but he had also begun a relationship with Dina Ruiz, a newscaster several decades younger than he (Eliot 2009, 293). They met in the early 1990s when she interviewed him for a Salinas, CA, NBC affiliate (Eliot 2009, 289). The couple married in March 1996 shortly after his final split with Fisher. It was only his second marriage. In September of that year, he finally severed ties with Locke. He settled out of court after it became clear that a jury might decide in favor of Locke in her fraud case against him. In December of 1996, daughter Morgan was born.

In the late 1990s and early 2000s, Eastwood did not make anything as pandering as *Firefox* or *The Rookie*, although *Space Cowboys* comes close, but neither did he reach the artistic high of *Unforgiven*. Instead, he directed and acted in thrillers and middle-of-the-road dramas like *Absolute Power*, *True Crime*, *Space Cowboys*, and *Blood Work*. They each display Clint Eastwood-style strengths such as timely plot lines and intimate dramas often shot in tones of green and shadows. In 1997, he directed but did not appear in *Midnight in the Garden of Good and Evil*. Its nonfiction source by John Berendt was a mid-nineties publishing sensation seen only once a decade or so. Expectations, including mine, were high. The book was rapturously received; the movie was a mess despite John Cusack's brave effort to lend it dignity. I had almost forgotten that Kevin Spacey played a flashy villain, but even his high screen wattage could not save the project.

Absolute Power is not one of Eastwood's better films, but its plot is pure Eastwood. The story concerns a jewel thief—Eastwood—who witnesses, in Eastwood's own words, "a murder involving one of the nation's highest officials, a man who feels that, because of his office, he can get away with anything" (Eastwood 1997). Eastwood's deep distrust in institutions and bureaucracies that grant power explodes here, while individual morality that operates outside legal structures asserts itself. Eastwood's thief is a criminal, but a principled one, whereas the president and his secret service quickly reveal themselves to be immeasurably corrupt. In a column to promote the film, Eastwood discusses the problems he sees in the government's abuse of power—whether the murderous cover-up of a president's affair that drives the plot of *Absolute Power* or the denial of a building permit in Eastwood's beloved Carmel, the incident that led to his own campaign for mayor.

He mentions the Nazis and the Nuremberg trials, but he also discusses the raid by the FBI and the Bureau of Alcohol, Tobacco, and Firearms of the Branch Dividian cult's compound in Waco, Texas, in 1993. "Abuse of power isn't limited to the bad guys of other nations, either. It happens in our own country if we're not vigilant. At Waco, was there really and urgency to get those people out of the compound at that particular time?" (Eastwood 1997).

Absolute Power was written by the legendary screenwriter and author William Goldman, whose other credits include *Butch Cassidy and the Sundance Kid*, *All the President's Men*, *The Princess Bride*, and *Marathon Man*. It was based upon a popular novel by famous crime author David Baldacci. *Midnight in the Garden of Good and Evil* fails as a film, but it is also an adaptation from a wildly popular book. *True Crime* is based on the novel by Andrew Klavan, also an author of crime novels, the type of book you might pick up from the airport bookstore. *Blood Work*, as well, is based on a crime novel by Michael Connelly.

With exception of *Space Cowboys*, all of Eastwood's films from *Bridges of Madison County* to *Mystic River* are based upon books, mostly in the crime genre. In 2002, a *New York Times* critic called the genre the "nouveau-noir" and notes that it was "enjoying a current renaissance" (Maslin 2002). She mentions Eastwood's adaptation of Connelly's *Blood Work* (Connelly cites *Dirty Harry* as an influence) and afterwards notes that Eastwood is preparing to adapt Dennis Lehane's *Mystic River*. The string of adapted popular source materials makes the arrival of *Mystic River* in 2003 the more stunning, devastating, and brilliant.

MYSTIC RIVER AND THE POETRY OF SUFFERING

When *Mystic River* appeared in 2003, critics and Eastwood fans felt that something new had happened in his work. If they had seen *Bird* in 1988, *White Hunter, Black Heart* in 1990, or *Unforgiven* in 1992, neither the concepts nor the tone would have seemed so strange. And if they considered the range of subjects Eastwood had explored previously—multiple facets of the American experience, from heavily stylized out-of-control capitalism in *High Plains Drifter* to down-close poverty, bust, and hope, as in *Honkytonk Man*—they would have perceived a slow yet marked shift from concerns with the workings of earthly justice (legacy of Eastwood's favored film *The Ox-Bow Incident*) toward increasing attention to events in his characters' lives that exceeded their ability to understand or their strength to bear.

　　Mystic River recalls the philosophical undertones of *The Outlaw Josey Wales*—the deaths of Josey's wife and little boy; the wrenching sorrow of the father, bowed like Job; and the inexplicable madness of war. Why should little children suffer? Who or what allows human suffering? Has the universe slipped out of control? Does a benevolent Divine inflict injury not only far in excess of perceived wrongdoing but also randomly on human creatures, little children, who know no guile and have done no wrong? Or does every violent act originate in human freedom and will?

　　In *Mystic River*, the viewer feels the weight of those questions, even if they are not expressly articulated. The spectator lives inside the head of an abused child, a grieving father, and a despoiled American neighborhood in simultaneously observed moments of the plot as it slips toward an unsettled conclusion.

　　During their decades as teachers and coaches, my mother and father fed and sheltered thousands of boys and girls—farm kids and children of immigrants who sought refuge in factory towns throughout the Midwest, displaced by the gross political upheavals of World War II. Mother and Dad welcomed little boys and girls who had too little to eat on their hardscrabble farms or in crowded flats from

Pittsburgh to northern Indiana to Detroit to Chicago. By day, they taught them the same skills—reading, writing, history, and critical thinking—that future generation of these children might learn at private schools. By night, they taught the kids' parents how to find a job, shop, and survive in an alien land. Ever the historian, my father continually reminded us that not so long ago our own ancestors had emigrated from war-torn parts of Europe to make a new life in the Promised Land, and that we should welcome our new neighbors and help them to find their own way.

In the world that Clint Eastwood portrays in *Mystic River,* rescue lines of the kind my parents offered do not exist for the three boys whose story the film follows, modern descendants of the Irish immigrants who landed in America as refugees from the massive Potato Famine of the mid-19th century. Instead, the movie quickly and hellishly descends through vivid images of borderline poverty (crowded houses, concrete play spaces, gaunt cheeks, absent parents) on the sensory level, into a grim narrative parable about the consequences of abandonment—of a neglected and abused child, a fragile neighborhood, and the lost sense of human decency.

If you or your child is harmed, who's going to avenge you? Not the police, but your kin—in blood sacrifice, a tribal response that still obtains in many parts of our world today. Distant news images of Afghanistan, Bosnia, Rwanda, Congo, Mali, or Sudan come to mind. Yet in the corrosive corner of contemporary South Boston captured in *Mystic River,* only your kinship network (a false and exclusive "community") "has your back."

In Eastwood's explosive 2003 movie, Dave Boyle, the child sufferer who escapes death at the hands of sexual predators, becomes a sacrificial victim to avenge another death in his own neighborhood within his own family. How can we understand "justice" in a lifelong death sentence like his? As the movie engages the religiously freighted justice-language of *Unforgiven,* "Deserve's got nothin' to do with it," *Mystic River* reveals a part of the universe that seems to lack a spectrum along which innocence and guilt can be tracked and punishment meted out by an all-seeing and benevolent deity.

In *Mystic River,* director Eastwood reverses the regenerative story of *Hang 'Em High, The Outlaw Josey Wales,* or *Gran Torino,* where a person who survives war, rape, lynching, or assassination ultimately finds vengeance endlessly debilitating and turns toward love, forgiveness, and reconciliation. *Mystic River* lacks the strong redemptive narrative of Eastwood's other films, in part because it lacks the empathetic voice of a chorus figure (a "normal" person) who witnesses and interprets events and contrasts them with a better way to live. Instead, the camera provides the commentary. It shows the barren space where the three boys play, unprotected; the intense unreality of the lush park where Katie is murdered and her father's violent vengeance is unleashed; the uncomfortable close-ups of Dave's delusional nightmares and jumbled thoughts; and the poison spit out hesitatingly with Celeste's confession of Dave's "guilt" or Annabeth's seduction of her remorseful husband.

It would be easy to misunderstand this harrowing and deeply disturbing movie by calling it a tragedy in the abstract, when its genius lies in its palpable, gritty particulars—the rumbling Bach-like bass line as Dave (Tim Robbins, in an Oscar-winning performance) rants about vampires and wolf-boys; the close-ups of a sorrowing father's face, ravaged by the murder of his child; and the film's deeply unsettling opening. In the brief opening scene, the director captures the confined, corroded atmosphere in which 11-year-old Jimmy Markum (Sean Penn, also Oscar-winning), Sean Devine (Kevin Bacon), and Dave begin to move out of childhood into adolescence.

The movie begins with a long, God's-eye aerial pan across Boston Harbor that sweeps past the lattice of backyard porches in South Boston's three-deckers, rickety havens that provide fathers with escape from the street out front where their boys play. We barely see or hear the men, who are not in our direct visual field. Theirs is a rudimentary culture of beer and baseball, with too little work to season the long summer days. These men, as a friend who grew up in Boston has remarked, are the "Southies" who threw rocks at buses when in the early seventies (approximately the same time as the movie) the courts had ordered busing to desegregate schools. It was *their* kids who retreated at the end of the day to tiny kitchens and cramped bedrooms, closed-in spaces that mirrored a social and familial world where nothing they ever did was right.

Eastwood's camera captures the peeling paint and claustrophobic interiors as markers of ever-increasing economic decline that hit parts of all American cities even long before the economic crash that occurred five years after Eastwood shot the movie. Whereas for generations the three-deckers we see in *Mystic River* provided "an affordable and reasonably spacious place to live," for late-19th-century immigrants in 2008, three-family homes "represent 14 percent of the housing stock but made up 21 percent of foreclosed property" (Goodnough 2009). (The article's author notes that Dennis Lehane, who wrote the novel *Mystic River* on which the film is based, grew up in Dorchester, a "tough neighborhood in East Boston.") Any "gentrification" of the world of *Mystic River* to which the adult Jimmy Markum refers early in the film does not appear in the movie's world, nor does any real threat of urban renaissance touch its doomed sense of place.

The camera turns toward three boys passing the time playing street hockey and talking about their future. For hooligan Jimmy, a future crime boss, being grown up means driving a car, even if he has to "borrow" one to drive around the block. Stuck in the here-and-now, though, a sewer abruptly swallows their ball—and their lives with it. Idled now, they draw their names in fresh cement, which provides an opening for two predators to invoke the image of The Law and The Church to punish their transgression.

With a few cinematic strokes—a black, luxurious car driven by one man with a badge, his passenger adorned with crosses around his neck and on his ring, young Dave, whose single mother lives on another street, disappears into the ominous cavern of the vehicle. The lovely child Dave, large and ungainly, poor, fatherless, innocent-eyed—his "difference" marked in every frame—gets into the car. The camera captures his plaintive gaze at his friends out the back window in a steady shot, echoed at the end of the movie when the adult Dave is similarly abducted by the men who will murder him.

After young Dave is kidnapped, the movie tumbles toward chaos. Eastwood refers in an interview on the *Mystic River* DVD commentary to child abuse, the "stealing of someone's life, someone's innocence," a subject he had explored 10 years earlier in *A Perfect World*. The shots that follow Dave's abduction flash before us with scant context or connection to other events: a murky glimpse of the neighborhood dads scrambling for help; a shadowed shot of legs descending basement stairs, the two men's faces revealed only by a sliver of light; and the sight of a little boy lying on a rumpled bed crying, "Please. No more." A delirium of nighttime images tears at the screen as the child darts and flees through a forest as though pursued by demons.

The screen blackness infects everything we see throughout the rest of the film, as the same lighting scheme appears whenever the narrative slides into nightmare. When Dave sits by his son's bedside and tells him about the wolves and vampires that haunt him, filmmaker and my former student Alex Schwarm notes that a sliver of light "exposes a portion of a face against a sea of darkness." The pattern of a stroke of light on a dark screen repeats when Dave tells Celeste of his dreams of vampires, "the undead," and again when Dave crouches at the edge of the river, as he recounts the murder of the pedophile and falsely confesses to Katie's murder.

The forest we see in the escape flashback becomes the lair of wolves, not picnickers resting from urban noise and concrete, just as the verdant park in the center of the neighborhood will harbor murderers, not playful forest sprites.

Amplified sound and discordant music (drumbeats, slashes, and howls) create a horror-film atmosphere, as in *Twilight*, that becomes part of the movie's sound design and anticipates its tragic trajectory. We feel the dull, sickening threat of something hideous hiding behind every corner, a lurking force in the movie that is never found or calmed. The alert listener will recall the discordant music and grotesque lighting that undercut the Stranger's and Preacher's false-savior identities in *High Plains Drifter* and *Pale Rider*. In *Mystic River*, the adult Dave's association with vampires and monsters complicates the spectator's sympathy for him as an easy victim—a key to the ways Eastwood exposes a spectator's conflicted fascination with and loathing of a sufferer.

Distanced by the camera and wrapped in an anonymous blanket, the child disappears into his shabby brownstone, with faceless neighbors watching, watching. The circular ascending and descending theme present from the beginning of the movie, CDBC/DEGEFD, assumes ritual resonance. Where is absolution and cleansing in the narrative configuration that follows Dave's escape? Eastwood elides scenes of reconciliation with mother or friends. Instead, we only hear a bystander pronounce that the child, seen at a distance from the back as he enters his house, "Looks like damaged goods."

The upstairs bedroom shade is pulled down, which effectively closes off the child from his community. Defiled, he must bear the burden of his stain. No communal rite of purification takes place. The child himself "must" be responsible for his own fate—a judgment often passed upon women who are the victims of sexual violence. Little Dave has been soiled, deprived of a chaste, innocent, idyllic childhood free from knowledge of good and evil.

Further, despite the movie's repeated images of washing—Dave's bloody hands; his stained clothes, scrubbed hastily by a frightened wife Celeste (Marcia Gay Harden); Jimmy intoning that Dave can be washed clean in the River—Dave can never escape the stain. In his beginning lies his end. His life prepares him to become the scapegoat 25 years later for the death of another child, Katie, daughter of his boyhood friend Jimmy, who will murder him.

As the movie unfolds, the viewer experiences Dave's suffering and escape from captivity through flashbacks mediated by his tortured memory, replays of the shots that immediately followed the kidnapping. We never learn whether he received medical care or pastoral counseling for his injuries. Of the years between his ordeal and the present, we hear little of his life. We infer the rest from the verbal and visual exchanges that populate the second part of the movie: Dave's isolation and intensifying nightmares; his flashbacks; his wife's fears; and the neighborhood's quick leap to accuse him of Katie's murder. He becomes the neighborhood's *pharmakos*, the scapegoat who must absorb its miseries. Whereas in older societies the defiled were carried outside the city walls to be tortured and killed, Dave endures a lifetime of suffering within the confines of the neighborhood and inside houses too small for his gangling body.

Moments after the grown-up Dave and his son Michael appear on screen, the pair round the corner onto Dave's old street. Terrified, he sends his child away and gazes at a cement sidewalk square where he and his friends had begun to write their names when the pedophiles drove up and their childhood ended. The colors in the frame disappear: the crowded houses (familiar to us from the film's opening shots) bleach out. A blinding light removes Dave from time and space as he glances around in confusion trying to reorient himself. Each time we see Dave from now on, the film's opening musical theme reappears in a new and discordant form, leading us deeper and deeper into his madness and pushing the tragedy toward its horrifying conclusion, a lynching in every way as repulsive as the one that climaxes *The Ox-Bow Incident*.

Neither the law nor divine power punishes the child rapists for their crime—as if any adequate punishment, even death, could expunge the memory of four days of repeated rape. But nevertheless, Eastwood the director engages vengeance itself—profound, primal, animal fury at other human beings and the universe—as though even the exhaustive, piercing brilliance of *Unforgiven*, with its complex take on vengeance, had not adequately explored the dark side of human nature. As Eastwood observed of *Unforgiven*, *The Outlaw Josey Wales*, and *Pale Rider*, "The past is often associated with a trauma, with a drama that has been repressed but keeps coming to the surface. The past poisons the present" (Wilson 2007, 161). Although the central characters seem to be related by blood or extended kinship bonds, the "blood" of kinship is replaced by raw, bloody violence. Primordial violence obliterates meaning.

In *Mystic River*, Eastwood focuses on the horror of the two events—the symbolic death of Dave and the real death of Katie, Jimmy's daughter. The apocalyptic events upend a comfortable, unreflective feeling about the neighborhood with its illusions of protective kinship and encroaching gentrification. The film is full of illusory visions of escape: Dave from his captors; Katie (Emmy Rossum) and Brendan (Thomas Guiry), her sweetheart, from a future in this decayed part of the city; Jimmy, from prison into the role of respected businessman and crime boss with control over the neighborhood; Sean from a poisonous past into a vocation as a police detective.

In a key scene, a Christmas tree twinkles in the background, shorthand in Hollywood mainstream movies for the promise of renewal (e.g., *It's a Wonderful Life*). At the end of *Mystic River*, the neighborhood celebrates the nation's birthday with flags, a parade, and marching bands as though all were well. But just as in *Heartbreak Ridge* and *Unforgiven*, sentimental religious symbolism and jingoistic patriotism will not save the day. The movie's troubling narrative heart cannot be soothed by a sugary ending.

The reality shown in the film shatters any hope for a better future. Eastwood does not insert a feel-good climax as in Tim Robbins's earlier film of literal imprisonment and escape, *The Shawshank Redemption* (1994), in which he and Eastwood stalwart Morgan Freeman use their time in prison to form indelible bonds of friendship. The young boy Dave escapes physically but not psychologically. Katie is murdered, her broken body lying in an abandoned bear cage, her suppliant hand upturned. Brendan, an engaging character and overlooked moral touchstone of the movie, remains trapped in his murderous family. Even the few stolen moments of the young sweethearts' happiness, when Brendan hides in Katie's car to surprise her (like Romeo and Juliet, children of two warring families), predict her tragic death and Dave's murder. Not many hours after their meeting, she will be surprised again, her car invaded—this time by her murderers. Katie's teasing words that Jimmy would "shoot" Brendan and then "kill" him if he knew they were dating anticipate Jimmy's murder of the innocent Dave.

Further, although through most of the film Dave seems passive and gentle, he is capable of erratic outbursts. At his breaking point, he paces like an animal in a cage. His allusions to vampires refer simultaneously to the forces of evil that increasingly suck his life from his spirit and to his own barely repressed murderous impulses.

Only Sean appears to have escaped the confines of the neighborhood. Not only is he a law enforcement officer, but he also has a strong friendship with Whitey Powers (Laurence Fishburne), a black man whose color, in the distinctive Eastwood tradition, is never an issue. At times, when Sean talks about his neighborhood, we expect his partner to speak about his own childhood in a Boston ghetto of a different and possibly far worse sort—perhaps Roxbury. But neither race nor bitterness infects Whitey's performance as a detective, team player, and wise counselor for his sorrowful partner.

Whitey and Sean's friendship alone transcends the grievously prevailing neighborhood norms. Whitey acts as a pastoral presence for Sean on two levels: he breaks through Sean's fear of the old neighborhood by well-placed questions at the time of the murder, and he urges him either to get on with his life or to reconcile with his wife by confessing that he has wronged her.

Eastwood resists the temptation to structure the relationship of Sean and Whitey as a replay of the *Dirty Harry* series or *The Gauntlet*, where the hero's partners too often end up dead. Nor is Sean like Dirty Harry in any way other than in his deep sadness and estrangement from his wife. Here, though, with Whitey's common-sense advice and constant support, Sean becomes the center of a small forgiveness drama, an interpolated tale in the style of Dickens. Alienated from his wife and child (perhaps also the tortured legacy of the neighborhood trauma), Sean's return to the neighborhood of his childhood finally gives him the strength to escape its cycle of destruction. Sean's reconciliation with his wife provides one of the few sources of hope in the film.

The other players in *Mystic River*—Jimmy and Dave, their wives, and Dave's child—are sucked into the sewer that devoured the childhood ball. The rituals of the Catholic Church, imaged ironically at film's beginning in a community Confirmation of bright colors and inspiring music to symbolize a child's welcome into the family of faith, offer neither consolation for Jimmy nor models for grieving. The movie alternates tight, dark, cramped urban spaces with green spaces, but unlike the poetic symbolism often associated with pastoral landscapes, the greenery in this movie hides misery—the forest through which Dave escapes; the lush park where Katie dies; the out-of-the way country bar where Dave receives his death sentence.

After Jimmy believes he has avenged his daughter's death with the blood of his childhood friend Dave, he discovers he killed the wrong person. He stands by his bedroom window and gazes onto the street. The tattooed cross that covers his back marks a symbol of continual suffering, not love, as though he has singled himself out as a sacrificial victim.

If, instead of Dave, Jimmy had been the one to get into the kidnappers' car, he never would have had the "juice" to court Katie's mother, he tells Sean in an eerie confessional scene in the sterile green cafeteria at the police station. But if he had not married Katie's mother, he continues, Katie would not have been born or murdered. He feels "at fault" for her death yet never links his own vengeful murder of "Just Ray," the father of Katie's murderer, to Katie's death. Spectators see it but he does not, obsessed as he is with his own sense of injury.

Where does *Mystic River*, philosophically profound and psychologically disturbing, fall in the overall pattern of Clint Eastwood's movies? It stands alone. Even in *Honkytonk Man* and *Gran Torino*, the two films where Eastwood's character dies, the entire movie, wasted lives and all, moves toward joyful release, full of hope for the main character's extended family, and for America as a whole. *Mystic River*, one of the great movies of the decade and of Eastwood's career, severely critiques the culture of blood vengeance, but even its pitying gaze at its characters and their environment, holds out little hope for regeneration for them or their world.

REFERENCES AND FURTHER READING

De Vries, Hilary. 1992. "His Own Man." *The Los Angeles Times*, August 2.

Dowd, Maureen. 1995. "Go Ahead, Make Him Cry." *The New York Times*, March 26.

Eastwood, Clint. 1997. "Absolute Power." *The Washington Post*, January 12.

Eliot, Marc. 2009. *Clint Eastwood: American Rebel*. New York: Crown Publishing Group.

Goodnough, Abby. 2009. "Hard Times for New England's 3-Deckers." *The New York Times*, June 19.

Junod, Tom. 2012. "The Eastwood Conundrum." *Esquire*, September 20. http://www.esquire.com/features/clint-eastwood-profile-1012. Accessed February 25, 2014.

Locke, Richard. 2008. "Grand Horse Opera." *The American Scholar*, Summer. http://theamericanscholar.org/grand-horse-opera/. Accessed February 24, 2014.

Maslin, Janet. 2002. "The Crimes They Are A-Changin'." *The New York Times*, May 13.

Simsolo, Noël. 2003. *Clint Eastwood: Un Passeur à Hollywood*, 2nd edition. Paris: Cahiers du Cinéma.

Wilson, Michael Henry. 2007. *Clint Eastwood: Entretiens avec Michael Henry Wilson* (Interviews with Eastwood). Paris: Cahiers du Cinéma.

Chapter 9

THE DIGNITY OF LIFE:
MILLION DOLLAR BABY

If *Mystic River* can be termed "harrowing" (its assessment by audience members with whom I first saw the movie), *Million Dollar Baby* simultaneously elevates a sport beloved by Americans, illustrates the myth of "social mobility through hard work" at work, and moves spectators onto the plane of compassion, an arena barely explored in mainstream political discussions, much less in movies.

Eastwood the artist overturns audience expectations for an invincible, powerful, disdainful hero, a return to the carefree sauciness of the iconic Man with No Name or the first Dirty Harry. The main character is dirt poor, talented, vulnerable, and a woman. The Eastwood character Frankie Dunn bears some Eastwood storytelling trademarks: an absent wife, an estranged daughter, a new daughter, a love of poetry in unexpected places, and a calming, wise sidekick. But *Million Dollar Baby* moves to a narrative and cinematic level in keeping with *Mystic River* and *Unforgiven:* a triumphant ascent and a deepening love relationship between a surrogate father and daughter slips from comforting darkness into the bright, unforgiving lights of the boxing rings and a hidden, destructive corner of mid-America.

In *Million Dollar Baby*, the poem "The Lake Isle of Innisfree" by William Butler Yeats holds a central place. Not only does Yeats's poem offer an image of natural beauty and peace—a sacred space far from the ravages of interstate highways, urban blight, and rural poverty—but it also sings with the rhythm of Irish bards and lone balladeers who celebrate the pulses of life even as death stalks outside the window.

> I will arise and go now, and go to Innisfree,
> And a small cabin build there, of clay and wattles made;
> Nine bean rows will I have there, a hive for the honey bee,
> And live alone in the bee-loud glade.
> And I shall have some peace there, for peace comes dropping slow,
> Dropping from the veils of the morning to where the cricket sings;
> There midnight's all a glimmer, and noon a purple glow,
> And evening full of the linnet's wings.
> I will arise and go now, for always night and day
> I hear lake water lapping with low sounds by the shore;
> While I stand on the roadway, or on the pavements gray,
> I hear it in the deep heart's core. (Yeats 1920)

The poem softens the nightmare in which the main characters are trapped after a beginning filled with triumphs in sports, personal relationships, and self-knowledge. Near the end of the movie, we watch Maggie Fitzgerald (Hilary Swank), a scrappy boxer out of Missouri, and Frankie (Eastwood), her trainer, in a moment where they must learn to cope with their world turned upside down. Maggie, woefully injured, sits motionless opposite her companion, listening to the lilting rhythms of the verse he reads aloud to her. Yeats's poem suspends time and space, creating a sacred corner shaped and colored by their imaginations.

For Maggie, newly introduced to poetry's power to transform a listener, the reading conjures up a real cabin where she could live with Frankie to cook for him and return the love he has given her. She knows such retreats exist, where seekers take refuge from injury and violence; he had told her from the first days of their friendship that she needed to protect herself, to buy a home where she would always be safe. Neither Maggie the boxer nor Frankie her coach and friend could have known that their home together would be in a hospital room, and that pain and death would claim her long before she could make peace with her troubled history, her battered body, and her crushed dreams. The "deep heart's core," Yeats's poetic summary of longing, contains all that the friends will ever know of a perfect world, a paradise on earth where love rules.

In *Million Dollar Baby*, Eastwood repeats the questions his other iconic movies address: What is a life all about? Which lives are to be valued, and why? What about suffering? How might we define "righteousness?" The tension between the desire for a perfect world and this world's wrenching imperfections appeared in Eastwood's earliest movies, *Play Misty for Me* and *High Plains Drifter* and became more defined in *The Outlaw Josey Wales* and *The Gauntlet*. In *Pale Rider*, the ethics of forgotten lives were forged against the backdrop of apocalypse, both imagined and real. The threat of end-times figured in the film's opening assault by faceless men on horseback and the violent death of the

Director Eastwood with Hilary Swank in Million Dollar Baby. *(Warner Brothers/ Photofest)*

protagonist in his past life. *Unforgiven* contains one of the most provocative lines in all of Eastwood's artistic work: "Deserve's got nothin' to do with it." And "deserve" figures heavily in *Million Dollar Baby*, a film suffused with darkness and light.

Although critics such as Richard Corliss (*Time*) and Jonathan Rosenbaum (*Chicago Reader*) joined Roger Ebert in pronouncing it "a masterpiece, pure and simple" (Ebert 2004), the movie works on multiple emotional levels simultaneously. In *Million Dollar Baby*, Eastwood defies stereotypes within the boxing genre and storytelling overall. We watch the story play out as "plucky heroine rises from trash" and as "small-time boxer makes good," but beneath this surface plotline, Eastwood offers a story infused with tightly focused compassion, grief, and love. A family takes shape: Frankie Dunn, a tough old manager; Scrap (Morgan Freeman), his former protégé turned janitor and only friend; and Maggie, a Missouri refugee who seeks a better life through competitive boxing.

Most of the film's work is done through manipulation of light and shadow. Faces and figures are often etched against a black or intensely colored background, or the film suddenly cuts to its aesthetic. As film critic Robert Kennedy emailed to me in 2007: "It's a darkened, extremely spare film style that utilizes the dimly lit edges of people in shadows or standing in the corners, never really in the picture at all, always just barely there. Overall, the tone is sharp, tightly scripted, dimly lit, like in the shadows of what's real, exploring the edges of the frame." The careful use of the narrative voiceover, heavy use of darkness and shadows, and stylized set pieces (the gym; the boxing rings; the visit to Missouri) give the entire movie a slightly unreal aura, a visual and sonic rhythm that continues throughout Eastwood, as though the images existed only in a dream world.

Equally, little welcome exists in the wasteland of shabby trailers and prefab housing we see in Missouri, either, where Maggie grew up mere steps away from the killing fields of the Kansas–Missouri border, wars that exist as the backdrop for *The Outlaw Josey Wales* and referenced repeatedly in *Unforgiven*. The cramped lowlight interiors and shabbiness of the gym echo the desolate cabin where Will Munny and his children lived or the damp campfire that barely warmed him and Ned, his travel companion in *Unforgiven*. The confectionary treats of Disneyland visited by Maggie's family lie just beyond the corner of Los Angeles's vast and untended city center—a center filled with plastic images of ideal image of a lasting city.

Eastwood is as much a city filmmaker as a chronicler of the vast terrain of the open prairie in sickness and health, or of the forests and deserts on the way to Texas, a strength that surfaces in *Million Dollar Baby* and again in *Changeling* and *Gran Torino*. That said, we do not see much of Los Angeles in *Million Dollar Baby*. The godlike aerial shots that repeatedly moved over Boston in *Mystic River* are lavished here on boxing rings. We see the confined interior of Frankie's house, where he squirrels away the letters his estranged daughter Katie returns to him, and where he witnesses distanced evidence of his defeat as a boxing coach: for instance, his star fighter's victorious championship fight under another manager. We retreat with Frankie to the comfort of his gym office, where he reads poetry, teaches himself Gaelic, and chats with his longtime friend Scrap. The office provides an island of dignity that soothes him in his losses.

The Hit Pit gym that Frankie and Scrap run provides a refuge for a few who have been left behind in our country, the lowest of the low, for the "oddballs, those pushed to the edges of American society," as Eastwood comments in the movie's DVD extras. Maggie is only among the latest of decades of American refugees from the failed promise of education and success whom the crotchety old team of Scrap and Frankie has woven into this small community. "She grew up knowing one thing," Scrap tells us in voiceover, "she was trash." Eastwood takes the opposite angle from Rocky and other boxing movies. This is not a typical American Horatio Alger success story, rags to riches. Rather, the movie forces us to ask: Why does such poverty exist in a rich country like ours?

Boxing may offer Maggie a chance to earn money and respect, both of which are woefully absent from her life, as we learn through flashbacks. Most of all, it provides her with purpose and meaning, a reason to keep on living. Even Billy the Blue Bear, Maggie's nemesis, was a prostitute before she became a boxer—one other way for a poor woman to survive. Hit Pit gym becomes Maggie's home, family, and community.

Frankie takes on Maggie and trains her as a boxer, despite his early loud refusals and the males-only sheen of the sport. Gender is always prickly with Eastwood. Despite his own macho image and the scarcity of female companions for his lonely male protagonists, the director portrays loneliness as a loss, not a warrior's badge. Harry Callahan suffers, as do Josey Wales and Will Munny, from appearances of their competent wives in dreams and visions. Even the Stranger and Preacher, disembodied and gun-happy as they are, need—and pick—clear-sighted women as lovers, and in *The Bridges of Madison County*, the thoroughly physical Robert Kinkaid (played by Eastwood) coaxes a full-blown sexual partnership from Francesca Johnson with his gentleness and kindness. More importantly than his heroes' particular shortcomings, Eastwood the director has given roles of substance to women, culminating in *Changeling* (2008). Maggie's character is one of the strongest, though; she fills the spots left empty by Frankie's wife and his alienated daughter while carving out her own place in his heart.

The relationship between coach and fighter builds slowly, as Frankie admires Maggie's increasing mastery of boxing skills. The progress is visualized through tight shots as he moves her feet to an unheard rhythm, with the camera staying close to their faces and bodies as the dance grows in confidence and partnership.

The poetry of the evolving relationship plays out on screen. The rapid montage of Maggie's knockouts is played almost for comic effect and balances the more somber exchanges between coach and pupil, which are more horizontal, more grounded, and shot in near darkness against moody green backgrounds in at least five sequences. Eastwood told interviewer Michael Henry Wilson that he approached and shot the film "as if it were in black and white" (Wilson 2007, 173), a strategy he also employed in *Unforgiven* and his war movies. The authenticity of the relationship is established by tactile closeness conveyed in close ups, the verbal exchanges that evidence Maggie's total dependence upon Frankie, and the magnitude of Frankie's grief over his lost daughter.

Even before the unthinkable accident that overturns Maggie's life, she and Frankie bond through the blood sport that is their common calling. They bond through and against the cheering crowd, through her opponents and against them—a refreshing change from the mostly male Westerns. Long before Maggie lies wounded and helpless, she offers herself and is offered as a sacrifice to bloodthirsty crowds who feast on the spectacle of spilled blood, mashed noses, and bruised kidneys. The matches are filmed with an elegance that masks the ugliness of the sport. Maggie's early bouts border on the burlesque, with crowds as raunchy as dancehall customers in a painting by Toulouse-Lautrec, or peasants in a painting by Pieter Bruegel, a 16th-century Flemish painter who like Eastwood delighted in crossing borders of social and economic class. The camera catches bits of bodies, snatches of overlit faces set against darkened spaces, faces like interchangeable masks hiding unknown desires. Maggie's body is on display, that is, until the camera hustles her out of sight when she strikes the winning blow.

Lest we miss both her meteoric rise in the world of boxing and the shadiness of the sport, Scrap's voiceover intervenes as a chorus and interpreter; the illusion of "reality" is broken. The camera pulls back to spot her before a fight silent, in a barely lit corner of the locker room, a view of her face and emotions obscured by the distance.

But as Maggie's career advances (and as the amount of money at stake increases exponentially, the ever-present theme of "commerce" that haunts most of Eastwood's films, like *Unforgiven*), the camera registers ever more stylized crowds viewed at steep angles and long shots from above. To underline the unreality that surrounds the matches, Eastwood begins to disjoin image and sound in almost silent-movie display that the a-synchronic sound design creates. The tonality, rhythm, and volume of the music interlace with the other elements.

Maggie's match with Billie "The Blue Bear" rips open the real-life world of competitive sports and exposes its corruption, extreme violence, and disregard for human life. The film's narrative structure initially encourages us to concentrate on Maggie's string of successes, creation of a new identity, and pursuit of recognition. But as the movie progresses, boxing is revealed to resemble human sacrifice more than economic or spiritual redemption. The unnatural, highly stylized, and surreal lighting punctuates and interrupts any smooth, linear progression of the plot. Human beings are put up for sale—not by Frankie, who protects his fighters, but rather by the underground managers who work in the shadows to cut deals and urge athletes to dope up and play dirty. Unlike the Hit Pit gym's office and club, which establish a protected space to nurture human interactions, the boxing ring in *Baby* is uncovered as a profane space, a contaminated space, a mockery where bodies are meticulously prepared for display before injury and possible death.

Return to our first sight of Maggie and follow the ways that she prepares herself for the sacrifice of her body. We see her first in a darkened and confined hallway, her clothes, hair, and face, shaded slightly green and marked by too little food and too much sorrow. The obscuring shadows make her look old and tired, even slightly cadaverous, almost undead, but nothing like the voracious, sexy vampires of contemporary popular culture.

As the film continues, an overhead shot captures only a part of her face as she devours restaurant leftovers in dim light, only a part of her body visible. The shots recall the framing and lighting of the vampire in F. W. Murnau's silent film *Nosferatu* (1922) from the novel by Bram Stoker, albeit an unauthorized adaptation, just like *Fistful of Dollars* was an unauthorized adaptation of *Yojimbo*. The visual reference raises a question sometimes posed by my students and other audiences: Is Maggie an angel or a devil?

A few scenes into the movie, the production design and cinematography shift into the mode that will be sustained up to the moment Maggie is injured: long shots of Maggie silhouetted sharply against the blue-green of the gym wall, punching the bag Scrap has loaned her. Such shots, held for long screen seconds, return with variations in three early scenes. The color bridges the prefight concentration, the locker room talks, and her apartment. The moments of preparation aestheticize her training, bringing the beauty of her inner life into the composition of the shots.

The stylized, gorgeous shots of her training, and the exchanges between her and her two mentors, Frankie and Scrap, take place in various shades of darkness that bring the "reality" of the shots into question. During the months of her training, the protected space of the old gym where Maggie trains becomes the home where she returns after each venture out to fight or waitress for companionship, counsel, and touch. She uses her earnings to buy a house not for herself but for her family.

Frankie links Maggie's need to find a "house of (her) own" specifically with his other mantra, "Protect yourself." Maggie uses her money not to protect herself and her economic future but rather to create a site where her family might remake itself into a loving community. Her gift is rejected. Harsh, uniform, filled white lighting (which could be interpreted as the untamed glare of the summer sun or as the director's severe judgment of what we are witnessing) evokes disgust. Maggie's family members pollute every space they enter. Nearly halfway through the movie, Frankie, the spectators' stand-in, witnesses the moral degradation of Maggie's mother and sister and suffers as Maggie is publicly humiliated ("People hear 'bout what you're doin' and they laugh," her mother says mercilessly. "They laugh at you."). Many shots of Maggie at the gym and later on her deathbed are highly stylized, not realistic; these sequences, too, seem overheated in almost an operatic way, underscoring their ugliness and heavily judging the family's selfishness, ignorance, and cruelty.

Some viewers have suggested to me that Eastwood has gone over the top with his portrayal of Maggie's family. Yet each harshly lit sequence develops her more fully as her family's scapegoat—the one who bears the sickness of her family, the one who is abused even as she gives everything she has. Sadly, the scapegoat motif parallels the sacrifice motif; we learn that Maggie gives her earnings to that same mother who neglects and humiliates her.

Those who consider the family scenes overly florid and unfair to American poor whites should remember Dostoyevsky's handling of the innocent Sonia's prostitution in *Crime and Punishment*. The parallels are nearly exact. Although Sonia sells all that she possesses, her body, to feed her family, her stepmother berates and even beats her in public. A tearful reconciliation between Maggie and her mother might have pushed more emotional buttons for spectators and sold more theater tickets, just as Eastwood could have altered his source material to have Maggie revive or to reunite Frankie with his lost daughter. Eastwood is making no general statement about "white trash." This may be the only film in which he presents any group of any color or class (except murderers and rapists) without compassion. If Billie the Blue Bear is a nightmare character, the actress/boxer who plays her, Lucia Rijker, coached Hilary Swank. On the DVD, Lucia cries when she recounts her own story, grounding the film in human experience. Like Maggie, she fought to buy decency for her family. Like the character Maggie, her gifts were refused.

Frankie and Maggie allow themselves to love and be loved by each other in an affection conveyed through wondrously lit intimate conversations. Among those luminous moments and to the low accompaniment of a guitar, Maggie relates a story about her father and her pet dog in almost total darkness as the refugees return to California from the disastrous trip to Missouri to see her family. (In retrospect, the story about Axel, a dearly loved pet put out of its misery by her much-cherished father, anticipates Maggie's own death.) The alternating shots are lit only by flashes from passing cars and shadows that pass across their faces as she declares, "I got nobody but you, Frankie," and he replies, "Well, you've got me."

The scene overlaps past, future, and present, but more: it is composed of equal parts of joy and sorrow, happiness and tragedy. As viewers, we are lost in time and space, light and dark, prepared and perhaps strengthened by the familial bond between Maggie and Frankie to bear the anguish that is to come.

Light softens and diffuses as the camera peeks through the dirty windows of Ira's Roadside Diner, where the friends share homemade lemon pie. The old Missouri board and batten structure may date to post–Civil War days, when Missouri spawned ravaging gangs and gunslingers like Will Munny in *Unforgiven*. Board and batten siding was originally put over log cabins to provide warmth and protection against the wind. Its vertical lines contrasted with the horizontal lines of the logs. The joints between the boards were covered over with strips of wood, or batten.

After a several-second shot of the diner lit against the pitch of the night, the camera observes Frankie and Maggie through a pane of glass before moving into a large, inviting space full of customers (notably, at least one black). Frankie's happy comment on the pie, "Now I can die and go to heaven," is greeted by Maggie's antiphonal response, "I used to come here with Daddy," a reference both to her relationship with Frankie and the return to moments in the past where she felt loved and secure. The sequence closes as the camera moves outside once more and the noodling of the guitar resolves. "Blue Diner" was written by Kyle Eastwood. Earlier songs were written by Kyle and Michael Stephens, with David Potaux-Razel. "Blue Morgan," written by Clint, plays under the end credits at first with single piano melody, then backed by a full orchestra score as if to underline Frankie's move from a solitary life toward a love relationship. The credits list "Music by Clint Eastwood" and "Orchestrated and Conducted by Lennie Niehaus."

Eastwood could have ended his movie with the tender conversation in Ira's. The diner envelopes Maggie and Frankie as father and daughter, each rescuing the other. It replicates the protected space of the Hit Pit gym, already established as a haven.

The scene that unfolds halfway through the film begins a new journey for Maggie, Frankie, and Scrap toward the title, a stunning climax to her boxing career complete with bagpipers and near-victory over a vicious fighter. Even before Maggie falls, the visuals become heavily stylized with a silent crowd of watchers. The scene is observed first in close-up and then from an overhead shot of the ring where Maggie lies. The music, until now elegant and spare, is further reduced, to strings. Maggie sees Frankie and the doctor and hears sounds as if she were underwater, recalling the frighteningly dreamlike sequences of Julian Schnabel's movie The Diving Bell and the Butterfly (2007). The lights spin, and the screen goes dark. Eastwood changes the camera's role from invisible observer to expressive and involved agent that aims to transport the spectator into another world.

The sequences that follow her horrific accident unfold the deepening love between Maggie and Frankie, as he strokes her head, feeds her, bathes her, and masterminds her care. They model a perfect healing relationship. She is helpless; he is ever-present, not condescending, never blaming her. He never reveals his overwhelming despair to her—he opens his heart only to his priest and to Scrap. The class and economic gulf between Maggie and Frankie has been crossed; he is teaching her Gaelic. "The Lake Isle of Innisfree," quoted at the beginning of this chapter, which he reads to her, captures a shared dream of absolute beauty and peace, a place (in reality or in a dream) where her broken body and his aching loneliness can be made whole.

Everything that follows in Million Dollar Baby should be viewed through the lens of that healing scene. The actions now tumble one after the other in every descending panic: the cruelty of Maggie's rapacious family, her disintegrating body, her sores and the loss of her leg, her passionate request to be released from pain, her suicide attempt, Frankie's struggle with the teachings of the Church (and his refusal of the priest's request that he "Leave her to God"), and his love. Frankie wants to keep her with him yet honor her wish to die. The bright, unforgiving light and static shots that exposed her family's greed now yield to a restless camera and close-ups of her face as she asks for the favor that would prove his love: to be released from this life.

Although Eastwood's score plays underneath this scene, it does not direct the spectator's response. Nor does Scrap's voiceover, which with its comforting and objective tone guides us toward the film's conclusion. The suffering, Michael Henry Wilson writes, "creates a spiritual community among the three principal persons, a kind of trinity of suffering where Maggie is the Christ figure" (Wilson 2007, 172).

What does Frankie's love for Maggie mean, and in what ways do his beliefs as a Catholic influence the expression of his love for her? Does Eastwood, as the director, support the actions he shows? In the scene between Frankie and the priest, the Church's teachings clash with the dictates of love and conscience. Frankie cries quietly and bitterly; he wants comfort—wants to tell someone of the depth of his love for Maggie—but the priest only chides him for the vague guilt he imagines Frankie to feel over his lost daughter and the peril that Frankie will face if he helps Maggie to die. The effective counseling, words that clarify Frankie's dilemma and identify with Frankie's sorrow, come from Scrap. We do not ask "How can Frankie save himself from damnation?" we ask, "Why does Maggie have to suffer?"

The film conveys the texture of love through Frankie's actions. As the representations of protected space multiply, the director suggests a life beyond this one, at least in the imagination, a theme he will explore fully in 2010's *Hereafter*. Since life must be lived in the here and now, whether or not we imagine a perfect world, we honor Scrap's presence as witness, interpreter, and manager of Hit Pit gym and its welcoming community.

Some critics deplore Frankie's removal of Maggie's breathing tube. Michael Medved and Rush Limbaugh are chief among those who sought to spoil *Baby*'s box office success by giving away its ending (Rich 2005). Frank Rich writes, "What really makes these critics hate *Million Dollar Baby* is not its supposedly radical politics—which are nonexistent—but its lack of sentimentality" (Rich 2005). These critics, however, should note that Eastwood adapted a short story that in its turn may or may not represent real actions taken by the author of that story. Eastwood the director, too often written about in movie reviews as though he were "really" Dirty Harry or the Man with No Name, exists at least three removes from the event presented on screen. He is Eastwood the man; Eastwood the director, who has adapted several short stories; and Eastwood as Frankie Dunn, who exists within a movie.

The voiceover further distances Eastwood the man from the plot that unfolds on screen. What we see and hear on screen visualizes Scrap's *interpretation* of the events he describes. To claim that what we see is "real," a real director creating a model for an action that he wants imitated, distorts the fundamental mechanism of storytelling, written or filmed. Narrative always reflects the shaping, filtering, and reflective act of creation.

Furthermore, the film never glorifies Frankie's action. He acts in "fear and trembling," to use the phrase popularized by Danish philosopher Søren Kierkegaard, in his 1843 book *Fear and Trembling*. He enters the hospital corridor quietly and reverently, fully aware that he is entering the presence of unimaginable and undeserved suffering. He emerges from darkness, his lithe movements contrasted with her nearly comatose body laid out against a white pillow. He explains (as he had promised) the meaning of the name he had given her, *mo cuishle*, "My darling, my blood," sealing their love with a gentle kiss close to her lips. To answer viewers' and critics' questions about the meaning of the phrase (and its correct form), I asked Eithne Ní Ghallchobhair, a scholar from Cambridge University. In a March 8, 2008 email to me, she explains: "To address a person, the speaker should use 'A,' unlike Frankie's 'Mo chuisle.'" She explains further:

> Irish has a vocative case which always begins, A . . . it lenites [weakens] the following noun and also slenderises the last consonant, if and when possible. Therefore cuisle, vein, becomes "a chuisle," meaning "my darling, or my life's blood" . . . along those lines. The A is the particle associated with the vocative case. *Mo* means my. It's a possessive pronoun and lenites the following noun." (E-mail to author, March 8, 2008)

So *Mo chuisle* would mean "my darling" also, but if he were speaking about, not to, her.

Eastwood the writer/actor never allows the scene to dissolve into hysterics, his or hers, even when he confesses that she is blood of his blood, heart of his heart. He exits the room, but the camera lets him slip out of the frame, pulling a black screen across our line of vision to shroud our access to the rest of his life.

The curtain pulls back to reveal our interpreter, Scrap, his watch-ful face etched against the edge of the frame, half in darkness and half in light, mirroring Frankie's face. Scrap, critic Michael Henry Wilson notes, is "not situated topographically"—do not reduce the scene to photographic realism. Eastwood himself commented: "It's a deliber-ately abstract space" (Wilson 2007, 173–74). Scrap, Frankie's rock and the movie's Greek chorus, offers not judgment but rather tender and sorrowful observation. My students, while they acknowledge that Scrap may not actually be present in the same space as Frankie, believe that he nonetheless witnesses the final act of love.

The final montage of nine brief scenes pulls the film away from trag-edy and back toward affirmation. The gym still runs as a welcoming community even without Frankie. Scrap's letter to Frankie's daugh-ter after his disappearance, which turns out to be the motor for all the film's images and sounds, may exist ultimately as her story using Scrap's voice—or Scrap's recasting of his memories, now half seen with his remaining eye. By the end of the movie, we, the spectators, must wonder who controls what we see on screen. Darkness suits per-sons, environments, and events Scrap half sees, with his blind eye and from the distance of memory. Still, we are party to scenes where Scrap was not present (the locker room; the hospital rooms; the Missouri visit). What consciousness gives us the information that the camera presents?

As the camera crawls in toward the grimy window of Ira's Diner, we may see Frankie perched at the counter savoring his memories of Maggie as he eats his lemon meringue pie and imagines paradise, his perfect world, where everything that is broken will be made whole. Eastwood told an interviewer, "I decided to use the little restaurant because it resembled a wooden cabin, something like the one Maggie and Frankie envisage living in together. But I muddied the windows so that no one could see who is sitting at the counter" (Wilson 2007, 174). As spectators, we scramble to reconstruct the whole of his body and this place. We desire what we cannot see and cannot have, the physical and spiritual healing imagined by Yeats's "Innisfree." In blackness or near blackness, our clear vision obscured, we reach beyond the realm of the senses toward the unknown. Memory, imagination, and hope coalesce.

Hollywood films rarely grant ethical issues the serious focus they deserve. Events are sanitized and, more critically (and unforgivably, as Frank Rich observed when writing about *Million Dollar Baby*), sentimentalized. "Eastwood's film," Rich continues, "has the temerity to suggest that fights can have consequences, that some crises do not have black-and-white solutions and that even the pure of heart are not guaranteed a Hollywood ending" (Rich 2005). Like a Greek tragedy, the movie offers no answers, only greater wisdom—a "stunningly drawn map of the human heart disguised as a boxing yarn" (Travers 2004, 170). The story operates in a realm beyond the senses. Wisely, Eastwood avoided Technicolor to bypass the appearance of crisply photographed reality and the temptation toward sentimentality.

The movie may not quite offer a catharsis as with traditional tragedy (*Oedipus Rex*); Frankie's act is muted, and then he disappears. The last words and images belong to the gym and to Scrap as he concludes the memoir, or perhaps to the dimly lit café, where dream might give shape to our longings. As Jonathan Rosenbaum wrote at the time of the movie's release, "In a bleak world, where neither family nor religious faith offers any lasting respite, *Million Dollar Baby* offers redemption that derives from the informal and nameless loving relationships people create on their own rather than inherit from family, church, or society" (Rosenbaum 2004). Eastwood, rejecting false sentiment, has created a vision of searing beauty—and a transformative vision of a perfect world. Film scholar Tania Modleski argues that, if conservatives looked closer at the film, they would find it deeply resonant with their own ideology. She lambasts the film on the basis of its portrayal of race and class, and its seeming blindness to its own politics.

As a director and actor, Eastwood continued to insist that his films tell individual stories without political relevance. To him, people who charge that *Million Dollar Baby* is a comment on disability rights, or on class, are simply reading too much into his films: this was the case with his previous films, as well as with this one: "I never thought about the political side of this when making the film," he says in a column by Frank Rich (Rich 2005). Critics on the right and left were wrong, Eastwood says: the film is not political at all. Nonetheless, Eastwood offered a fresh way to look at the American experience.

REFERENCES AND FURTHER READING

Corliss, Richard. 2004. "*Million Dollar Baby* Review." *Time*, December 27, 179.

Davis, Lennard. 2005. "Why '*Million Dollar Baby*' Infuriates the Disabled." *The Chicago Tribune*, February 2.

Dostoyevsky, Fydor. 1992. *Crime and Punishment*. Translated by Richard Pevear and Larissa Volokhonsky. New York: Vintage Classics.

Ebert, Roger. 2004. "*Million Dollar Baby* Review." *The Chicago Sun Times*, December 14, 2005. http://www.rogerebert.com/reviews/million-dollar-baby-2005. Accessed February 25, 2014.

Kierkegaard, Søren. 1986. *Fear and Trembling*. Translated by Alastair Hannay. New York: Penguin Classics.

Modleski, Tania. 2010. "Clint Eastwood and Male Weepies." *American Literary History* 22, no. 1 (Spring): 136–58.

Rich, Frank. 2005. "How Dirty Harry Turned Commie." *The New York Times*, February 13.

Rosenbaum, Jonathan. 2004. "A Little Transcendence Goes a Long Way." The *Chicago Reader*, December 24. http://www.jonathanrosenbaum.net/2004/12/a-little-transcendence-goes-a-long-way/. Accessed February 25, 2014.

Toole, F.X. (Jerry Boyd). 2000. *Rope Burns: Stories from the Corner*. New York: HarperCollins.

Travers, Peter. 2004. "*Million Dollar Baby* Review." *Rolling Stone*, December 30/January 13, 170–71.

Wilson, Michael Henry. 2007. *Clint Eastwood: Entretiens avec Michael Henry Wilson* (Interviews with Eastwood). Paris: Cahiers du Cinéma.

Yeats, William Butler. 1920. "The Lake Isle of Innisfree." In *Modern British Poetry*, ed. Louis Untermeyer. New York: Harcourt, Brace, & Howe. http://www.bartelby.com/103/44.html. Accessed February 25, 2014.

Chapter 10

THE WAR CYCLE: *FLAGS OF OUR FATHERS; LETTERS FROM IWO JIMA; GRAN TORINO*

In 2006, Clint Eastwood—a household name since *Rawhide*, *A Fistful of Dollars*, and *Dirty Harry*—startled those who loved his Rowdy Yates character hotheaded and simple, the Man with No Name anonymous and yet dangerously nonchalant, and Dirty Harry reckless and depressed. He deserted the Western terrain, wild or urban, and abandoned the iconic screen persona (or seemed to, until 2008's *Gran Torino*) that made him famous whether he was clothed in a dirty poncho, a drover's dusty jeans, a policeman's polyester slacks, or the open-shirted casuals of the itinerant photographic journalist. He made two war movies in one year, itself an impressive feat that put his efficient shooting schedules to good use. He starred in neither one, despite his recent successful acting turn in *Million Dollar Baby*. One of the films, *Letters from Iwo Jima*, was even shot in Japan using Japanese actors speaking Japanese and subtitled in English. With *Letters* and its companion, *Flags of Our Fathers*, more than setting his own persona aside, Eastwood dared to challenge myths about The Greatest Generation and traditional American perspectives on the politics and history of the World War II—the "good war" evoked by Studs Terkel's oral history of the same name.

It was always tough to separate the plot of a given piece from its famous driving force—the actor, director, producer himself—surely one of the reasons that many confused spectators misunderstood and underestimated him for four decades. So powerful and pervasive is the Eastwood presence on-screen or offscreen that the subtlety of his performances, precision of his directing, and profundity of his thematic engagements frequently were overshadowed by his perceived dark double, the *Doppelgänger*, the beautiful but deadly gunslinger condemned to haunt the corridors of peace-loving consciences until the Last Days. In any philosophy of perpetual or "endless" war, the Dark Knight stalks the forces of evil. War is inevitable, if not hotly desired.

"Never before have I seen such a waste of lives," quips the Man with No Name in *The Good, the Bad, and the Ugly*. The look on his face as he gazes across fields of torn blue- and gray-uniformed bodies is not one of a detached observer but rather a gaze of sadness and disgust, a moral statement placed in words and sight within one of the greatest antiwar movies. Forty years after his Spaghetti Westerns, Eastwood seized the chance to film a waste of lives similar to that of America's Civil War, this time on a faraway Pacific island, with boys too young to leave their mothers and wives (the Japanese soldiers on Iwo Jima were as young as 16, and many American soldiers were no older than 19) and too poor to buy a pass out of mass slaughter. Yet the director turns away from the telescopic despair of the Death Angel toward the watchful bard who, in the lyric of the Civil War song, "looks for the right/To see the dawn of peace." He leaves the *Pale Rider* and Revelation 20's dark seductions behind.

Remarkably for any mainstream movie, Eastwood shows two sides of the battle, separate films, not only the heroic and triumphant American one, unlike the unified approach used in *All Quiet on the Western Front* (Lewis Milestone, 1931), *The Battle of Algiers* (Gillo Pontecorvo, 1966), or even *The Thin Red Line* (Terrence Malick, 1999). The filmmaker pities young men, hardly more than children, caught in brutally mismanaged battles and exposes the ugly side of the generals and politicians who support wars for their own gain.

Director Sam Fuller once wrote: "There's no way you can portray war realistically, not in a movie nor in a book. You can only capture a very, very small aspect of it. For moviegoers to get the idea of real combat, you'd have to shoot at them every so often from either side of the screen" (Fuller 2002, 123). The nightmares of Doc Bradley in *Flags*, hallucinations of Will Munny in *Unforgiven*, venomous outbursts of Walt Kowalski in *Gran Torino*—the men attempt to give voice to their recurring nightmares.

FLAGS OF OUR FATHERS AND *LETTERS FROM IWO JIMA*

Flags of Our Fathers begins with the stunning immediacy of a chaotic battle that cannot be won. Critic Scott Foundas wrote at the time of the movie's release, "*Flags of Our Fathers* is to the WWII movie what Eastwood's *Unforgiven* was to the western—a stripping-away of mythology until only a harsher, uncomfortable reality remains" (Foundas 2006). He continues: "With *Flags*, Eastwood has made one of his best films—a searching, morally complex deconstruction of the Greatest Generation that is nevertheless rich in the sensitivity to human frailty that has become his signature as a filmmaker" (Foundas 2006). Indeed, the movie systematically exposes in the machinery of war the layers of willful misunderstanding and calculated cruelty that fuel, then exploit, young men's agony.

As the film opens, we hear the gentle lyrics of "I'll Walk Alone," so huskily sung that the vocalist could be Eastwood himself, conjuring images of an abandoned wife and children at home. We imagine that we see a uniformed boy scarcely out of knickers pausing on a railroad platform with his knapsack slung over his shoulder, and a sweetheart with her ear to the wireless hungry for news from the front. News of the individual rarely comes in wartime—only officers with black-banded letters or unit mates bearing tales of a son bravely fallen, an aura of saintly sacrifice surrounding the telling. (*The Messenger* directed by Oren Moverman in 2009 visualizes the delivery of the dreaded letter and its aftermath.)

We shudder in *Flags of our Fathers* as Doc Bradley (Ryan Phillippe), one of the flag-raisers in the famous Iwo Jima photograph, is served an ice-cream sculpture sundae covered with strawberry syrup at a State dinner. He sees not a mound of confection but rather a hill covered with blood—rivers of blood spilled over the raging hot island which for

The iconic photo comforted suffering families, but in Flags of Our Fathers, *Eastwood exposes the multilayered exploitation of our soldiers. (DreamWorks/ Photofest)*

Japan symbolized its mystical essence as a nation, a people, and a divine power in the world. To the young Japanese boys trapped in the island's hewn thermal caves or to the young American boys who rushed up those rocky beaches and cliffs, neither the divine sheen of Japan as an imperial idea nor the concept of a just war waged by a divinely blessed America saved their arms, eyes, or sanity.

Letters from Iwo Jima, which emerged at the end of 2006 not long after the release of *Flags of Our Fathers* and the rerelease of *Army of Shadows* (Jean-Pierre Melville, 1969), further developed Eastwood's wish to get into the skin of the enemy outside. Doc Bradley in *Flags of Our Fathers* cries out for his hapless buddy Iggy, a simple boy dragged out into the fog of war who vanished in the darkness and was sucked into emptiness. Try as the political machine may to paint the bright face of cheerfulness and patriotism on World War II, *Flags* exposes the execution of the war as a crime against children. War resembles the hideous schemes of the serial murderer who stalks the plot in

Changeling in all but the mind-numbing numbers of boys whose bodies are mutilated, parts of their leg bones still left in their shoes, their chests ripped open, and their blood soaked into the barren ground.

The operation that sends 100,000 soldiers (United States) or 22,000 (Japan) to take or defend Iwo Jima—a barren rock in the middle of the ocean—discounts their individual lives. It forces the young and unseasoned men to murder close at hand or from a detached distance, by proxy, crazed by sorrow and terror, unhinged by vengeance, unmanned, and stripped of all that makes them human. The flags displayed so brazenly in the two movies (American in *Flags* and Japanese in *Letters*) ultimately cover coffins, masking the mutilated remains of schoolboys in the bright public colors of heroic fantasy. Eastwood shot the two movies in desaturated color film. The rambling, sorrowful, and pain-filled plot of *Flags* is transformed with *Letters* into a tightly structured narrative with almost silent opening and closing contemporary frames enriched in the central tale by a subtle exploration of "memory." As my student Ben Rudofsky put it in our 2009 class, its restless camera lives among and dies with its doomed subjects, young Japanese soldiers, as it roams through the labyrinthine passageways of the island's deadly thermal caves or nests with the boys as they huddle to write letters home, dodge debris, or meditate upon their approaching deaths.

As *Letters* opens, a modern-day archaeological team treads upon a blasted beach dotted by rusted artillery that testifies to earlier, unhappy times—a futile battle suppressed in the Japanese collective memory and absent from its record books—post-apocalypse terrain reminiscent of Andrei Tarkovsky's *Stalker* (1976) or Alfonzo Cuarón's *Children of Men* (2006). Probing a mysterious labyrinth of caves and tunnels, the investigators uncover a buried trove of letters that we wish we could read. Buried secrets fill Eastwood's movies, as in *Bridges of Madison Country* and *Gran Torino*. Just as the letters to an Iowa farmwife from her lover find visual expression in the heart of *Bridges*, the dusty letters we glimpse at the start of *Iwo Jima* suddenly wipe into the sepia of soldiers' uniforms and the dust from the excavated ash.

The "detective" frame of *Letters* encircles an inner plot marked by controlled displacement in time and place. From the beginning of the movie until the return of the contemporary frame two hours later, the unyielding volcanic rock of Iwo Jima, multiple intrusions puncture the isolated inner story. The soldiers construct elaborate subterraneous hiding places; the illusory tight world of the island is penetrated repeatedly by entries from an unseen outside—the battle's general, Tadamichi Kuribayashi (Ken Watanabe), an Olympian equestrian, Baron Nishi (Tsuyoshi Ihara) with his horse, and an assortment of officers. Further, flashbacks in color or in black and white repeatedly interrupt the inner plot's forward movement and disturb the monochromatic image of an island of graves.

Spurts of color come and go in abstract artistry that plays in antiphonal rhythm against the film's unfolding human stories. The Japanese flag, for instance, which in the film is obscurely positioned, could easily be mistaken for an American flag. Fires and explosions have been treated on film to "bring them into the foreground acutely, their bright orange hue cutting across the black and grey landscape and lending them a surreal quality," as Rudofsky wrote. One flashback, warmly colored and underscored with chamber music, simultaneously marks Kuribayashi's happy sojourn in the United States and reveals an inner split between West and East not only in the general himself but also in the presentation of the film.

Most shocking of all, after nearly an hour's immersion in the caves' dark and silty hues with young soldiers we have come to love, the spectator's surrogate Saigo spots the massive American fleet through an opening in a wall of the cave, massed offshore on the blue, blue sea ready to begin a battle that will kill or inalterably scar everyone it touches. Yet after this storm of exits and entrances, deaths, confessions, and redemption scenes, the final shot of the movie's interior plot alights upon a still image of the setting sun.

The concept for *Letters from Iwo Jima* sprang from the director's chance discovery of a book of letters and drawings belonging to Kuribayashi, *Picture Letters from Commander in Chief*, collected and translated into English by Tsuyuko Yoshida. Though viewers are never allowed access to the collection, its central conceit, letters written long ago by a father to his daughter from great physical and cultural distance, picks up on Eastwood's persistent theme of the rupture of parent and child as part of the movie's particularly complex engagement with memory. In *Flags*, a son reconstructs his father's anguished wartime experiences from shards of artifacts: a newspaper article, a photo, a medal, a few interviews with

his father's acquaintances, a bit of historical research, and ample imagination. The *Letters* script was written—or rather absorbed, filtered, and
recast—by a Japanese American writer, Iris Yamashita (with Eastwood's
valued earlier scripter, Paul Haggis), designed to place the viewer inside
the Japanese boys' anguished experience within their island prison and
acutely aware of the Imperial madness that will consume them.

Letters was a daring, risky, artistic, and commercial move for Eastwood. Raised on war films and rejecting most as "classic propaganda,"
Eastwood decided when he was shooting *Flags* to "show the two sides
of a battle," portraying the effects of war on both sides—a feat never
attempted by any other filmmaker, he commented on NPR, except perhaps by Lewis Milestone in *All Quiet on the Western Front* (Gross 2007).
Eastwood's choice to make a film in Japan with Japanese actors and
dialogue seems natural for a director who was familiar with the movies
of Kurosawa.

Eastwood sets up the audience to identify with some of the young
soldiers, focusing upon their individual stories and their unfolding relationships. The inner plot begins with the voiceover of the conscript
Saigo (Kazunari Ninomiya), a narrative device that immediately draws
the spectator into his thoughts. The young soldier's criticisms about the
war are unprecedented in Japanese war films, as Eastwood commented
to NPR. Certainly they violate a consistent cultural representation of
Japan, positive or negative—that is, the men within the plot are allowed to exhibit a human, rather than a monolithic, range of attitudes
toward their country, their predicament, and their fellow soldiers. It
reaches for something larger than nationalism: to cross borders into
another's being and absorb his suffering as your own.

Letters builds upon the fierce antimilitarism of *Flags* even as the director visually creates an underground prison that houses child soldiers
ripped from their human attachments and sent to die in the name of
a national religion. The characters we follow and love in *Letters*, not
only Saigo but also Kuribayashi, Nozaki, and Shimizu, resemble Jamie
and Josey, star characters in *The Outlaw Josey Wales*, who also suffered
in a futile and endlessly perpetuated earlier American war. They also
recall Doc and René and Ira, young kids in *Flags of our Fathers* whose
suffering was sold as propaganda to fuel an ongoing war on the Euro-
pean front of a world war.

Eastwood interlaces the claustrophobic caves with flashbacks to Saigo's warm home space and loving wife, giving texture to the young man's backstory to underline the loss in wartime of everything that sustains human life. Even deprived of their means of survival, their bakery, the young couple lives for the future—their unborn child.

In his dying moments, the general recalls a world of reason and hospitality, his own and his American hosts', where perceived peace allows chamber music, wine, and laughter, and the thought of war disappears into the abstract.[1] Peace could have been forged during the months when East met West. But whereas peace needs engagement, reconciliation, and connection to flourish, as in *Invictus*, *Letters* shows the collapse of communications. Soldiers fire upon their own men, as with the death of Pat Tillman in the early days of Iraq; commanders fail to relay battle orders, and hundreds are accidentally killed, as in the botched battle operations at the start of World War II (name a few) or the Civil War and the manic scrambling by American commanders to fix upon a plan for Iwo Jima.

In *Letters*, the "letters" in the title go unsent as far as we know. Even though we see the soldiers writing their families and glimpse Saigo taking yet another letter to his wife to the island dispatcher to be mailed, even though we hear the texts of letters home recited in voiceover by Saigo and Kuribayashi, neither the letters nor the men can leave the island. His fellow officers feud with him and with each other. He discovers to his alarm that the army and navy do not share information. His orders are either disobeyed or never reach their intended audience.

The few phone and radio connections, telegrams, letters, and messengers from the far-distant Emperor only intensify the sense of absence and abandonment. Inside the island compound, just as the war is nearly lost, the piercing tones of schoolchildren singing about the "imperial land" crackle over the barely audible radio waves to underscore the

---

[1] I am not sure when this episode is supposed to have taken place, but certainly the thirties. The United States—at least the American public—would have been oblivious to Japan's imperial ambitions or to events such as the "Rape of Nanking." The United States did not declare war against Japan until our mainland was bombed on December 7, 1941.

Empire's mindless recruitment of child soldiers. Even more painfully, the schoolchildren come from Nagano, Kuribayashi's own hometown. The brittle transmission taunts its listeners, as the few survivors gather to hear the bitter reminder of an outside world they will never see again and cannot save.

With the first voiceover of reluctant soldier Saigo, spectators have been drawn into the human tragedy seen from the soldiers' side— suffering both abstract, as the young men serve as sacrificial offerings to the god of war, and deeply individual, with the flashbacks to clean, well-lighted places. Through Saigo's eyes, we witness the sight of an entire platoon's grenade suicides—bright bursts of orange against the caves' dank grey—the deaths of young men we have come to know and pity as they found themselves cruelly outnumbered. Eastwood's direction allows us to witness not only this remote corner of the war from the inside of a cosmic heart—children needlessly massacred—but also to feel the firebombing of Tokyo (Kuribayashi 2007, 175) and the on-the-ground horror of the atomic bombs dropped not long after the Battle of Iwo Jima ended.

Terry Gross asked the director about the timing of his war movies. "It is difficult not to think of Iraq (a war that Eastwood opposed) upon seeing the two films," he said (Gross 2007). "Each war calls up comparisons," he responded when asked in 1976 about the resonance of *The Outlaw Josey Wales* to the by-then thoroughly discredited Vietnam War. "Most of the films on war," he has commented, "convey propaganda. I prefer those which try to avoid it." I can hardly think of a more insulting term for Eastwood to use to describe a film than "propaganda": propaganda is everything he hates—filmmaking about politics rather than people, filmmaking aligned with a particular agenda, party, or group. Citing war films that came closer to the truth, Eastwood mentioned *Battleground* (*Bastogne*, William Wellman, 1949) and *The Steel Helmet* (Samuel Fuller, 1951), films that "aged well because they are based upon what the characters have lived" (Wilson 2007, 183).

In *Letters*, Eastwood probes justice and reconciliation through a unifying poetic prism of images, words, and music—a daring artistic choice to defuse centuries of demonizing Japan. The Japanese soldiers, young and powerless and driven to madness or suicide, find their human counterparts in the American boys drafted out of poor homes like Harlon

Block's in Texas or those of Ira Hayes, René Gagnon, and the other soldiers from *Flags of our Fathers*, all from families who had not yet recovered from the devastations of the Great Depression or racism or the assaults of nature.

Letters' muted color palette with its oppressive look of half-light given neither to sun showers nor to restful dark, suggests a prison and a graveyard. *Letters* begins with the voiceover of Saigo, the spectator's surrogate, as he asks his absent wife, "Are we digging our own graves?" The film's ending—thousands of corpses and wounded stretched along the island's beaches—not only echoes the death-strewn hillside in *The Good, the Bad, and the Ugly* but also exposes the difficulty of telling one wounded man from another. The wounded Americans and Saigo, the Japanese prisoner, could be brothers, even twins, to echo a phrase from *All Quiet on the Western Front*, one of Eastwood's most admired war movies.

Has *Letters* attracted worldwide fame through American viewers' thirst for bloody action? No. You only need to watch its opening frame, listen to its haunting piano melody, and give yourself to the unfolding stories of Saigo, Kuribayashi, and their friends. You will never see "the enemy" the same way again. You will prepare yourself for the next two installments in Eastwood's war cycle, "Oneself as the Other," *Gran Torino*, and *Invictus*.

Flags of Our Fathers and *Letters from Iwo Jima* marked another critical and creative high point in Eastwood's long career. Both films were critically lauded, and reviewers were quick to note the ways the films resonated with the contemporary political moment. Manohla Dargis, a major champion of Eastwood's work, calls *Flags of Our Fathers* "a work of its own politically fraught moment," particularly in its focus on the disjuncture between images of the war—which can be mobilized for political or even commercial purposes—and the lived reality of the war itself (Dargis 2006). Noting that the film works as a "gentle corrective to Steven Spielberg's *Saving Private Ryan*, with its state-of-the-art carnage and storybook neatness," Dargis sees *Flags of Our Fathers* as a film in whose story "ambivalence and ambiguity are constituent of a worldview, not an aftereffect" (Dargis 2006). The moral certainty epitomized by the phrase "good war" and demonstrated in countless war films, including Spielberg's, is nowhere to be found here. Dargis is even more effusive toward *Letters from Iwo Jima*, which for her:

> confirms his reputation as one of the greatest directors working today, and one of the few for whom filmmaking is a moral impera-
> tive. . . . In "Iwo Jima," Mr. Eastwood humanizes the Japanese without evading their barbarism; rather shockingly, neither does he flinch when it comes to the Americans. (Dargis 2006)

For Eastwood, the two films show the futility of war. By exposing the humanity as well as the moral failings on each side, he depicts the violence of war unmoored from its political motivations.

In the war films, however, some in the conservative press detected a moral equivalence between the Japanese and American forces, one that ignored historical realities such as the Rape of Nanking. In a column in *The Weekly Standard*, a conservative journal, Jonathan Last critiques the two films for suggesting, as Eastwood puts it, that "there were good guys and bad guys everywhere" (Last 2007). He cites documentation of Japanese atrocities that far outstrip anything conducted by Americans (in his view), and notes that "Contrary to Eastwood, there were not 'bad guys' like this 'everywhere'" (Last 2007).

Reactions like Last's resemble earlier reactions to Eastwood's films. Eastwood continually denies the political resonances of his films, and with the war films, he framed the narrative as a story of individuals rather than a commentary on the specific politics of the two belliger-ent sides. In the past, his refusal to see that his films could have politi-cal implications has drawn the ire of liberals (in the *Dirty Harry* films especially), but with films like *Million Dollar Baby*, *Flags*, and *Letters From Iwo Jima*, conservatives were quick to cry foul, as though he had betrayed the conservative cause.

GRAN TORINO

It was now 2008. Although Clint Eastwood was well over 70, over the past five years he had created some of the most ambitious and thought-ful work of his career, a remarkable illustration of what Dargis called his "moral imperative" to make films. Perhaps the relative calm in his personal life allowed him to retain focus, for during his seventies, Eastwood's life was indeed calm, thanks in part to Dina's influence. In 2009, he told GQ: "Good. I like myself better than I did," a striking admission (Hainey 2009). Although the couple separated in 2013, Eastwood spoke effusively of their relationship and the conciliatory tone Dina struck toward his many exes and children. "She's friendly with my first wife, friendly to former girlfriends. She went out of her way to unite everybody. She's been extremely influential in my life," he said in a 2008 interview (Fussman 2008). (Perhaps Sondra Locke was not among the exes with whom Dina was friendly, however.)

Eastwood's relationship with his children also changed around this time: Scott, his son with Jacelyn Reeves, appeared briefly in *Gran Torino* and now goes by Scott Eastwood rather than Scott Reeves. He appears in splashy photo spreads in magazines like *Town & Country* and, doubtless due to his striking resemblance to the young Clint, has quickly become something of a sex symbol. Eastwood's daughter with Reeves, Kathryn, served as "Miss Golden Globe" during the 2005 ceremony, a position bestowed annually on the daughter of a film or television star (Miss Golden Globe ensures that winners shuffle off the stage in the right direction after their speeches). Francesca Fisher-Eastwood, his daughter with Frances Fisher, performed the same role for the 2013 ceremony. The public face of the expansive Eastwood brood that began to gain prominence around the time of Kathryn's appearance at the Globes veers wildly from earlier, more guarded instances of public exposure—a few rare behind-the-scenes profiles of Eastwood the family man and roles in his films for his children with Maggie, Kyle and Alison. It certainly marks a change from the 1990s, when his two children with Reeves were acknowledged publicly only in the unfortunate context of his testimony in the legal battles with Locke (Eliot 2009, 252). Eastwood's comments about Dina imply that she motivated his change of attitude.

Eastwood's public persona hardly went soft, though. On the contrary. Even approaching 80, some still discussed him as though he were Harry Callahan incarnate, not an actor who had played that role a few times decades earlier. His gruff, Dirty Harry-esque persona made its usual appearances in places like *Esquire* and GQ magazine, staffed, I assume, by a bevy of longtime fans of the kind of unabashed masculinity Eastwood modeled for them. Although *Esquire* quotes him speaking fondly of his children and waxing poetic about Velázquez (although I'm pretty sure he means Goya), in general Eastwood is at his Dirty Harry best: showing a disdain for overthinking and careful planning ("It keeps coming back to 'We've come this far, let's not ruin it by thinking.'"); complaining about overstepping government regulators (about a trip to Iceland, where a platform to view a waterfall did not have a protective fence: "I said to myself, You know, in the States they'd have that hurricane-fenced off, because they're afraid somebody's gonna fall and some lawyer's going to appear. There, the mentality was like it was in America in the old days: If you fall, you're stupid."); and pondering the change in attitudes regarding fighting and bullying ("We live in more of a pussy generation now, where everybody's become used to saying, 'Well, how do we handle it psychologically?' In those days, you just punched the bully back and duked it out" (Fussman 2008)).

WHAT HAPPENS AFTER THE WAR IS OVER?

When rumors started to circulate that his next movie would resemble *Dirty Harry*, no one should have been completely surprised. Even though a return to the old growler would have broken with his recent string of artistic shockers, Eastwood liked to mix up genres and modes, even within the same film. Note, too, that all Eastwood fans are not alike. Some fans of Dirty Harry may still not know that he directed *Mystic River*, *Changeling*, *Invictus*, or the war movies, since he did not star in any of these.

The movie that sparked the rumors, of course, was *Gran Torino*. Dirty Harry no. 6! For months I waited, enthralled by the trailer that played for months before its December 2008 opening. The title came from the protagonist's car, a 1972 model—it came out in late 1971, right around the time of the first *Dirty Harry*. The trailer features Eastwood's Walt Kowalski taking the law into his own hands, to protests by others that he should just leave that to the police—all very Dirty Harry. Eastwood's furious snarl, "Get off my lawn," gun in hand, comes across as the perfect near-octogenarian summation of a Harry Callahan ethos: "Go ahead, make my day" for the Life Alert generation. I guess

Eastwood had to make another Dirty Harry revenge movie, I sighed to myself. He has so many children to support.

But what a pity! Eastwood had spent the past 30 years acting in and sometimes directing movies with abundant audience appeal, like all five Dirty Harrys, *Every Which Way But Loose*, and *Every Which Way You Can*, and course and always, the Spaghetti Westerns. He alternated big movies with "personal" but little-seen movies that he directed and funded himself like *Honkytonk Man* and *Bronco Billy*. *The Outlaw Josey Wales* in 1976 and *Bridges of Madison County* in 1995 had a little more traction, in part because he still was a bankable movie star. But he didn't begin to get major art-director's press until *Unforgiven* in 1992 and *Mystic River* in 2003. Since then it's been one brilliant movie after another, including *Changeling*, with Angelina Jolie. So why, I asked myself, was he doing another Dirty Harry?

What a relief to discover that he didn't. Not that the Man with No Name, Dirty Harry, the Stranger in *High Plains Drifter*, and the Preacher from *Pale Rider* have gone away, replaced by the soft, gentle, and sympathetic Robert Kinkaid in *Bridges of Madison County* and vulnerable and affectionate Frankie Dunn in *Million Dollar Baby*. All the Dirty Harry standards appear in the first half of the new movie, *Gran Torino*, all wrapped up in the figure of Walt Kowalski, the movie's central character (played by Eastwood). But they must be dealt with nonetheless.

The mythic apparatus of the Superhero is present in Walt's acid one-liners and in the giant rifle he packs not too far out of reach. The one man American superhero model hasn't worked out too well: look at Iraq and Afghanistan. But vigilante justice, so hot a topic in some circles in 2010? I had to wonder what Eastwood would do with the vigilante response in this movie. He had rejected that model for a long time in his "personal" movies, but audiences and the press mostly did not grasp what he was doing when awards season came around. They were stuck back in the seventies and eighties looking for the *Man with No Name* or *Dirty Harry*.

The plot is set in a formerly booming, now run-down American industrial city, Detroit, with formerly all-white pristine neighborhoods overtaken by waves of immigrants—like a destroyed Norman Rockwell painting. The protagonist, Walt, embodies the dreams of a better life of one immigrant strand, Polish. For his whole life, he worked on a Ford assembly line and took pride in his craft and his tidy home. He is now re- tired. Blacks and Hispanics have drifted into his neighborhood, and now, heaven forefend, an extended Hmong family has moved in next door.

In this timely movie, Eastwood links depression and spiritual uncer- tainty to a past history of violent acts, associating markers of personal disintegration with larger economic and social instability indirectly or directly caused by war. *Gran Torino* explores the terrain upon which Eastwood examines spiritual and social dislocation: Walt and the war memories that poison his life; the collapsing city within which he lives; his rebirth through the embrace of Sue and Thao, his new Hmong neighbors; and the fashioning of a wider human community.

The movie has two main parts, isolation and reconciliation. The events and persons in the first part mirror events and persons in the second in rhythmic antiphony: call and response. Funeral echoes funeral; meal scenes in one section return in another with startling variations; buried secrets surface unexpectedly and yet, in the movie's elaborate structure, fit into the larger redemptive scheme. In the first, Walt is newly widowed and is afflicted with sons and grandchildren who seem to inhabit the world of *commedia dell'Arte*, fools galore, or at least seem to be playing in a different movie from ones we've expected from Eastwood since *Mystic River* and *Million Dollar Baby*. Walt hates immigrants, dirt, shoddy workmanship, laziness, and the world in gen- eral. His flag flaps crazily outside his porch, where he sits most of the day and chugs beer from his cooler, alone with his regrets, whatever they are. Isolation is established visually and thematically as surely here as in the beginning of *Flags of Our Fathers*, where a young soldier stares desperately around him, unmoored in a grey and pitted battlefield.

Gran Torino begins with alienating devices that anticipate its later exposure of buried secrets. A long God's-eye sweep of the camera alights upon a modest church building surrounded by grass and cement. The camera dips inside to investigate the building's interior, where a massive organ fills the sanctuary with solemn music. It's a funeral, but for whom? It might as well be for the tall, gaunt man who stands beside a coffin, a poor creature whom the camera isolates as it begins to rove around the gaping spaces trying to catch a snarl here, a yawn there, or a few words of irreverence or kindness.

With whispered dialogue, we learn that the funeral is for the man's wife, yet we hear his sons scorn him, and his grandchildren admit that they feel no sense of gravity or loss at their grandmother's death. One friend, Al, comes forward to console Walt, for that is his name. Otherwise, he stands alone, comfortless. Rather than the classic organ background that plays at the funeral, the film could have opened with "I'll Walk Alone," the wrenching period song that underscores the beginning of Eastwood's problematic, sad antiwar movie of 2006, *Flags of our Fathers*. Instead, we are face-to-face with the deep wounds that scar a former soldier, and the isolation he suffers even within his own family.

In Eastwood's previous two movies, *Flags* and *Letters from Iwo Jima*, he engages the horror and senselessness of war through the eyes of two innocent conscripts, Doc Bradley the student and Saigo the baker. One is American, the other Japanese, each haunted by what he saw and did during the war. *Gran Torino* signals the thoughtful director's further reflection upon "what war does to men's souls."

The artistic agenda of Eastwood across his long career as a director has stimulated spectators to see through the eyes of the other person, most radically in *Letters from Iwo Jima*. Like confession, practical acts of mercy and love defuse hatred. Eastwood the director defies the rhetoric of heated screeds that aim to divide Americans from one another by opening his audiences to women, the poor, the oddballs, and minorities, and with *Gran Torino*, marginalized immigrants such as the Hmong.

So begins the friendship between a teen under siege to local gang members, Thao, and a victim of a far-distant war with another victim of a U.S.-fueled war who sadly needs to be reborn. Eastwood does more than throw one-liners and comedic scenes at us. He undercuts everything with rich and complex people such as these, interacting in community, as Yoga teacher Rachel Koontz suggests.

Walt's transformation begins with a meal and heats up when he does some matchmaking with Thao and Youa, an echo of his romance with his now-dead wife Dorothy. The women bring the unhappy stranger into their midst for a birthday celebration. Even better, the event itself—a ritual celebration—offsets the depression that often afflicts elderly immigrants in America (Brown 2009). The meal follows Walt's recognition of what he holds in common with the Hmong.

The camaraderie of the meal challenges isolation. At the beginning of the movie, Walt seems immobilized by life's experiences and sorrow. When he crosses the threshold of Sue's house and enters into relationship with the Hmong, he shifts out of the past toward confession and release.

Actor Clint Eastwood had played a lonely man without a sweetheart many times before *Gran Torino*. Despite the presence of strong women in many of the movies he has directed (*The Gauntlet*'s Gus; *Unforgiven*'s Strawberry Alice; *Gran Torino*'s Sue), the iconic Clint enshrined in the public imagination for good or for ill slinks through his roles, big gun or not, with a dead or estranged wife in the background.

Eastwood's assorted characters carry around loss as part of their persona. "I once knew someone like you. No one was around to help," the Man with No Name says to the Mary figure Maria he has rescued from sex slavery in *A Fistful of Dollars*. Ditto for Dirty Harry, Josey Wales, Will Munny, and the protagonists in *True Crime and Blood Work*. Rootlessness may add to his appeal—"a rolling stone gathers no moss," as my husband sang to me on my honeymoon—or it may signal the end of the isolated hero-savior as a life model for Eastwood characters. As the director told Michael Henry Wilson in an interview, "You can only go so far with a solitary hero. If you create family connections for him, you give him a new dimension" (Wilson 2007, 47). Walt Kowalski builds family connections in *Gran Torino*. But it takes time—115 minutes in this movie—for a damaged person to emerge from depression and isolation.

Gran Torino gave director/actor Eastwood yet another chance to rescue the forlorn man without a family: Josey Wales with flames of loss imprinted in his dreams; Will Munny with only a photo of his dead wife to sustain his sense of rightness with God and the social order; Charlie Parker, a black man adrift in a white world and his own demons; and Frankie Dunn keeping vigil at his adopted daughter's bedside. *Gran Torino*'s emotional landscape cannot be divorced from its political and social message. Its humanistic message emerges organically from Eastwood's criticism of nearly 40 years of America's failure to love. In *Gran Torino*, Eastwood mobilizes another story, another set of characters, a transformed version of all his former selves to open America's mind and heart. And he does it in the most unexpected way—self-sacrifice.

In thousands of movies, myths, and stories, self-sacrifice has been the special domain of the powerless female. At the end of *Gran Torino*, however, Eastwood uses weakness as strength, also a theme in multiple narratives: David and Goliath; *Scheherazade*; the little tailor and the giant. The dark night sky shrouds Walt's figure as he emerges from his house with a shotgun early in the film—as ready as Dirty Harry, it seems, to take swift action against the murderous Hmong gang's threats. "Get. Off. My. Lawn," he growls in that gruff and low voice Clint-watchers know all too well. Walt, significantly enough, ratchets up the action here and in the sequence where three young black men mock-threaten Sue and her dopey boyfriend, Trey (played by Eastwood's own son Scott). Walt first pulls a mock gun, his cocked finger, and then a real one. So silly are all the confrontations in the movie that we are shocked when first Sue, then Walt, are actually harmed.

Darkness at movie's end, however, signifies an emotion rooted in deeper emotion than anger or despair. It signals the warm embrace of a death that comes before new life can begin—a warmth conveyed by the soft light and full score in the ending frame sequence in *Unforgiven* or in the "Eastwood shots" of two people connecting their lonely lives in *Million Dollar Baby*, *Bridges of Madison County*, and *Breezy* (YouTube 2009).

Unlike the unkempt professional killers who slept in their clothes and looked it (the Man with No Name in the Spaghetti Westerns, for instance, and *High Plains Drifter*'s Stranger), Walt Kowalski prepares for his latest showdown by getting a haircut and a shave, mowing his lawn (seen in a God's-eye shot), crafting a new will, buying a tailored suit (which he leaves back in his closet), and making a gift of his beloved dog Daisy to his irascible female counterpart, the Hmong grandma next door. He prepares to sacrifice himself in radical response to the violent assault and gang rape of the redemptive and life-giving figure of Sue, his neighbor and friend. She herself has been sacrificed to all the violence in the unstable, cruel, and tragic world of an economically ravaged city where hatred and fear have trumped welcome.

The two types of sacrifice call for differing reactions from the spectator. Sue exists in relationship to others—sister, daughter, granddaughter, cousin, neighbor, and girlfriend. Her violation is real, visceral. She possesses a centered sense of herself and her ambitions ("Hmong girls go to college," she tells Walt), and in one scene after another, she shows uncanny insight and maturity. Nonetheless, as a woman and a minority in a decayed part of a great American city, she is unprotected. In solidarity with the millions of women throughout our troubled globe, she suffers from the war that America wages upon its marginalized citizens and the displaced citizens wage upon one another: sexual violation.

Walt, however, gives up his life voluntarily. Critic Karina Longworth comments that the film's "fairy tale" ending would never solve the problems shown earlier in the film (YouTube 2009, now offline). But the ending reaches for a spiritual response to violence: derail retribution to allow agents of law and policy to address the serious social problems the film shows so graphically. In Eastwood's earlier films such as *The Gauntlet*, *Pale Rider*, and *Million Dollar Baby*, the main characters absorbed the violence of the life around them with compromised hope for a better world. In *Gran Torino*, *Flags*, and *Letters*, the characters and the fabrics of the films point toward a reconciled world free of war and war's memories.

Gran Torino's core story far surpasses the petty, mean-spirited emptiness of Walt's clueless sons and their wives and children, who consider Walt as an easy source of favors now (the Lions tickets) and of money and his car (once he's dead)—a nuisance to be warehoused, not a parent to be cherished. As throughout his career, Eastwood goes for the jugular: an apocalyptic wasteland (the war zones on Iwo Jima and in urban Detroit); a brutalized innocent (Sue, Ira Hayes, Shimizu, and Saigo); and a willingness to risk financial disaster (Eastwood the producer's possible economic ruin by making *Bird*, *Letters*, and *Gran Torino*, a movie that ends of the death of the Eastwood character). At its magnificent end, though, justice and peace prevail in *Gran Torino* through Walt's intentional martyrdom.

REFERENCES AND FURTHER READING

Bradley, James, and Ron Powers. 2006. *Flags of Our Fathers*. New York: Bantam.

Brown, Patricia Leigh. 2009. "Invisible Immigrants, Old and Left with 'Nobody to Talk To.'" *The New York Times*, August 30. http://www.nytimes.com/2009/08/31/us/31elder.html. Accessed February 25, 2014.

Dargis, Manohla. 2006. "A Ghastly Conflagration, a Tormented Aftermath [review of *Flags of Our Fathers*]."' *The New York Times*, October 20. http://www.nytimes.com/2006/10/20/movies/20flag .html? Accessed February 25, 2014.

Eliot, Marc. 2009. *Clint Eastwood: American Rebel*. New York: Crown Publishing Group.

Foundas, Scott. 2006. "Print the Legend." *The Village Voice*, October 10. http://www.villagevoice.com/2006–10–10/film/print-the-legend/full/. Accessed February 25, 2014.

Fuller, Samuel. 2002. *A Third Face: My Tale of Writing, Fighting, and Filmmaking*. New York: Knopf.

Fussman, Cal. 2008. "Clint Eastwood: What I've Learned." *Esquire*, December 15. http://www.esquire.com/features/what-ive-learned/ clint-eastwood-quotes-0109. Accessed February 25, 2014.

Gross, Terry. 2007. Interview with Clint Eastwood. *Fresh Air*. National Public Radio. http://www.npr.org/templates/story/story .php?storyId=6781357. Accessed February 25, 2014.

Hainey, Michael. 2009. "Clint Eastwood: Icon." GQ, December. http://www.gq.com/entertainment/men-of-the-year/2009/ badass/clint-eastwood-legend-invictus-director?currentPage=1. Accessed February 25, 2014.

Kuribayashi, Tadamichi. 2007. *Picture Letters from the Commander in Chief: Letters from Iwo Jima*. Edited and translated by Tsuyuko Yoshida. San Francisco: VIZ Media.

Last, Jonathan. 2007. "Eastwood Goes to War." *The Weekly Standard* (blog), February 12. http://www.weeklystandard.com/weblogs/ TWSFP/2007/02/clint_eastwood_on_war.asp. Accessed February 25, 2014.

Terkel, Studs. 1997. *The Good War: An Oral History of World War II*. New York: The New Press.

Wilson, Michael Henry. 2007. *Clint Eastwood: Entretiens avec Michael Henry Wilson* (Interviews with Eastwood). Paris: Cahiers du Cinéma.

YouTube. 2009. "Eastwood Critics Roundtable Part 2: *Gran Torino*." *Film Society of Lincoln Center*, January 3. http://www.youtube .com/watch?v=gWun9zSQYvg. Accessed February 25, 2014.

Chapter 11

THE WEAK SHALL BE STRONG:
INVICTUS; CHANGELING

INVICTUS: VIOLENCE IS NOT THE WAY

A book I once read about the failure of Irish Christianity assailed forgiveness as a cunning and callow way to exact revenge by guilt. If American movie sales weigh in, revenge, not forgiveness, sells big. Forgiveness belongs to small art films such as *Atanarjuat* (Zacharias Konuk, 2001) and *Dead Man* (Jim Jarmusch, 1995), or foreign films such as *Le Fils* (*The Son*) and *L'Enfant* (*The Child*), by the Belgian directors the Dardenne brothers, or to *Invictus* by Eastwood. According to Aristotle's analysis of audience response in *The Poetics*, spectators need catharsis, release, and the restored feeling of purity (*katharos*) that a plot with a violent climax might produce. They need revenge. As critic Stanley Fish wrote on the website of the *New York Times:*

> Once the atrocity has occurred, the hero acquires an unquestioned justification for whatever he or she then does; and as the hero's proxy, the audience enjoys the same justification for vicariously participating in murder, mayhem and mutilation. In fact, the audience is really the main character in many of these films. You can almost see the director calculating the point at which

identification with the hero or heroine will be so great that the desire to see vengeance done will overwhelm any moral qualms viewers might otherwise have. (Fish 2009)

In my opinion, Fish completely misreads both *Gran Torino* and *The Outlaw Josey Wales*, but he is right that revenge is pervasive. It would be dramatically easier for the director—it always is, in American movies— but Eastwood tackled the harder task of dramatizing reconciliation.

Mandela (called Madiba, his tribal name) was a hero to those who still grieved the murder and the unifying mission of Martin Luther King Jr., but he was hardly the universally adored figure that he became late in his life, and in his death. Although in hindsight American politicians are quick to praise Mandela's struggle, many politicians in the United States at the time of his imprisonment were not nearly as accommodating toward him. After Mandela's death, amid the outcries of grief and appreciation, liberal commentators like *Forbes*'s Rick Ungar were quick to note that many, including Dick Cheney and Ronald Reagan, refused to support sanctions against the apartheid regime in the 1980s and refused to use their political influence to call for the release of political prisoners. Reagan believed Mandela's group was a terrorist group; Cheney defended his vote against the sanctions during the 2000 presidential race whereas the Congress overrode Reagan's veto and passed the sanctions with bipartisan support (Ungar 2013). Sam Kleiner notes, similarly, that while politicians and public officials on the left and the right all opposed apartheid as a matter of policy, Republicans and Conservatives in the United States favored preserving economic relations with South Africa, even if that meant undermining attempts to end the racist policies (Kleiner 2013).

It was only in the 1990s, after his release and election as South Africa's president and with his appearances on *Oprah* and other programs, that he became the elder statesman figure with whom politicians on the left and right liked to associate themselves. Even then, Mandela always belonged to the other side of the globe—known as a symbol of commitment and justice, but known less so as a person. Eastwood, whose films (in his view, anyway) always privilege the human over the political, sought to humanize Mandela the person, with his own life, world, and concerns, back into focus with *Invictus*. As Eastwood told

GQ interviewer Michael Hainey, "the world needs this kind of story nowadays . . . he's in prison twenty-seven years, he had a lot of time to think. He philosophized. He came out almost as this perception . . . of what Christ would be like if he existed: a guy who would forgive" (Hainey 2009).

In *Invictus*, we see and breathe this world and ask: What might we learn from Mandela's life, events, and circumstances? How did Mandela rise to power, and in what ways did he use that power? Perhaps more intriguing, given the radical nature of the actions that Eastwood depicts in the movie, what was he taught as a boy? What did he read? Where, when, how, and why did he develop an attitude of inclusivity—not only including women but also Communists in his early African National Congress (ANC) operations? How did he come to internalize the philosophy of Gandhi and the theology of King but other activists did not? The story world of this movie assumes such expansive questions. Ever the economic film director, Eastwood concentrates on specific action and utterance that deepen our concern for such questions without using fleeting screen time to ask about or elaborate on them.

Morgan Freeman long considered making a film from Mandela's autobiography, *Long Walk To Freedom*, and although Freeman was not involved, a film version of that book was released in 2013. Freeman, for his part, wisely backed away from such a daunting task. Whoever tackled the full burden of the Mandela story would have to pick carefully to capture not only the man's actions once he took office, but also his core motivations—whatever gave him strength to reject violent reprisals and insist upon peace and reconciliation.

From 70 plus years and an overabundance of significant life events, he selected only the one year, 1994–1995, and lavished as much attention on Mandela's new Afrikaner citizens and colleagues as on his black citizens and longtime partners in the antiapartheid struggle—which is, of course, exactly as Mandela had done. Accordingly, Eastwood pays much more attention to reconciliation than to revenge in the new South Africa.

With a movie that caps the career of one of America's most prolific and perceptive readers of the moral, social, and political landscape, consider what Eastwood includes, what he alludes to, and what he excludes altogether. As his personal movies have always tackled seemingly intractable ethical problems—how human beings should live together with justice and mercy—this film in particular should be judged by what the director portrays on screen and what he indexes by words, music, gestures, and other signs, not by what he chooses not to show.

For starters, Eastwood pared away several key characters in the story of Mandela's life and ascent to the presidency. The film does not show Winnie Mandela, his wife and collaborator, or Thabo Mbeki, for years his partner in negotiations with the white government and in 1999, his successor. Their absence signifies the rift between Mandela and his former associates. Winnie betrayed him personally and politically. She was unfaithful, and she also endorsed violence against whites. Mbeki, so central to the negotiations that brought Mandela to power, badly damaged Mandela's hard-won social unity as soon as he himself became president.

But if these central black characters are missing, Eastwood selected a curious role and color reversal with Mandela's ever-present, highly efficient personal assistant. Beginning in 1995 and continuing at least until 2011, Zelda la Grange, a young white woman, ran Mandela's affairs. In the film, Zelda's role of gatekeeper, schedule maker, and fellow strategist "Brenda" is played by a black actress, Adjoa Andoh. His personal secretary, Mary, is played by Leleti Khumalo. The historical Mandela chose Zelda in part because, as an Afrikaner reared in a Pretoria suburb and the Dutch Reformed Church, she embodied the multiracial entourage Mandela wanted to gather around him.

Eastwood does not need to portray the complete backstory. The "whole" background and history of violence lurk behind what at first appear to be the film's throwaway scenes. Under cover of the ordinary, spectators sense Mandela's black bodyguards' fear when the white detail (whom Mandela wisely retained, not only for reconciliation but also to retain institutional knowledge and ensure safety) enters their control room and the unreasoning panic and hatred shown by a white couple as they watch Mandela's investment ceremony on television. South African expert and Oxford University professor William Beinart notes that Mandela wanted to win over the armed forces because he was worried about a possible power base in the military (2001, 302). For these and other details, the movie draws heavily from John Carlin's 2008 book, *Playing the Enemy: Nelson Mandela and the Game that Made a Nation.*

Eastwood's Invictus *honored Nelson Mandela's shrewd peace-making through the medium of rugby. From left, former rugby player Francois Pienaar, cast member Morgan Freeman, director Clint Eastwood, cast member Matt Damon, and chairman and chief executive of Warner Brothers Entertainment, Barry M. Meyer. (AP Photo/Matt Sayles)*

The dramatic segments point to a wider range of issues: the events and history that lie behind the white couple's near-hysteria at Mandela's release, events that they pretend not to know. The television announcer who spews out poison and fear to incite whites to hate their new president harkens back to the confidence man from *The Outlaw Josey Wales* (the physical resemblance is striking) who hawks deceptive advertising and hatred of the outsider. We hear Mandela's own daughter, Zindzi, recall the white policemen who threw her family out of their own home while Mandela was in jail. We hear whites refer to the revenge taken by other newly independent peoples against their white colonial oppressors (as in the civil wars in nearby Mozambique that ended in 1992 after 15 years of violence) as reasons to fear for their lives under the new regime.

Further, as spectators, we witness the disbelief of whites and blacks alike when, instead of exacting revenge for more than a century of unconscionable violations of property, liberty, and life, Mandela embraces the country's rugby team and keeps its name and colors. Mandela understands the power of sight and language—the synecdoche that references the unstated yet fully sensed whole. The green and gold team colors, the proud or despised name of Springbok, and the mostly blond Afrikaner Springbok players themselves symbolize what the world was late to recognize—but South Africans knew in their hearts—as apartheid itself. If Mandela were to refuse vengeance and transform the tortured past into a positive future, what more economical symbol could he choose than to turn to green and gold—colors of unity—from colors of blood? As William Beinart writes, "Although rugby was largely a white sport, the event was specifically used by Mandela as an arena to emphasize reconciliation and shared values" (2001, 341). Eastwood called it correctly. Sanctions did not budge the entrenched apartheid government until the rest of the world laid sanctions on *sports*. The government had to free Mandela.

CHANGELING: THE POWER OF HOPE

Changeling, one of the most probing and astute of Eastwood's movies, marks yet another Eastwood exploration of the uneasy earthly face of justice, where the universe seems off balance and imperfect humans struggle to bring it right. On the surface, the movie exhibits basic elements of a crime drama (suspected murder, manhunt, innocent man or woman wrongly accused, a constant Eastwood as well as Hitchcock theme since *Hang 'Em High*), corrupt cops, clever detective, and attempted rescue. Its rich visual texture (ominous rain-soaked exteriors, low-light interiors) will not allow the plot's apparent contradictions to be superficially dismissed, though. The story's philosophical and theological undertow is too strong and relentless to shrug off. We the spectators are forced to look, listen, and feel the rhythms of the bond between Christine and Walter Collins, mother and son—their daily life together, her little personal triumphs despite her husband's desertion, and her richly depicted but limited means.

Eastwood's juxtaposition of real-life tragedy and fairy tale allusions increases the existential sorrow in the one and the unbounded horror in the other, for within one short Saturday Christine's Walter disappears and the police, after weeks of maddening delays, replace him with a boy she knows is not hers. The identical mystery of uncertainty and almost certain loss are attached visually to *Flags of Our Fathers*, where images of lost and murdered boys abound off and on screen.

Changeling, which Eastwood took over from director-producer Ron Howard due to scheduling problems, may lack the "nuanced" and "ambiguous" spin of other Eastwood movies, as Kent Jones suggested in an online round table discussion at the time of the film's release (YouTube 2009). But nonetheless, whether Eastwood was involved in its genesis or not, he dared to make a movie that centers on a woman's life, a mother's anguish, without a hint of sentimentality or melodrama. If few directors ever presented the other side of a military conflict as he did in *Letters from Iwo Jima*, few male directors have so thoroughly and honestly captured a woman's innermost anguish.

Despite the presence of two high-octane stars, Jolie and John Malkovich, and the enthusiastic reception of the film at Cannes, where it opened the festival, *Changeling* received little attention in the United States. It played in limited theatrical release across the country and soon vanished from public consciousness.

But *Changeling* enters a different realm of reason and emotion from *Torino*, or indeed from most movies about the American experience. Christine is a victim of oppression and perhaps of fate, but she does not fall into the prostitute/sacrificial victim trap of so many stories. *Changeling* does not fall into any preset female genre formula; it is based upon a much-publicized but soon forgotten real-life incident.[1] But rather than being dismissed as a tawdry tabloid news item of the time, the filmmaker considers the woman's story as spiritually foundational. He and the screenwriter Michael Straczynski believe her; she is not a hysteric, as the police lieutenant accuses or the psychiatric ward doctor concludes, or a commodity to be marketed, as we suspect when the newspapers get hold of her story. He gets inside her skin, living her terrible loss and sorrow, dwelling with her as she lives with a changeling in her household, eating at her child's spot at the table, sleeping in her little boy's bed.

Eastwood could have made an entire movie simply about American life during the years a bare decade after the Great War, the years between Charlie Chaplin's *The Circus* (1928) and Frank Capra's *It*

---

[1] The screenwriter, J. Michael Straczynski, played with a number of structures as he crafted the script from over 6,000 pages of documents from the period. But Eastwood liked his original script and made few changes to it.

Angelina Jolie's character in Changeling *lies at the heart of an intricate
narrative of love, loss, and hope.
Here, Jolie and director Eastwood at
Cannes. (AP Photo/Evan Agostini)*

Happened One Night (1934), the end of the silent era and the beginning
of film sound. The post–World War I boom created monstrous wealth
for a few and left the rest just a few steps behind its burgeoning tech-
nological advances, much as Christine runs a few tragic steps behind
the bus to take her home to Walter after a long day's work. Unknowingly, her life will soon become tangled in a world she previously had
no idea existed: the great city, its little hell holes, prison/asylums, the
countryside outside the city where murderers prey, news sensational-
ism, the Church, the court system, and systemic corruption right in the
heart of the law. Once the protected circle of her fragile family of two
is broken, she is thrust into the widening, enveloping circles of a dark
social order—unfolding layers of abuse. She becomes the victim of a
corrupt and uncaring police force, backed up by doctors and a psychiatric hospital. She also becomes the unwitting darling of the moment
for a grandstanding preacher, Gustav Briegleb (Malkovich), and the
masses that turn out to see her and her supposed son.

Later in the film, the crowds who follow the preacher also come out to
see Christine vindicated in the courts of law. The world does eventually
become involved in her story. Yet Eastwood the director continues to

focus on the mother's loss. By movie's end, what remained with me was not the wild-eyed face of the serial killer, the weird resonance of Malkovich's crusading preacher of a type Eastwood remembered from his childhood (Merigeau 2008, 64), or the satisfying sight of corrupt Los Angeles cops sentenced for their malfeasance—Curtis Hanson's L.A. *Confidential* (1997) had already cornered the market on bad California cops.

Neither do the mechanisms of the modern world—a runaway car or a ski-lift hoist or a badly executed war—take her son from her. The machinations of the modern world do not steal the child away in a dull blur of customary movie-style sensation or horror, although *Changeling*'s screenwriter and Eastwood could have turned the script to focus on the murders. The movie does not punctuate the death that way. Eastwood's vision horrifies us with the underlying knowledge that only a short car ride from Los Angeles's clanging streetcars and humming phone lines, a madman murders children with an axe and his own hands. This is primitive fear, primal as a mother's love for her child.

The film's idyllic opening remains in all its tangible details of lived life. I cannot forget Christine's uneasy mixture of disbelief, grief, and sympathy as she sits on the bedside of the boy who claims to be her lost son (a shot lit almost exactly like one in *Mystic River* where Dave sits on his son's bed and begins to ramble about vampires). The aerial shot of a cold, frightened, deserted Christine also remains with me, as she lies on a slab in the psychiatric hospital awaiting her possible death the next day. A similar aerial shot pulls together a sympathetic Detective Ybarra and the young boy who led him to Walter Collins's probable burial spot. Most of all, I cannot shake the questions that hover over the movie: What kind of society have we created where the innocent are persecuted? What kind of universe gives birth to and harbors a child murderer?

Across 40 years as a director, Eastwood has seized upon the permeability allowed by screen artifice to suggest by image (seven bullet holes in the back; a cloud of mist; a radiant sunset over a single grave; a shadow seen through a dusky windowpane) and sound (howls and wails; a simple guitar or piano line) what mortal dangers might lie behind the everyday veil of reality. Again and again he has imaged profound loss, as, again and again, courageously and confidently, he has violated the unofficial movie commandment, "Never harm a child."

Josey Wales drags the burlap shroud of his son across the ground and sobs and moans over the fresh grave. The opening shots of *Unforgiven* visually echo the burial segment in *Josey Wales*. Will Munny, his shadowed figure etched again a sunset sky, digs a hole to place the beloved wife who restored his soul. But the little boys' bodies in *Changeling*, and the soldiers, lie untended, unmourned, forgotten.

Jimmy in *Mystic River* howls when he hears of the murder of his cherished daughter Katie, as I heard the father of a seven-year-old boy crushed by a runaway car howl at the heavens when his child was lowered into the ground. Further, *Mystic River* is driven not only by the search for Katie's killer but also by nightmares that Dave, a grown version of the Walter Collins who might have escaped, endures. (I owe the visual and thematic connections between *Mystic River* and *Changeling* to filmmaker Alex Schwarm, who took a class of mine in winter 2009.) Frankie in *Million Dollar Baby* kisses the face of young Maggie, light of his life, his own heart's love, as he eases the woman-child into the unknown.

Doc Bradley in *Flags of Our Fathers* cries out for his hapless buddy Iggy, a simple boy dragged out into the fog of war and who vanished in the darkness and was sucked into emptiness. Try as the political machine may to paint the bright face of cheerfulness and patriotism on World War II, *Flags* exposes the execution of the war as a crime against children. War resembles the hideous schemes of the serial murderer who stalks the plot in *Changeling* in all but the mind-numbing numbers of boys whose bodies are mutilated, parts of their leg bones still left in their shoes, their chests ripped open and their blood soaked into the barren ground.

In "the perfect world" imagined and posited repeatedly in Eastwood's iconic movies—the green and fertile farm of Ned and Sally in *Unforgiven*, the peace pact between Josey and Ten Bears in *The Outlaw Josey Wales*, the little cabin that Maggie and Frankie dream about in *Million Dollar Baby*, or the warm, well-lighted spaces in *Letters*'s flashbacks—no child would suffer abuse, be abandoned, or die young. No man or woman would be disdained for poverty, gender identity, ethnicity, race, or lack of power. No human being would ever endure loss or loneliness. Each person would flourish; all stories would be told and heard. *Changeling* adds to the long list of Eastwood films that give us a glimpse of perfection, if only to give us a sense of the scale of how far our world has fallen from that elemental state of grace. Yet it is precisely in the portrayal of small, everyday acts of brave and moral heroism that Eastwood honors the forgotten ones overlooked in their time and passed by the sweep of history.

But this is not a perfect world. "In a perfect world," Laura Dern's character Sally Gerber comments in *A Perfect World*, "such things wouldn't happen," referring to the tragic waste of the childhood abuse, prison stint, and senseless death of Butch Haynes (Kevin Costner). Eastwood tells tales that bubble up from this imperfect world—tales that rarely surface in a power-and money-driven social order. He sets stories of the forgotten ones in dialogue with the evanescent thoughts and images of a perfect world—a place of welcome, comfort, and healing toward which all humans might yearn—a place where traditional equations of power are overturned and the weak and powerless are finally known by name.

Changeling lacks a Hollywood happy ending, even if the character of Christine Collins lives in hope. The film, a litany of questions, moves from the chronicle of a real-life story into the realm of transcendent meditation that affects the way we live together as citizens and members of the human community. The "perfect world" (if it existed) cannot be cordoned off from the real world, an oasis that belongs only to a few. Neither should those who suffer in our contemporary world wait for the next world. Peace and justice belong to the world in which all creatures make their home. Eastwood has brought forward a tale of one woman's suffering and loss and extended it to the vulnerability of mothers all around the world who have been subject to rape and the murder of their children.

REFERENCES AND FURTHER READING

Beinart, William. 2001. *Twentieth-Century South Africa*. Oxford: Oxford University Press.

Carlin, John. 2008. *Playing the Enemy: Nelson Mandela and the Game that Made a Nation*. New York: Penguin Press.

Fish, Stanley. 2009. "Vengeance Is Mine." *The New York Times* Opinionator blog, December 28. http://opinionator.blogs.nytimes.com/2009/12/28/vengeance-is-mine/. Accessed February 25, 2014.

Hainey, Michael. 2009. "Clint Eastwood: Icon." GQ, December. http://www.gq.com/entertainment/men-of-the-year/2009/badass/clint-eastwood-legend-invictus-director?currentPage=1. Accessed February 25, 2014.

Kleiner, Sam. 2013. "Apartheid Amnesia." Foreign Policy, July 16. http://www.foreignpolicy.com/articles/2013/07/18/apartheid_amnesia_gop_nelson_mandela. Accessed February 25, 2014.

Mandela, Nelson. 1995. Long Walk to Freedom: The Autobiography of Nelson Mandela. New York: Back Bay Books.

Merigeau, Pascal. 2008. "Dans l'atelier d'Eastwood" ("In Eastwood's Studio"). Le nouvel, November 6–12, 63–64.

Ungar, Rick. 2013. "When Conservatives Branded Nelson Mandela a Terrorist." Forbes, December 6. http://www.forbes.com/sites/rickungar/2013/12/06/when-conservatives-branded-nelson-mandela-a-terrorist/. Accessed February 25, 2014.

YouTube. 2009. "Eastwood Critics Roundtable Part 2: Gran Torino." Film Society of Lincoln Center, January 3. http://www.youtube.com/watch?v=ELN12EkMAO4. Accessed February 25, 2014.

Chapter 12

HEREAFTER; J. EDGAR; AND *JERSEY BOYS*

With *Jersey Boys* out in theaters June 20, 2014, Clint Eastwood has announced his next two directorial projects. *American Sniper* is scheduled to appear in 2015, followed by a remake of the classic Hollywood film *A Star Is Born* (date of release not yet known). Since he does not act in the film, his cult fans may seek another icon to love or simply watch reruns of *The Good, the Bad, and the Ugly*. Yet he has adapted an intriguing subject: the rise of the singing group The Four Seasons, made into a Tony-winning musical production a few years ago. I will be there. I may watch *Bird* again before I see the movie on the big screen, or I may play some Four Seasons songs again to remind myself how much of contemporary pop music culture owes its life to the still-vital energy of 1960s music.

But before 2014, Eastwood made four first-class movies that simply did not catch box office fire or attract merited critical attention: *Changeling, Invictus, Hereafter,* and *J. Edgar*. Will *Jersey Boys*, in which Eastwood neither stars nor sings, come and go like those? Has the mega-franchise industry ruined the reception of any small, offbeat project?

Indeed, in the new millennium, Eastwood's type of film has become more and more difficult to produce in Hollywood, even for a successful director. In the industry, moderately budgeted studio films for adult audiences have become increasingly rare in favor of high-budget franchise "tentpoles" that play well in China and elsewhere and extremely low-budget films (microbudget horror films, say) that cost only a fraction of an Eastwood production.

Hereafter certainly has struggled to find an audience. It is not difficult to guess why. Its title suggests a religious film, a horror movie, or a fantasy flick—all movie genres with long and in a few cases distinguished pedigrees. Despite its potential to disappoint die-hard Dirty Harry fans, though, *Hereafter* contains all the elements of a good story: disaster, death, and grief; winsome characters; and a gentle, quiet, hope-filled ending tinged with romance. But it has suffered the misfortune of opening on American screens at a time when violence and fear of "others" coincides with the increasing availability of guns. The presence of a buff Matt Damon may trigger expectations about finding another Jason Bourne, who might stop jumping through windows and open the doors of heaven itself, but in *Hereafter*, Damon plays a quiet, reclusive, sad man damaged by a brain disease—not unlike veterans of America's wars or contact sports, whose brain injuries have destroyed hope for a peaceful life.

· *Hereafter* braids three narrative strands: the near-death and spiritual transformation of a French media star, Marie LeLay (Cecile De France), who (she believes) dies when she is swept into a tsunami and returns to life; a lonely young man, George Lonegan (Damon), whose disease-disturbed brain curses him to cross into the world beyond; and a young boy Marcus (Frankie McLaren), who wants to connect with his beloved dead twin brother, Jason (George McLaren). The movie follows the story lines as they interweave. The "hereafter," an imaginative construct that intriguingly seems to lie just beyond our grasp, inserts itself into every part of the movie.

In addition, as the three main characters' paths increasingly interconnect, the movie slowly reveals—almost as throwaway scenes—multiple layers of a commercialized "hereafter" industry. George's brother peddles his "skills" as a medium for money. Marie's former lover and her publisher, so admiring when she was shallow and flashy, disdain her story about an encounter with death, even as her television station continues to sell images of disaster like lollypops. Dozens of mediums whom the resourceful Marcus locates on the Internet and experiences in public seances show the extent to which frauds prey upon the sufferings of vulnerable and grieving men, women, and children.

True to Eastwood's career-long emphasis on lived experience, each of the plot strands attends to the particulars that drive each character's story. He films George's sections largely in black and white and green, except for the cooking class scene. When George is forced to give a reading, darkness (low-key lighting) shrouds the figures (note the scene with Marcus in particular), another Sergio Leone echo in the *Dollars* trilogy common to the murder settings. He often eats alone, like *Gran Torino's* Walt Kowalski before a transformative meal with his Hmong neighbors.

Marie's story line varies in color and movement as she is swept away by a tsunami and continues to see visions. Marcus remains more resolutely outside the door of paradise, as befits a smart kid who determines to discover what an "afterlife" might look like.

Eastwood, however, has toyed with the idea many times before. Leone's "resurrection" of the Man with No Name in *Fistful* is revealed as a hoax when the near-dead hero flips aside his serape in a "reveal" like the pulling aside of the trickster's curtain in *Wizard of Oz* (1939). *Hereafter* fits easily within a career of a director who plays with mysticism and the possible existence of a life beyond this one (*High Plains Drifter; Pale Rider*); Will Munny imagines that he sees into the afterworld in a frighteningly realistic near-death scene in *Unforgiven*.

Moreover, the director often has alluded to a "paradise" or "perfect world" that his characters dream about and long for: for instance, in *The Gauntlet, Bird, A Perfect World, Million Dollar Baby*, and *Letters from Iwo Jima*. Suffering needs a vision of a better, if not a perfect, world—as he has put it, a "what if" scenario. What if, instead of waiting for a lone savior, the "hero" (whether a god or a gifted human), to save the day, we could see into the life hereafter? Would that change the ways we live our lives in the here and now?

Hereafter is a hopeful movie, its lovely ending—fittingly for a philosopher who reads hundreds of scripts and stories a year—brings the three storylines and its characters together at a London Book Fair. The honored British actor Derek Jacobi reads from *Little Dorrit*, as a rapt George listens. Eastwood chose the reading carefully: it's the story of scandalous commercial fraud defeated and despair transformed by the love of a young woman, Amy, for an older man, Arthur. (A nice touch: Eastwood surely noticed parallels between himself and his much younger wife Dina at the time of when the movie made—2010.)

Hereafter asks: What if the future entered the present, as happens with the "ghost of Christmas yet to come" in Charles Dickens's "A Christmas Carol"? Ebenezer Scrooge is transformed spiritually and practically by what the ghost reveals will happen to him if he does not change the ways he behaves toward other human beings. A parallel character in Eastwood's work is Walt Kowalski, who confronts his poisonous memories to cleanse his guilt by giving his love and his life to his new friends, the outcast Hmong family. The young priest who stalks him and later becomes his friend offers confession and communion— that is, to participate in the blood sacrifice of Jesus Christ (Walt is a Polish Catholic in a parish rapidly changing ethnicity)—as a way to release his toxic memories.

The near-death experience of Marie in *Hereafter* opens her heart to seek a new way to live, the premise upon which Dickens (George's much-loved author) built his greatest works. The artistic work wrenches truth from falsehood, stripping away layers of image from consumerist contemporary life: as in Alejandro González Iñárritu's *Amores Perros* and Krzysztof Kieślowski's *Red*, where heavily marketed women's images on billboards correspond to emotional and physical collapse, the giant billboards in Paris that bear Marie's image are removed as soon as she is no longer a salable commodity.

Charles Dickens makes a fitting visit to and becomes a silent partner in the movie's exploration of the concept of the hereafter. Dickens struggled with many of the themes we see emerge in Eastwood's iconic work: the tension between a dark, unforgiving world of poverty, social isolation, and grief; and the wish for renewal, welcome, and joy. Whereas Dickens's early novels imagined that paradise or a perfect world might be realized through the love of one person for others (*Pickwick Papers*, for instance), as Dickens's career unfolded, the worlds he imagined became bleaker; the power of love (either Christian or romantic) became less effective; and a small cottage surrounded by a verdant terrain became less of a possibility.

"A Christmas Carol" also plunges into the heart of evil, identifying ignorance and poverty as the death dealers of the society Dickens's readers knew. But the story ends with Scrooge's journey toward a chance for a new life. The instruments of his transformation, the Spirits, guide him to tap into the restorative past, immerse him in the horrific present, in which most English men, women, and children lived out their miserable days, and glimpse into life after death, life without *metanoia*, life without a softening of his hard heart.

The three narrative strands join as the once-restless hands of George and Marie touch each other, and a happier Marcus, now friends with both, reenters a family. The characters no longer need the certitude of knowing what lies on the other side of death. They have opened their hearts to the world around them, the world, as critic Kent Jones has written, of "Physical Evidence."

J. EDGAR: A WEB OF SPIES

When I watched the mildly vilified and largely ignored *J. Edgar* for a second time, I meditated further upon some questions the movie raises. Eastwood's 2011 film, a masterpiece of period, mood, and understatement, features strong performances by Leonardo DiCaprio as Hoover and Armie Hammer as Clyde Tolson, his partner. The distaste of the critics did not surprise me because *Changeling, Hereafter,* and even *Gran Torino* and *Invictus* were sadly overlooked in the United States. How dare Eastwood ("Dirty Harry") abandon the tough American hero template to focus upon a woman, three damaged fools, a crazy old kook, and a mythologized political figure in a far distant land! And with *J. Edgar:* how dare he make a biopic on a reviled and shadowy "G-man" who ruined our country without painting him in the colors of pure evil!

Rather than starting with J. Edgar Hoover's early life and marching toward his death, though, Eastwood begins the film as the powerful director of the untouchable FBI (Federal Bureau of Investigation) dictates his life story to a young FBI agent, who busily types away without comment. Speech quickly fades into images of an ambitious young man (J. Edgar, played by Leonardo DiCaprio) determined to protect his country from anarchists like the ones who overthrew the Russian Czar and his government—or so he tells everyone. The rest of the movie follows the same pattern: the older Hoover dictates his memoirs to a series of young agents; we then see almost cartoon-like plot illustrations of the "facts" the older man has given his transcriber.

As the movie progresses, the cartoons reveal not a great American hero (the dramatic G-man image Hoover presented to the outside world) but rather a paranoid, power-hungry figure who terrifies presidents and attorneys general, disregards the Constitution, and spies upon hundreds of thousands of American citizens. The glamorized story begins to fall apart. Hoover's own colleagues and confidents criticize him at first covertly with disapproving body language and later quite openly. Eastwood shows Hoover on an insane rampage against Martin Luther King Jr. and President Kennedy. Even his devoted secretary Helen (Naomi Watts) and his inseparable friend Clyde, no. 1 in Hoover's life (Armie Hammer), become horrified and disgusted by his lies.

The real-life J. Edgar Hoover did irreparable damage to freedom of speech and assembly during his years as head of the FBI. My husband and I and our friends were among his hundreds of thousands of targets. Hoover justified any means (perjury; torture; spying; violence) to "protect our country" even as he trampled on democracy in the process.

Hoover's actions, though deplorable, are also curiously old-fashioned in the era of NSA surveillance and digital espionage. At least Hoover's obsessions are recognizable as obsessions. In the modern world, even individual surveillance is abstracted to the level of "metadata," far removed from the realm of lived experience. For Eastwood, who so privileges the experiential over the abstract, the intuitive over the calculated, Hoover's hands-on obsession was perhaps more alarming, and was certainly more psychotic, than the ones and zeros that characterize surveillance in the 21st century.

The movie delivers much more than a cinematic biopic such as the excellent *Ray*, about Ray Charles. It resonates with current events—the illegal war in Iraq, with thousands of our soldiers and Iraqi civilians dead; prejudice and violence toward immigrants and others whose religion, skin color, or sexual orientation differ from our own; assaults upon freedom to assemble. The search to define and deliver justice in our democracy continues, and Clint Eastwood the director is on the case—not with guns but with a cinematic appeal for fairness, transparency, and decency.

REFERENCE AND FURTHER READING

Jones, Kent. 2007. *Physical Evidence: Selective Film Criticism.* Middletown, CT: Wesleyan University Press.

GLOSSARY

Ambiguity—lack of a clear meaning. Uncertainty.

American Exceptionalism—belief that the United States of America fundamentally or essentially differs (usually for the better) from other countries. American Exceptionalism undergirds the philosophy of Manifest Destiny.

Antiphony—alternation of one scene with another of similar theme; echoes of one character with others; or mirrors of one scene or character with another. The term is borrowed from religious ritual and early music.

Camp—celebration of the artifice of cultural texts. A movie draws attention to the artificiality of its portrayals. This is why critics called Eastwood's Spaghetti Westerns "camp"—they highlight the conventions of the Western genre.

Canted Angle—camera angle tilted to allow the horizon—or the floor-line—to cut diagonally across the frame, rather than parallel to its bottom.

Catharsis—purification or, in literature or film, release of tension in the narrative.

Color Saturation—intensity of an image's color. Highly saturated colors are rich and vibrant; an image-desaturated color, often used in Eastwood's film, is nearly black and white.

Commedia Dell'Arte—Italian theatrical tradition developed in the 1500s, featuring "stock" characters, usually masked, that recur across performances.

Diegetic and Non-diegetic Sound—sound with a source in the story-world ("diegesis") of the film, as distinct from non-diegetic sound, with no source in the story. If characters can hear the sound, it is diegetic.

Ethical System—way to live that may or may not be attached to religious faith and practice.

Fictional Modes—way to speak about fictional narratives first formulated by Northrup Frye. Frye's five modes, myth, romance, high mimetic, low mimetic, and ironic, pose different relationships between a protagonist, the world in which he (almost always a "he") finds himself, and the audience. In the "mythic" mode, the protagonist has godlike power over his environment, and audiences view him as in a position of superiority, whereas in the "ironic" mode, the audience looks down on the impotent protagonist. In *Unforgiven*, Will Munny (Clint Eastwood) begins the film dragged through the mud. His age and weariness (ironic mode) contrast with the image of him as a hero of legend (myth and romance combined). The final shoot-out in the saloon switches from ironic or low-mimetic mode (the storytelling mode of the rest of the movie) into mythic / heroic mode.

Film Noir—term applied after World War II by French critics to describe American crime films of the 1940s, especially those with low-key lighting schemes, bleak tone, women with sexual agency ("femmes fatales"), and stories of sexual duplicity. The films almost always portray masculinity in crisis, with weak men and powerful women.

Framing—in cinematography, framing refers to what appears in the final, projected image. Factors in framing include shot distance (how far away the camera is from what is in front of it) and camera angle (whether the camera is above, below, or level with the subject). In narrative, a "frame" refers to a plot's introduction, perhaps by a narrator (*LA Confidential*, *American Hustle*) or by a scrolled text (*Unforgiven*).

Hays Code—movie industry's self-censorship that dominated from 1934 until the introduction of the ratings system in the late 1960s. It allowed the industry to censor its own films and avoid final cuts by individual municipal or state censorship boards. The influx of edgy foreign films in the 1960s, which included Sergio Leone's Spaghetti Westerns, precipitated the Code's demise.

Icon (Art History; Religion; Pop Culture)—an "icon" corresponds to an imagined ideal. Eastwood's iconic image in the popular imagination may function simultaneously as actor (Dirty Harry; the Man with No Name); director; representative of American power (heroic movie images); and ideal American masculinity.

Index—one event references others in the past or references broader social and political implications of other events. In the Dirty Harry films, *The Outlaw Josey Wales*, or *Million Dollar Baby*, for instance, Eastwood insists his films do not "index" political meanings beyond a "good story."

In medias res—plot in literature or film begins in the middle of a story without any backstory.

Lighting—aspect of mise-en-scène. A typical film lighting setup contains three major types of lights: a key, the primary light that shines on the subject from the front; fill light, which shines on the subject from the front but from the opposite side of the key to lessen the sharpness of shadows; and backlight, which shines from behind to help distinguish the shadow from the background. *High-key* and *low-key* lighting refer to the ratio between the key light and the fill light. If little difference in brightness exists between the key and the fill, there will be little contrast between the brightest and darkest areas of the frame. This is known as *high key*. *Low key* refers to a lighting scheme in which the difference between the key and the fill lights is stark, leading to dark shadows and high contrast. Many of Eastwood's films use low-key lighting systems, sometimes abandoning the fill light altogether to which leads to dramatic contrasts between light and dark portions of the frame.

Liminal—transitional, between two states of being or places. Often "liminal" applies to discussions of rituals or ceremonies, but other places or states can also be "liminal." Eastwood uses liminal figures in *High Plains Drifter, Pale Rider, Hereafter,* and *Unforgiven,* when Will Munny "sees" his dead wife.

Long Take—shot with long duration, in general, or when compared to the typical shot duration for a given film. Not to be confused with "long shot," which refers not to the duration but rather to the distance between subject and camera. Famous long takes occur in *Touch of Evil, Goodfellas,* and *Children of Men.*

Manicheism—belief in moral dualism, with sharply contrasted total evil and complete goodness. Film critic Michael Henry Wilson notes of Eastwood's films: "He learned from his earliest film mentors, Don Siegel and Sergio Leone, themselves '*contrebandiers,*' ways to turn movie codes and conventions to his profit. How to circumvent the Manicheism of genre cinema."

Manifest Destiny—belief that Americans were destined to settle the entire westward span of the North American continent, providing "religious" justification for westward expansion and the conquering of Native Americans and their land. Its problematic tenets inform much of the Western genre.

Melodrama—genre of films sometimes derisively termed "weepies" or "women's pictures," in which emotions are heightened to trigger emotional reactions from viewers. Melodrama as a mode of storytelling may be used in any genre as an approach in which social questions—for example, sex, class, race, and so on—are displaced onto emotionally charged relationships among individuals. Some of Eastwood's films (e.g., *Million Dollar Baby*) operate in the melodramatic mode.

Metamorphosis—change of shape.

Metanoia—Greek word *metanoiein,* for "change of heart," usually meaning a conversion or radical change in a person's life. A more narrowly focused word than "metamorphosis," change of shape.

Mise-en-scène—"placed in the scene." Refers to the aspects of filmmaking that appear in front of the camera: lighting, set design, costumes and makeup, and staging (the placement of actors, props, etc.). Mise-en-scène includes elements common to filmmaking and live theater, as distinct from cinematography and editing.

Montage—the editing of a film, in which meaning is created by the ways individual shots are juxtaposed against each other. The final step in a film. Eastwood insists it is not the only element, as a film depends upon many collaborators.

Pan—short for "panorama," a movement in which the camera rotates horizontally on an axis. It mimics the effect of turning one's head, as though to survey a landscape.

Roman à Clef—novel based on a real life, but with a fictionalized veneer. If readers know who the characters represent in real life, they have the "key" ("clef" is French for key) and can understand the story behind a plot.

Screwball Comedy—subgenre of romance popular in the 1930s and 1940s that featured fast-based, comedic banter between men and women, challenges to gender roles (women often dominate men in humorous situations), and romantic unions during the final scenes. Screwball comedies are sometimes called "comedies of remarriage" because central couples usually have a romantic history.

Sound Design—composite audio track (or tracks) of a film, which can include recorded music, synchronous sound recorded at the time of filming, sound effects produced for the film specifically, asynchronous sound (sound which does not have a source visible in the frame), dubbed voices recorded after filming, and other elements.

Story vs. Plot—in the context of film analysis (and literary analysis), a story is a sequence of chronological events that grounds a narrative. A plot refers to the ways the events are presented in a particular film. Is the film told chronologically? Are there flashbacks? Are certain events in the story implied but not shown? Does the narrative perspective (point of view) change?

Synecdoche—figure of speech in which a part refers to a whole: for instance, "heads of cattle."

Tabula Rasa—"clean slate," a term popularized by philosopher John Locke that also translates to "a clean start."

Tilt—movement in which the camera rotates vertically on an axis to mimic the effect of nodding one's head.

Track—movement in which the entire camera moves, usually on a device placed along a track, and usually following a subject in the frame, or moving in to highlight a particular part of the frame. It mimics the effect of walking toward, alongside, or away from a subject. Most colloquial references to "zooms" are actually tracks (in a zoom, the camera itself remains stationary). A tracking shot is also called a "dolly shot" because the camera must be mounted on a dolly or other wheeled device that allows it to move smoothly.

Trompe-d'oeil—French term for "sleight of hand," literally a trick of the eye, where an image is designed to fool the spectator's initial glance. *High Plains Drifter, Pale Rider,* and *Hereafter* use this visual device.

Utopia—place or community of perfection. It means literally "no place," although it also connotes "good place." The idea was explored during the Renaissance by philosopher Thomas More.

Western—on its most obvious level, a work set in the West (though defining "the West" is often difficult) during the era of American westward expansion, especially the late 19th century: the decades that followed the Civil War. The genre explores what it means to be American and projects an ethos of individuality and self-reliance. Many Westerns dramatize the conflict between civilization (assumed to be white settlers) and wilderness, with a lone, wandering cowboy linking the two. He rides into towns to impose law and order, assisting in the march of "civilization," but he rides off into the sunset at the end, not at home with civilization's strictures. Western films were extremely popular throughout the Classical Hollywood era (roughly 1915–1960) and were also the most popular genre on television in the late 1950s as well as in other media (radio, print). Many Westerns now considered classics, however, are "revisionist," as they rework the conventions of the genre in a self-conscious and critical way. Classic Westerns were often "B films," produced to fill out a theater's film schedule, though there are exceptions like *Stagecoach* and *The Big Trail*. Eastwood's iconic Westerns (the ones he directed) all upend the genre.

Zoom—shot in which the length of the lens changes over the course of the shot. A zoom in gives the effect of enlarging a portion of an image without giving the sense of moving closer to its subject.

SELECT BIBLIOGRAPHY

The following lists only a small portion of the vast number of essays, books, and interviews about Clint Eastwood and his work. They are among the more useful and insightful sources. See "References and Further Reading" sections for more material.

BOOKS

Avery, Kevin, ed. 2011. *Conversations with Clint: Paul Nelson's Lost Interviews with Clint Eastwood, 1979–1983*. New York: Continuum.

Beard, William. 2000. *Persistence of Double Vision: Essays on Clint Eastwood*. Alberta, Canada: University of Alberta Press.

Eliot, Marc. 2009. *Clint Eastwood: American Rebel*. New York: Crown Publishing Group.

Engel, Leonard, ed. 2007. *Clint Eastwood: Actor and Director*. Salt Lake City: University of Utah Press.

Foote, John. 2009. *Clint Eastwood: Evolution of a Filmmaker*. Westport, CT: Praeger.

Jones, Kent. 2007. *Physical Evidence: Selected Film Criticism*. Middletown, CT: Wesleyan University Press.

Kapsis, Robert E., and Kathie Coblentz, eds. 1999. *Clint Eastwood: Interviews.* Jackson: University Press of Mississippi.

Knapp, Laurence. 1996. *Directed by Clint Eastwood: Eighteen Films Analyzed.* Jefferson, ND: McFarland and Company.

Locke, Sondra. 1997. *The Good, the Bad, and the Very Ugly: A Hollywood Journey.* New York: William Morrow and Company.

McGilligan, Patrick. 2002. *Clint: The Life and Legend.* New York: St. Martin's Press.

Schickel, Richard. 1997. *Clint Eastwood: A Biography.* New York: Vintage.

Simsolo, Noël. 2003. *Clint Eastwood: Un Passeur à Hollywood,* 2nd ed. Paris: Cahiers du Cinéma.

Vaux, Sara Anson. 1999. *Finding Meaning at the Movies.* Nashville, TN: Abingdon Press.

Vaux, Sara Anson. 2009. "Eastwood's Theology." In *The Common Review,* publication of The Great Books Foundation.

Vaux, Sara Anson. 2012. *The Ethical Vision of Clint Eastwood.* Grand Rapids: William B. Eerdmans. The chapters on *The Outlaw Josey Wales,* the war movies, *Unforgiven, Mystic River,* and *Million Dollar Baby* have been adapted from chapters in *Ethical Vision.*

Wilson, Michael Henry. 2007. *Clint Eastwood: Entretiens avec Michael Henry Wilson* (Interviews with Eastwood). Paris: Cahiers du Cinéma.   ,

ON EASTWOOD'S EARLY CAREER

Frayling, Christopher. 2000. "The Making of Sergio Leone's 'A Fistful of Dollars'." *Cinéaste* 25, no. 3: 14–22. Also see Frayling, revised paperback ed. 2006, *Spaghetti Westerns: Cowboys and Europeans from Karl May to Sergio Leone.* London & New York: I.B. Tauris.

Michaels, Len. 2007. "Fugitive from a Spaghetti Factory." *The Chicago Tribune,* November 15.

Slack, Sara. 1967. "United Artists Star, a Staunch Rights Advocate." *New York Amsterdam News,* September 2.

Tepper, Ron. 1959. "First Big Break: Clint Eastwood Thrives on Never-Ending Cattle Drive." *The Los Angeles Times,* April 26.

Warga, Wayne. 1969. "Clint Eastwood: He Drifted Into Stardom." *The Los Angeles Times,* June 22.

ON THE 1970s

Fayard, Judy. 1971. "Who Can Stand 32,580 Seconds of Clint East-
     wood?" *Life*, July 23, 44–48.

Knight, Arthur. 1974. "*Playboy* Interview: Clint Eastwood." *Playboy*,
     February, 57–72, 170–72.

Lukas, Karli. 2004. "On Hell's Hero Coming to Breakfast: Clint East-
     wood and *The Outlaw Josey Wales*." *Senses of Cinema* 31 (April).
     http://sensesofcinema.com/2004/cteq/outlaw_josey_wales/. Ac-
     cessed February 27, 2014.

Thompson, Richard, and Tim Hunter. 1978. "Clint Eastwood, Auteur."
     Film Comment 14, no. 1: 24–32.

Vallely, Jean. 1978. "Pumping Gold with Clint Eastwood, Hollywood's
     Richest Actor." *Esquire*, March 14, 38–45.

ON THE 1980s

Cahill, Tim. 1985. "Clint Eastwood's American Dream." *Rolling Stone*,
     July 4, 18–23.

Gentry, Ric. 1989. "Clint Eastwood: An Interview." *Film Quarterly* 12,
     no. 3 (Spring): 12–23.

Grenier, Richard. 1984. "The World's Favorite Movie Star." *Commen-
     tary*, April, 61–67.

Holmlund, Christine. "Sexuality and Power in Male Doppelganger
     Cinema: The Case of Clint Eastwood's 'Tightrope.'" *Cinema
     Journal* 26, no. 1 (Autumn, 1986): 31–42.

Stempel, Tom. 1984. "Let's Hear It for Eastwood's 'Strong' Women."
     The Los Angeles Times, March 11.

Vincour, John. 1985. "Clint Eastwood, Seriously." *The New York Times*,
     February 24.

ON THE 1990s

Bingham, Dennis. 1990. "Men with No Names: Clint Eastwood's 'The
     Stranger' Persona, Identification, and the Impenetrable Gaze."
     Journal of Film and Video 42, no. 4 (Winter): 33–48.

Breskin, David. 1992. "Clint Eastwood" (Interview). *Rolling Stone*,
     September 17, 66ff.

Howell, Georgina. 1993. "Cool Clint." *Vogue*, February, 220–25, 299.

Plantinga, Carl. 1998. "Spectacles of Death: Clint Eastwood and Violence in 'Unforgiven.'" *Cinema Journal* 37, no. 2 (Winter): 65–83.

Prats, Armando. 1995. "Back from the Sunset: The Western, The Eastwood Hero, and *Unforgiven.*" *Journal of Film and Video* 47, no. 1/3 (Spring–Fall): 106–23.

Verniere, James. 1993 "Clint Eastwood: Stepping Out." *Sight and Sound,* September, 6–10.

ON THE 2000s

Hainey, Michael. 2009. "Clint Eastwood: Icon." GQ, December. http://www.gq.com/entertainment/men-of-the-year/2009/badass/clint-eastwood-legend-invictus-director?currentPage=1. Accessed February 25, 2014.

Merigeau, Pascal. 2008. "Dans l'atelier d'Eastwood" ("In Eastwood's studio"). *Le nouvel,* November 6–12, 63–64.

Modleski, Tania. 2010. "Clint Eastwood and Male Weepies." *American Literary History* 22, no. 1 (Spring): 136–58.

INDEX

2, 9–14; education, 10, 13; employment before entering show business, 10–12; extramarital affairs and infidelity, 23, 58–59, 61, 69, 110; iconic status, 1–8, 27–28, 38, 45, 60, 61–62, 141; luck and, 12, 14, 35; military service, 12–13; personal life, 2–3, 23, 33–34, 40, 45, 57–59, 61, 69–70, 110, 152; physical fitness, 11, 36, 59; political beliefs, 1–5, 63–65; salary and wealth, 24, 26, 40, 45, 58–59; stardom and iconic status, 1–6, 20, 23, 26–28, 33–34, 40, 52, 57–59, 83, 154; survival of airplane crash, 12–13. *See also individual film titles*

Eastwood, Clint Sr. and Ruth (parents of Clint Eastwood), 9, 10, 36, 101

Eastwood, Dina (Ruiz), 3, 110, 152, 175

Eastwood, Maggie (Johnson), 13, 23, 33, 40, 58–59, 61, 110, 152

The Eiger Sanction, 59–60

Elevator to the Gallows (Malle), 74

The Enforcer, 60

Ethics. *See* Morality and ethics

Euthanasia, in *Million Dollar Baby*, 133–35

Every Which Way But Loose, 61–62, 154

Family (in films): in *Gran Torino*, 157; in *Hereafter*, 176–77; in *Million Dollar* Baby, 130–32; in *The Outlaw Josey Wales*, 5, 52, 54–56; in *Pale Rider*, 68–69; in *A Perfect World*, 107–8

Firefox, 62, 110

Fisher, Frances, 69, 110, 152

A Fistful of Dollars, 23–27, 130, 157, 175. *See also* Spaghetti Westerns

Flags of Our Fathers, 51, 55, 93, 99, 141–47, 150–51

Fleming, Eric, 17, 19

For a Few Dollars More, 26. *See also* Spaghetti Westerns

Ford, John, 22

Freeman, Morgan, 93, 100, 119, 126, 163

The French Connection (Friedkin), 38, 42

The Gauntlet, 25, 60–61, 74, 75, 79, 95, 119, 125, 159, 175

The Good, the Bad, and the Ugly, 24–25, 26, 50, 142, 150, 173. *See also* Spaghetti Westerns

Gran Torino, 6, 50, 51, 52, 55, 62, 95, 113, 120, 127, 151–59

Great Depression, 9, 61, 150

Hackman, Gene, 93, 100

Hang 'Em High, 32, 62

Heartbreak Ridge, 6, 65, 118

Hereafter, 13, 173–77

Heroes: in *Gran Torino*, 154, 157; in Westerns, 22, 25, 51, 86, 88–91, 96–98, 142

About the Author

SARA ANSON VAUX, PhD, a lecturer in the Department of Religious Studies, is the Director of the Office of Fellowships at Northwestern University. Her published works include *The Ethical Vision of Clint Eastwood* (Eerdmans Publishing, 2012); *Finding Meaning at the Movies* (Abingdon Press, 1999); "Film and Catholicism" in *The New Catholic Encyclopedia Supplement* (Gale Press, 2011); and numerous articles on religion and film. She also edited *Covenants of Life: Contemporary Medical Ethics in Light of the Thought of Paul Ramsey* (Kluwer Academic Publishers, 2003). She is currently completing a book on "Food and Film."